Vietnam: No Regrets

One Soldier's "Tour of Duty"

Vietnam: No Regrets

One Soldier's "Tour of Duty"

J. Richard Watkins

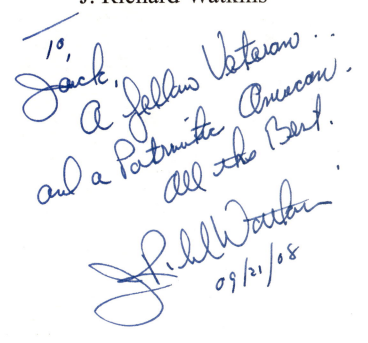

To,
Jack, a fellow Veteran ..
and a Patriotic American.
All the Best.

Richd Watkins
09/21/08

Library of Congress Cataloging-in-Publication Information
Watkins, Joel R.
    Vietnam No Regrets / Joel Richard Watkins   1st ed.

TX6319103   2006
ISBN#: 978-0-9793629-0-3

BAY STATE PUBLISHING

Dedicated to My Mother
Kathleen P. Watkins

And

Sandra J Crowley

"You are my heroes and you always will be."

And to the men who served with the
1/27th Wolfhounds 25th Infantry Division, Vietnam.

Special thanks to the following individuals for without their support and encouragement this book may never have been completed.

Harold Watkins

William Wallace

Kellie Manzone

Karen Flanders

Louise Waladis

Robin Rodenbush

Keary Watkins

Atty. Albert Flanders

Melanie Sullivan Florio

The Brockton, MA Vets Center

"Midnight"

Table of Contents

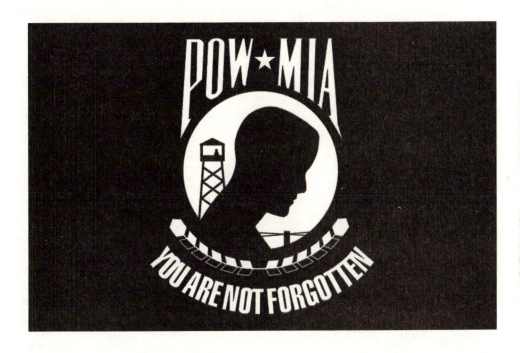

Chapter 1

Leaving on a Jet Plane

It was a cold and foggy Northern California evening, and I was waiting to board my flight to South Vietnam. I was part of a group of GIs heading off to the war zone. We didn't know one another, but we were about to share this once-in-a-lifetime experience together. We'd had our training for war, and we were ready to go—not eager mind you, but ready nevertheless. As our plane got ready to load up, I glanced over to a bank of phones where soldiers were making their last calls home and I thought about making one last call myself. But it was after two o'clock in the morning back in Brockton, Massachusetts, and my parents would have to be up early for work, so I let it go and got in line to board the plane for Vietnam. It had come as a surprise to me that it was a United Airlines flight; I had expected a military plane. But no, there it was right in front of me: a big United Airlines 707 Jetliner bound for Vietnam. I would be making the trip with approximately one hundred and sixty other soldiers of all ranks, but not knowing anyone on board, I felt quite alone.

The flight to Vietnam takes approximately fourteen hours, with stops in Hawaii and Guam along the way. It was one hell of a long flight, and we were glad to see the coast of Vietnam appear on the horizon. We arrived in the Republic of South Vietnam on a bright sunny morning made much brighter by the fact that we had left the States at night and had not been off the plane for quite a while. On our final approach for landing at Tan Son Nhut Air Base, we came in very low and very slow. From the windows of the plane we could see all the shell holes around the airport; they looked like craters on the moon, except they were on a very bright green wet surface. Flying in, we could also see the small shacks that the local people called home, alongside the gun emplacements of our troops. GIs waved to us or gave us the finger as our plane flew over their positions. Our final approach was so low and slow that all that was going through my mind was *Let's get this plane on the ground before we get shot out of the sky.* Thankfully, we landed soon enough.

As the back door of the plane opened and the outside air penetrated the interior of the plane, we immediately felt the heat and the humidity and the smell of Vietnam. As I looked at all the sober faces of the men aboard our flight just in from the States and then looked at the stewardesses saying goodbye to us, I knew that these girls might be the last American girls I ever saw.

It struck me how surreal this experience had become; the stewardesses knew we weren't going on any vacation, and we knew we weren't either. So what were all the smiles for? Some of the guys they were saying goodbye to would never board a plane again—alive, that is. As I look back on it now, I guess these girls were just doing a very tough job the best way they knew how. It couldn't have been an easy flight for them to make either. The flight over, that is: the trip back must have been great. But it took me a while to realize that, for my flight home would be a long time in coming, and I would change tremendously before my tour would end and I too would be taking this freedom bird home.

We disembarked and started down the stairs. Off to our right, waiting to board the same plane, was a line of soldiers with clean, new uniforms on, just like us. But they were not like us at all; if you really gave them a closer inspection, they looked older than we did, even though you knew they weren't. What was it, then? I guess they had that shallow-eyed look, the look you get when you work for days and days without enough sleep, that faraway look, that nothing-seems-to-matter, I-don't-give-a-shit look. But this look was even more so. They had a blank stare that was to become all too familiar to me in the coming months. These men just stared at us, not saying a word, even though we passed within a few yards of one another. A few smiled, and a few shook their heads, but not one word was exchanged between us. I found this strange, very strange indeed. In the coming year I would come to find out why this was so—the hard way.

These soldiers were waiting impatiently to board this very special plane that had just brought us in from the world, a world they had dreamed of for the past year and had missed very, very much. I envied them their return flight back to the world, but for Christ's sake, who was I to envy them anything? Hell, I'd just arrived. I would have to earn my flight back to the world that these men had missed so very much, a world I too would come to miss in the coming year. These guys had earned their flight home. Some had earned it more than others, for the Vietnam experience was not equal in respect to what each and every one of us had to endure in order to earn his flight home.

I was glad for them nevertheless. These guys had beaten the odds, they had served their country, and now they were going home to their families and loved ones, and I for one was very happy for them.

Chapter 2

My Orders Arrive

It was November 20, 1969, and my orders had finally arrived. I'd been in-country for all of three days now, and it felt good to have my orders in my hand. I now knew where I'd be going. It would be up-country to join the Twenty-fifth Infantry Division, Alpha Company 1/27 Wolfhounds. The First Wolfhounds were made up of approximately 600 soldiers, and their motto was "No Fear on Earth." The "Wolfhounds" came with quite a reputation as a very tough outfit. I mentioned to another soldier that I'd be going up to Cu Chi and would be attached to the Twenty-fifth Division, 1/27 Wolfhounds. He just gave me one of those looks that you really don't want to get, and smiled, and said good luck. Good Luck! Boy, that wasn't particularly encouraging.

There is one thing about the army: No matter where you are stationed, no one seems to know—or perhaps cares to tell you—much about anything. Given the fact that I was so new and didn't know what the hell I was doing, every little bit of information about my destination would have been welcomed; after all, it would have such a direct affect on my life. In the army it always seems to be hurry up and wait, and Vietnam was no exception.

This really was Vietnam. I still couldn't believe I was actually here. Being such a new soldier in this situation was more than a bit worrisome, to say the least. My great Vietnam War experience that I had looked forward to was about to begin for real.

This test of manhood, which I felt I had to go through in order to prove myself to myself—as well as to my brothers, friends, and relatives who had gone off to war before me—had truly begun after all. My feelings at the time was that if I didn't go to Vietnam I would never truly know if I had the right stuff or if I could hack it in "combat". Would I run? Would I freeze up? And most of all, would I let my fellow soldiers down? Well, now I had my opportunity. I'd gotten what I wanted, a combat assignment. Vietnam was for real now; it was no longer something I'd only read about or seen on TV. It was so very real that I could see it, I could feel it, and yes, I could even taste it. It was here, and it was now, and I was ready and eager to prove myself. Up until this time it had seemed so unreal; after all, a mere seventy-two hours earlier I was just getting off a United Airlines flight in from the States. I hadn't had my uniform on for thirty days prior, as I had been officially on leave.

Before leaving for Vietnam I'd driven cross-country with my best friend, Bill Wallace. He happened to be going to Vietnam the same time as I, the only difference being that he was in the Marines and would be shipping out as part of a unit from California a few weeks after I did. We were to spend some time in Vietnam together at the end of my tour, but I'll touch on that later.

Vietnam was such a very strange and foreign place. Words to describe it were hard to come by then, as they are today. Some words that do come to mind are *lush, tropical* and *very green,* as do *hot* and *humid.* The air also contained a red clay dust that you could never seem to wash off, no matter how hard you tried. I know that sounds like a contradiction, but that's what Vietnam was, on many levels: a contradiction. I think this fact alone was responsible for many deaths; if you were not on your highest alert at all times the land itself would find a way to take your life.

As we prepared to board the truck that was to take us north I was told that Cu Chi was the home of the Twenty-fifth Infantry Division, also known as the Tropic Lightning Division. This division was stationed in Hawaii and was personally ordered over to Vietnam by General Westmoreland himself. The division was highly trained in the art of jungle warfare, and I was proud to be a part of a group held in such high regard. As I was leaving, I took a good look around and realized just how big the base I was leaving really was. Bien Hoa Army Base was huge and I wondered if I would ever see it again. I realized then that this base would be my gateway home, back to my world, back to the States, and I resolved to do my damnedest to pass through its gates again.

The ride up to Cu Chi was very scary. No one really told us anything about where we was going or what to expect; all we could do was take our directions by the actions of the solders we were with. Some of the soldiers that were on the truck with us had been in-country for a while—you could tell by their tans as well as their worn uniforms. I would rely on my own instincts to survive this first trip to Cu Chi Base Camp. These instincts, as well as my training, would come into play more and more to help keep me alive as my time in the "combat zone" passed. This strangest of all places was called South Vietnam (The Pearl of the Orient) by the people back home, but to the guys who fought here it was just plain, Hell.

The trip north to Cu Chi Base Camp took only about an hour. Passing through the small villages along the way enlightened the senses as to how different this place called Vietnam really was. The people were so much smaller than we were, and, not to be mean, but they were not very good looking either. What struck me most, though, were all the young teenage boys we saw along the way. I thought, *If we are here to help these people fight for their freedom from their enemy, and we had come twelve thousand miles to do so, then why aren't these guys in uniform fighting for their own country?*

As our convoy pulled up to the Cu Chi base camp I couldn't help comparing it with an old Western army fort with guards on the towers and all. The only difference was that this base was made out of sandbags and barbed wire rather than poles of wood. But it was a "Fort" nevertheless. I was real glad to get off the truck and into the base camp; I felt a little safer behind the barbed wire. Barbed wire would become a friend as my tour of duty progressed. Cu Chi Base Camp was the home of the Twenty-fifth Infantry Division, housing approximately seven thousand soldiers. As my fate began to gain clarity, I grew increasingly concerned about my assignment to the 1/27 Wolfhounds.

My first night at Cu Chi Base Camp was confusing, as I was not immediately assigned to any outfit. I guess I just assumed I would be, but that wouldn't come until early the next morning. My first night at Cu Chi would pass without incident. This I can attest to personally, as I didn't sleep a bit, what with the constant artillery shelling and the flares hanging in the night sky to light up the perimeter, along with the machine guns shooting out their red tracer rounds. Christ, I thought that we would be overrun at any time. Here I was with my M16 rifle by my side, but I had no ammunition if the enemy were to attack. I felt kind of stupid to have a machine gun by my side with no bullets to put in it.

The next morning couldn't have come early enough for me. The base came alive and things started to happen. I was told to have my weapon and gear in order as I was moving out to Fire Support Base Chamberlain, ten miles further up-country and closer to the Cambodian border, a border that would have a profound effect on my life.

My short and tense truck ride up-country accompanied by a few other new guys was to be my morning's adventure. As the ten of us crossed the wire into Fire Support Base Chamberlain that morning, I just knew I was in deep shit. There couldn't have been two hundred soldiers stationed there. Now I was really getting concerned for my immediate safety. I had gone from Bien Hoa Army Base, with over twenty-five thousand guys, to the base at Cu Chi, with seven thousand guys, to a base manned by two hundred guys at most. I was to learn later that Chamberlain was named after a first lieutenant that had been killed in action in 1967 in this very same area.

Upon our arrival we were greeted by the First Sergeant of the base camp. He was a big, powerfully built black man, the kind of career soldier you would want to be with in combat, for you just knew nothing was going to happen to him over here. His name escapes me now, as many names would as my tour progressed. One of the unwritten rules of the war in Vietnam was *Don't get too close to the new guys,* as the odds were very good over there that if you were going to get killed it would happen in the first thirty days or so. As my tour in Vietnam proceeded I found this rule to be quite practical.

I had been trained in the States as a map-reader and a forward observer (an observer on the front lines who calls in artillery fire from distant fire bases and naval ships and also directs pilots where to drop their bombs) for the Infantry. This extremely small base was as far as I wanted to go into the combat zone. I figured the base was so small it was only a matter of time before the enemy would overrun us, but at least here I thought I had a fighting chance. The more I thought about it, the more I wondered where I would go if I were to be sent elsewhere. My mind must have been confused by all the heat and humidity because, yes, there was one last place I could go. Unbeknownst to me, my fate was being decided by that very same First Sergeant that I had met upon my arrival at Base Camp Chamberlain.

Chapter 3

I Meet My Team

As morning broke on my sixth day in-country I was awakened by a Buck Sergeant, who gave me the word that I would be leaving the relative safety of Fire Support Base (FSB) Chamberlain and would be going into the field. I was to have my shit ready in fifteen minutes; at that time a helicopter would be picking me up outside the main gate. Wow, helicopter! I thought. This would be my first time in a chopper and I was looking forward to it.

Back in basic training, the army had given all of us a battery of tests to see what we would best be suited to do. I had passed all the tests to go on to Helicopter Flight School; but going on to flight school had a hitch: you had to commit to the army for six years. I still might have taken them up on their offer but for one thing, and that was a big one: If you were to flunk out of flight training you would still have to fulfill your six-year commitment to the army. Hell, I was twenty-two years old, and the thought of six years in the army as opposed to what I was now committed to (two years), just seemed like a lifetime. I had no interest in making the army a career, so I turned down the Army's offer of learning to fly a helicopter. Looking back on it now, it may have been the biggest mistake of my life.

As I stood and waited for the chopper to arrive, I couldn't help but wonder where I would be going now. It had been quite a ride so far, and my tour had just begun. As the chopper came in I noticed that it was a small, four-man chopper with just the pilot on board. This seemed strange to me, but what the hell did I know anyway? This was going to be my first flight in a helicopter and I was very excited. The chopper landed, and I got on board. He motioned for me to put on the helmet that was on the seat beside me so we could communicate with one another in flight. This I did; he introduced himself, and I did the same. He mentioned we had to make one stop before we would reach our destination and that it wouldn't take very long. What did I care? Hell, he could've taken all day if he wanted to. After all, this was my first time in a chopper, and I was having a great time.

The sun was rising above the horizon now, revealing a breathtakingly beautiful countryside, with it's numerous shades of greens and browns. Water reflected off the rice paddies and I could clearly see the reddish browns of the small roads and trails that interconnected the villages below us. It was all so new to me and so exciting! With the cool wind blowing through my hair at three thousand feet, what more could I have asked for? I could have flown all day.

The stop we had to make was to pick up some mail. The mail was always in a big bright red bag. Why? Who knows, it's just the way it was. We were on the ground for only a few minutes, and then we were off again. This time we would be flying a lot closer to the ground, since we were not going very far. Off in the distance I could see some yellow smoke rising from the rice paddies. This signaled to the pilot where he was to put me down. As we landed I grabbed my weapon, jumped out of the chopper, and waved a farewell to the pilot as he lifted off into the bright morning sky.

After the chopper was gone I was left standing alone in a rice paddy in the middle of Vietnam. I must have stood there for only thirty seconds, but it sure as hell felt like a lifetime to me before someone came out of the tall elephant grass and bushes that were at the end of the rice paddy and waved me over to his location. As I breathlessly ran over to his position I was never so glad to see a fellow American as I was to see him. He shook my hand and said, "What's up, new guy?"

I was so relieved to see him I didn't know what to say. We made our way over to a small clearing, and there stood six other guys. They all came over to greet me as well. As I greeted them back I looked around for more soldiers, but there weren't any. I just stood there in shock. Here I was in the middle of Vietnam, and this was the team? Just the eight of us? Now the question was how was I going to survive this? Within the last twenty-four hours I had gone from a camp with upwards of twenty-five thousand men, to a team of eight. This was to be the Vietnam War I would know, and these were the men I would begin to fight it with. I made up my mind right then and there that I would suck it up, and I would survive Vietnam. What other choice did I have, now that I was here? And boy was I ever here, with a capital *H*.

The team leader was Captain Lewis; he was the commander of Alpha Company, and this was the company's command team. The other members of the team were from all over the country. One of the guys was right from my own back yard, Salem, Massachusetts. His name was Phil; he was a small, wiry, solidly built guy with dark, wavy, black hair. We got along right from the beginning—after all, we shared the same New England accent. Another guy was from Providence, Rhode Island. Butler was his name, and he was tall and thin. The other guys were from down South and out West. The Lieutenant that I would be working with was Lt. Baker. He had come all the way from Oklahoma to serve in Vietnam. Lt. Baker was older than the rest of us: all of twenty-eight. The Lieutenant was also assigned to the artillery, so in essence he was my boss. He would be my mentor in the field as well: I would learn more from him in a few weeks than I had learned in the past year of training to come to Vietnam. I would become so grateful for his teachings—and you know what? I don't remember ever thanking him; surely what I learned at his side helped me survive my tour.

The day was a couple of hours old now, and it was only 7:00 A.M. It was already getting hot, and having just arrived in from the States I was feeling the heat and humidity a lot more than the others. The sweat running down my back was proof positive of that. It would take me a while to get used to it.

We were packing up and getting ready to move out when Lt. Baker came over to me and gave me a canvass belt that held ten clips of extra ammo for my M16, with each clip holding twenty rounds. At this time I was also given a large Bowie Knife, six canteens of water to add to the couple I had brought with me, and a rucksack to keep my stuff in, along with a PRC-10 radio with an extra battery. The rucksack and the radio both had some dried blood on them. That was the reason I was here: the last guy that carried this stuff had been wounded and flown out the day before. Soldiers carrying radios were always the enemy's first target, because they were the ones who had the communications link with the outside, and it was best to eliminate them right from the beginning of any firefight. The weight of the stuff I was to carry must have been sixty pounds; if you add six canteens of water, food, and extra ammo for the M60 machine gun, I guess I was humping over eighty pounds on my back, and I felt every pound of it. It would seem to get heavier and heavier as my day progressed. The temperature during the day in Vietnam was always up in the high nineties. This only made the going that much more difficult for the grunts that called the jungles of Vietnam home.

Everyone was up on his feet now getting ready to move out, but no one was really saying very much. It was kind of like they knew just what to do and began to move out as a team, for their morning patrol. As I stood there trying not to fall over backwards, I found this to be of some comfort.

Phil moved out first; he had the point this morning. Being on point in Vietnam was by far the most dangerous position to be in. The point-man would be the first to contact the enemy, as well as the most likely to trip a booby trap, but he was also the most experienced, so it only made sense that he should draw the assignment. We moved slowly through the thick underbrush and high grass trying not to make too much noise, but with all the gear we were carrying that was pretty much impossible to do at times. We probably sounded like a herd of elephants smashing our way through that thick jungle, but for the most part we did okay. We did the best that we could—we didn't want to alert the enemy to our presence. What we were doing was searching for the enemy in our area of operations (AO). If we found any we would then make up our minds whether to engage them or to wait and call in for reinforcements. The situation would dictate what we would do, and every situation would be different.

Our AO (area of operations) at this time was twenty miles west of Cu Chi, bordering the Vam Co Dong River that ran along the Cambodian border. This area was known in Vietnam as a "Free Fire Zone", which meant anything that moved was considered the enemy and would be shot on sight. The local populace knew this, as well as we did and they would stay out of this area, kind of a Vietnamese "No Man's Land".

We'd been on the move for over an hour now, and my pack along with the radio and the rest of my gear was really starting to dig into my shoulders. It was just so goddamn hot, and the humidity was starting to rise. It seemed like I had one of my canteens of water at my mouth at all times. I just couldn't seem to get enough to drink, at times I thought I was going to pass out. I needed to get off my feet and take a rest before I did, but it wasn't time yet to take a break, so I would just have to gut it out until it was. I just prayed that we would stop soon.

The sun climbed higher in the sky as we walked along between the high grass and the tree line. We always found the tree line area the safest to be in, because we wouldn't be so exposed from a distance, but it did have the disadvantage of the possibility of ambush from the tree line itself. It was a tradeoff, as so much of our activities would be in the jungles and rice paddies of Vietnam.

As we slowly made our way down the trail that would take us closer to the river, three shots rang out in quick succession, very sharp and very loud. It took me completely by surprise and scared the hell out of me. Within a microsecond, so many things raced through my mind: What was I supposed to do? What was my function going to be? Who was doing the shooting? Was it the enemy, or was it our point-man? Lieutenant Baker scrambled back to my position, keeping as low a profile as he could. He could see the scared look on my face—Hell, I was petrified. I was down on one knee, sweat was running down my face and dripping off my nose, and my heart was beating a mile a minute. I had needed a break, but this wasn't what I had in mind.

The jungle had gone quiet—deathly quiet—and not a sound could be heard. My eyes darted about, and my ears strained to pick up the slightest sound to help me make a decision, as to what my next move should be. I strained instinctively not to move a muscle. Lt. Baker leaned over and whispered for me to keep my head down and to follow his lead, as we had just run into a Viet Cong patrol. Our point-man Phil had surprised the enemy and had gotten off a few rounds as they fled. They were looking over the situation as to what our next move should be. In the meantime he would call our position into FSB Chamberlain for artillery cover, just in case we needed it.

Captain Lewis had decided to take a look at what he thought we were up against. We would not call for reinforcements at this time, for he felt secure with his decision to search out and engage the Viet Cong (VC) by ourselves. The mere fact that there was no return fire from the enemy after Phil had spotted them, helped him make this decision. He didn't feel the enemy force would be too large for us not to handle. What was he talking about, for Christ's sake—there were only the eight of us, I thought. We began to move up to where Phil was kneeling down waiting for us. As his position was only about twenty yards in front of us, we got there rather quickly. As we raced up to him he motioned for us to stay low, as he thought there could be more of the enemy in the area. The feeling was that the lower we could keep ourselves the less of a target we would be, and thus the likelihood of one of us becoming a casualty would lessen. The whole situation was so new to me and so scary, that all I could do was follow directions to the best of my ability. And hope I didn't get shot doing so.

As we searched for the enemy we would move very slowly and keep as low a profile as we could, taking care not to make a sound. We would use hand signals to communicate with each other. We searched for fifteen minutes, and no contact with the enemy was made. All we found was some fresh blood trails leading off into the thick underbrush and followed them for a while, but they faded off into the jungle. As we continued our search for the enemy it was beginning to feel like a dance: They would go one way, and we would follow; we would go another, and they would follow. We felt they were close, real close. The fact that they didn't want to expose themselves to us was frustrating; we knew from the blood trails that Phil had wounded one or more of them. But we didn't know how many there were, and they probably didn't know how many of us there were either. We were dancing, dancing with the enemy, as a moth will dance with a flame, taking care not to get too close.

And so would the enemy dance with us throughout my tour. We knew that unless they had us outnumbered by three or four to one they would be crazy to engage us, because with our artillery and helicopter support only a call away, they would be annihilated if they did. It was estimated that the kill ratio was thirty to one in our favor during any engagement with the enemy during the Vietnam War, and I believe it.

After an hour or so we ended our search. The dance was over for now, and it looked as if we had won this one; at least we thought so, and that was all that really mattered to us. As for me, it had been my first encounter with the enemy, and I was relieved that it was over. The fact that all of us were in one piece was a great feeling as well, because that fact could have changed in a matter of a heartbeat. We took a break and made our plans to hook up with the rest of the platoon, which was patrolling within a couple of clicks (two thousand yards) of our position.

It only took us about forty-five minutes of constant walking to reach the rest of First Platoon. They were out in the same area as we were but just a little further north of us. If we had really run into a large force of VC this morning, they would have been able to reach our position within a short time. The one thing about our movements as a platoon, as well as a company was the fact that we would always have one another covered at all times. There was a hell of a lot of comradeship and pride amongst the men of the 1/27 Wolfhounds, and I was now part of them.

The platoon had on any given day twenty-five men attached to it. This figure could go as high as thirty if everyone was on-line, but with sick calls and leaves and of course R & R (rest and recuperation) there were usually twenty to twenty-five men in the field. Today in the platoon there were twenty-six of us. I was attached to the captain's command team. Captain Lewis would spend some time with each team and each platoon. He was the commander of Alpha Company, and this was his prerogative. For this reason I would be moving around a lot, because as a member of the command team I would have to go with the Captain and Lieutenant Baker. This would have its down-side, because I was never really with any one platoon long enough to become close to them. On the other hand, it let me get to know the whole company, and I believe this is why the captain liked to move around all the time.

The other thing about being with the command team was that we would always go where the action was. The Captain would always want to be with his men whenever and wherever the fighting was taking place. If the action was far enough away from us, he would think nothing of calling in a chopper to pick us up and take us into the battle. This would have its good points and its bad points, as well.

After just one day in the field and some contact with the enemy, I was starting to feel like I was part of the team. I knew I would have a long way to go to prove myself to my fellow soldiers, but at least I felt I was on my way to doing so.

Chapter 4

Taking A Break

After a short walk in the hot noon day sun we reached the stand-down area and met up with the rest of the platoon. There was some good-natured kidding all around about the gooks we let get away that morning; after all we were out there for the body count. A large body count meant something to everyone. It made the captain look good to his superiors. Given the fact that he was a lifelong army man and a graduate of West Point, it was important for him to look good-- if he was going to move up the corporate ladder; anyone could see that. Even so, it kind of rubbed me the wrong way that someone had to die for someone else to look good. I was new in-country and it would take a while for that feeling to leave my head—but leave it would.

The team with the highest body count that week got to rotate into FSB Chamberlain for a couple of days of guard duty, which was a hell of lot better than sleeping out here in the jungle—and a hell of a lot safer, to boot. The body count was all-important for many reasons, not the least of which was that there would be less of the enemy to contend with. Less of the enemy? That was a joke; they would just keep on coming, no matter what the body count was. We would find that out the hard way in the coming months.

The better part of each day we spent checking all of our equipment to make sure everything was in good working order. The heat and humidity of this country really did a number on it. We would clean our weapons, and I also had the responsibility of making sure my radio was in perfect working order, as well.

As an RTO (radio transmission operator), my duty would be to communicate with the Artillery Batteries in the area to call in artillery support as needed. There were two RTOs on the command team; the captain's RTO communicated with the Infantry division headquarters to call in more troops as needed and to maintain a direct line with the Colonel in charge of the Battalion.

I really didn't mind carrying the radio that much; it had its good points and its bad points. One of the good points was that I was always in contact with my base as well as any helicopters or jets that were in the area. The bad thing about it was that I would be the logical choice for the enemy to shoot at in a firefight. The radio had an eight-foot antenna protruding out of the top of it, and that was very hard to hide while out on patrol. It also made walking through the thick jungle pretty darn near impossible at times.

Our food would be delivered in twelve meal boxes whenever we were in a stand-down situation, as we were at this time. Given the fact that we had to carry everything we had, what we would do is pick the food out of the boxes that we wanted or thought we wanted to carry; this would help to keep our load as light as possible. For the year I was in-country I think I lived on fruit cocktail and hot chocolate and pound cake for my entire tour. What we didn't want we would shop around and trade with one another; whatever was leftover would be destroyed. We were great at destroying things we didn't want. What other choice did we have? Everything came in cans, and we didn't want to leave anything for the enemy to use against us. (The enemy would pack those cans with explosives and use them as booby traps against us). It was just a shame that all this food had to go to waste. The little kids we would see in the villages we would go through during the day looked so thin and malnourished that they could have used that food. But this was war, and we were under orders.

It was noontime now, and everyone was taking a break. We had been up for most of the night, and we had earned it. A perimeter was set up around us with listening posts set out fifty yards or so; this was our usual procedure—we didn't need any surprises. This was also a good time for Lieutenant Baker and I to get together and go over the dos and don'ts of radio procedure.

I was new to the radio, and he showed me everything I would have to know. He explained to me that at this time our radio call signs were the following: Our base camp call sign at this time was "Two Eight," and he was "Two Eight Echo," and I was "Two Eight Echo Bravo." These call signs would change many times during my tour. We would have to say these call words every time we were on the radio. It was very important that we follow correct radio procedure, as there were other platoons using the same radio frequency, and the guys back at the fire support base would need to know to whom they were talking. Even though after a while the guys at the base would come to recognize my voice and know it was me by my "Boston" accent, I would still always use the call signs whenever I had any communication with the base.

As my tour progressed I became a lot closer to a couple of the guys I was with at our first stand-down. One of these soldiers was Phil, who was from north of Boston. Phil would take me under his wing and teach me some of the finer points of surviving the jungles of Vietnam. He would show me what to watch out for and explain to me the importance of always using my instincts and my common sense in combat.

I may have received some of the best jungle training the army had to offer, back in the States but being here and living it would be very different indeed. Phil was a great guy, and I'm glad I got to know him as well as I did. We were approximately the same age and kind of wanted the same things out of this place: to survive and go home and get on with the rest of our lives. We really didn't talk about anything in particular, just general things, but that was how it was over here, you didn't want to get too close to each other. I really don't know why; I guess it was in case one of you got killed, the other guy wouldn't mourn as much. But that really wasn't it, because all of us were so close that we would've done anything for that not to happen. There's a saying that there is no bond greater than that forged by men who have faced death together in combat and I believe that is true. So as much as we may have tried to keep some personal things to ourselves and not share them with each other, it just didn't work out that way. When a fellow soldier went down, it would hurt—and hurt a lot. It would be something that you would never completely forget; just when you thought that memory was fading into the past it would come and visit you during the night, more vivid than ever, and would never completely release its ugly grasp on you.

I must have dozed off for a few hours, which didn't surprise me; I don't believe I had gotten more than a few hours sleep in the past week. Phil came over to awaken me and asked if I wanted to go out on a little patrol with him, Jackson and Bernier. At this time our location was very close to the river, and there were always tunnels and hiding places that the enemy would use during the day to take a break in. Phil was getting kind of bored with just hanging out, waiting to go out on the night's ambush. So what could I say? I was new and I had to learn everything I could, as fast as I could in order to survive. And after all, isn't this why I was here, to find the enemy and kill him before he had an opportunity to kill me? So I said sure, even though I could have passed on this one. I grabbed my M16 and off we went in search of the enemy.

Phil said we wouldn't be going out too far. This was reassuring to me, as I didn't know what the hell I was doing and I really didn't want to get killed my first week in the field, now did I? Our patrol took us along the riverbank; we kept as quiet as possible looking to surprise the VC if we could, and it didn't take long to find him. We were only two hundred yards from our stand-down area and the rest of the company, when Phil who was up front as usual on this small four-man patrol put up his arm and motioned for us to stop; he had spotted something along the river's edge. He motioned us up by the use of hand signals. As we moved very slowly and quietly towards him, I could see a large mound of dirt, mud, and small tree branches in front of us. We had not spoken a word since Phil put up his hand. I'd maneuvered myself into a position to be able to see what Phil was up to. Phil was now right against the mound and had a hand grenade out and was preparing to pull the pin on it and throw it into a small opening on top of the mound. From my vantage point I could see the very small hole that he was aiming for just on the other side. Phil looked back at us and kind of smiled—this was why he was out here: to find the hiding places of the enemy and destroy them before they had a chance to destroy us.

He pulled the pin and threw it right through that small hole in the mound. He ran back to us, and we all took cover as the grenade went off. The blast wasn't as loud or destructive, as I would have imagined. The earth only rose up a little and settled back down, with some black smoke coming out of the hole in its side. Phil and Bernier ran up to the position and let go with a couple of bursts of machine-gun fire into what was left of the mound. If there had been anyone alive after that grenade went off, there certainly wasn't now. The four of us checked it out a little and moved on. We weren't going to go poking around in that mound for fear of any booby traps that may have been set inside. Phil felt pretty sure if there were anyone in there now they wouldn't be bothering anyone anytime soon.

We made our way back to the stand-down area and started to get our gear in order for the night's ambush patrol. Phil was feeling pretty good about himself right about now; he surmised if anyone had been in that hiding place they wouldn't be out tonight to ambush us on our way to our night's position. And that was just fine with him; this was a war, and people get killed in war—better the enemy than one of us. I had to agree with him on that.

When dusk arrived, it was time for us to move out. We checked our gear and locked and loaded our weapons, and applied a dark creamy camouflage to our faces at this time—anything to take the shine off our skin and help us blend into the jungle better. We would take great care to move as quietly as possible so as not to be detected by the enemy on our way to our ambush site. The patrol wanted to be in position so that by the time it got dark we would be all set up. A group of soldiers moving to their ambush site in the dark would be in a very vulnerable position, for there would be other patrols out in our area as well.

The other men of First Platoon were also getting ready to move out; there would be three ambushes put into position by First Platoon this evening. Lieutenant Baker came over to me to make sure I had everything in order for my first night's patrol. I believed I had, but it was very nice of him to come over and check me out anyway. The area we wanted to set up our ambush in was out about five hundred yards from us. We figured it would take us about thirty minutes to get there, and we wanted to arrive just as it was getting dark. The timing could be critical for us, as we wanted to set up shop without the enemy being able to see us doing so. But we didn't want to be moving in the darkness, as they might set up an ambush of their own, and then we would be in a world of shit. As we moved out, I checked my communications with Fire Support Base Chamberlain and with the other radiomen on the other ambush patrols.

It was kind of like coordinating a stage production. Everyone had to be in their right positions at the right time for it to come off with the least amount of danger to any of the troops of Alpha Company. I could see by how smooth it was all coming together that these guys had done this many times before and were very good at it.

We found the area that Captain Lewis had designated as our night's ambush position. It was at the intersection of two trails. We were able to position ourselves so that we could see what was coming along both trails; it was perfect and right where we wanted it to be. We had ourselves situated behind a small stone wall, where we figured we could see them before they could see us. It would be Phil's responsibility to come around and give out the guard times for the night. Two guys would be awake at all times.

We would get two hours' guard duty and four hours' sleep throughout the night. This came out just about right, as there was a good eight hours of real darkness for us to contend with during the night.

As we settled in for the night, Lieutenant Baker came over and wanted me to call in our position and our artillery points. These points of reference were of the utmost importance to our patrol. They would give the artillery back at Chamberlain the points on the map to shoot at if we needed them. We would call in a number, such as number two, for example. The guys back at the base would already have this point of reference plotted on their map and could get us out the support we needed in the least amount of time possible. In combat, sometimes seconds can mean the difference between life and death. After the points were given to the fire support base, we settled in for the night's ambush.

Being out on an ambush felt kind of strange; after all, hadn't we all grown up with the idea that ambushing one's enemy was the coward's way of fighting? In all the cowboy movies I had ever seen, the cowboys never ambushed anyone—only the bad guys did that! The good guys always gave the other guy a fighting chance, a warning to come out and fight like a man, if you will. Win or lose, the fight always had to be fair, right? Well, I was to learn that this was as far from Hollywood as one could get, and fair had nothing to do with reality. In the jungles of South Vietnam, it was kill or be killed. So we did whatever it took to survive.

The VC (Viet Cong) were springing ambushes on us every chance they got, either by shooting us outright or by setting up booby traps that were designed to maim us by taking our legs off or worse. All we were trying to do was beat them at their own game, and whatever worked was fine with us. This wasn't Kansas, Toto—this was the real deal, and we were going to do whatever it took to stay alive for 365 days and then go home and try to forget all about the things we had done in order to survive. If we were lucky enough to make it home, that is. It would then be important to put this place behind us and get on with our lives after experiencing this madness called Vietnam.

As I leaned back and looked up into the sky that first night on ambush, for the first time I took note of how quiet it was and how dark it had become. The sky was big, clear, and full of stars; I'd never seen so many stars. The sky was also moonless this night—maybe that's why there were so many stars out? The Vietnam sky at night was always full of flares off in the distance, lighting up the areas around the numerous fire support bases that dotted the countryside. And almost nightly there would be B-52 strikes to contend with as well. Let me tell you, a B-52 strike will get your attention and get it real fast. The tremendous, earthshaking explosions that they would unleash upon the earth were so powerful and of such inconceivable force that it is impossible for me to explain them adequately. But on this night, at least for a while, everything was very quiet.

As I sat there, I started to take stock of my situation. Here I was, over twelve thousand miles from home, sitting in the pitch darkness on ambush, waiting for the enemy to walk by, so I could kill him. That was the reality of my situation, and it was starting to weigh on me. I wondered why I was here and how I ever got here? I mean, how did I really get here? To answer that question I would have to go back, back to my upbringing, as that was truly the beginning of the path that would take me here, here to the killing fields of Vietnam.

Chapter 5

How Did I Really Get Here?

I was born December 10, 1946, in the city of Brockton, Massachusetts. My parents' names were Frederick and Kathleen Watkins. At the time of my birth I had a brother Frederick and a sister Louise waiting for me, and I would soon have another brother named Harold, who was to come along fifteen months later. My brother Harold and I are what you would call classic post–World War II babies, in that we were fathered by a soldier who had just come back from fighting the Good War, the Just War, World War II, and was in a hurry to get back to normal and either start a family or increase the one he already had before he went away.

My upbringing was typical for the times. I was born into a family of the working class poor of this country. We didn't seem to want for much, but we didn't seem to have very much either. We were just very normal for the neighborhood I was raised in. Everyone seemed to be in the same rut of living from paycheck to paycheck, never really having anything extra without taking it away from someplace else. It's a very frustrating way to live, and I can now see why alcohol played such a large part in everyone's lives. No one seemed to know any different, nor did they seem to care; you don't miss what you have never had.

My father drove a truck for a living and seemed to be on the road most of the time. When he wasn't working he could always be found in some barroom with his buddies. I never seemed to see him all that much when I was growing up. Consequently, I really didn't get to know him as well as I would have liked. My father eventually left the family when I was ten years old and went to live by himself. That was a very sad day in my young life. But I guess his drinking had become too much for my mother to take on a daily basis.

My mother was a very patient woman, but my father's drinking finally just wore her out. Knowing the financial hardship this decision would bring upon the family and herself, she very bravely made the decision to ask my father to leave the house. I remember the relief I felt; living in that house with all the fights that the drinking brought about became unbearable at times. As I look back on the situation now, I can see why he did what he did and acted the way he did; with the passing of time I have learned to understand and love my father more than ever, even with all his faults. If I have one regret in life, it's that I never really sat down with him and told him how I really felt about him deep in my heart. I'm not making excuses or condoning his behavior—or mine, for that matter—it's just that I can better understand him now. It took me years to figure it out, but now I know and I'm glad I do.

I never really got that close to my father. Maybe I didn't try or maybe he didn't, I don't really know; but it was probably a combination of both. For the longest time I thought he just plain didn't like me, and I dealt with the rejection, as painful as it was, the best I could. I now have a much better understanding as to what his troubles were and where they came from; I only wish I could have been of some help to him. But what could a ten-year-old boy do to help his father? To this day I miss him and would give anything to sit down with him and have a nice, heart-to-heart talk. But I can't, and I wish I could, and that bothers me.

It seems like a lot of things I have done—whether they were good or bad, right or wrong—were an attempt to reach out to him to get him to recognize me and give his approval or just acknowledge the fact that I was there and that I loved him. I don't think I was asking for so much: just a pat on the back for a job well done and the words *I love you* would have gone a long way; in fact, they would have lasted me a lifetime.

My mother, thank God, was another matter. I have always felt loved and appreciated by her. As tired as she must have been after working all day in a shoe factory and then coming home and taking care of the family, she always seemed to have some time left for me. She would at least listen to me and try to understand the little problems that I may have been having at that time in my life. She may not have been able to relate to them, or to me for that matter, but at least she listened; and for that I am forever grateful.

My mother had her faults, just like the rest of us, but she was able to keep a lot of her thoughts to herself. I always thought everything was just grand with the family. It was only years later that I was to realize all she had sacrificed and gone without in order to keep us all together. As I look back on it now, I think she must have been a pretty good actress because I never saw it. But what does a teenage boy really see besides his own wants and desires anyway?

There were times after my father left home that we would all go without, but none more so than my mother. Here was a woman in her mid-forties, with her own wants, desires, needs, and dreams, which she literary sacrificed for us—a woman who was at the top of her class in high school and who dreamed of going on to college and becoming a teacher (and a great one she would have made, too). Here she was, working all day in that hot, dirty shoe factory, so tired by the end of the day that it was all she could do to walk home and fall into bed—all so she could get the energy to get back up the next morning and do it all over again, day in and day out. My mother had sacrificed her personal dreams and aspirations in life to be a full-time mother to us, her sometimes very ungrateful children. They just don't make mothers like her very often. To think how lucky I was to have had her as mine: I feel so very special and so very grateful. Without her teachings and her to look up to over the years I don't know what would have become of my siblings, or me either.

One thing my mother always had time for, no matter how tired she was, was a good game of cards. Any kind of cards would do: whist, rummy, poker—it didn't matter, she would always be there ready to play. She didn't win very often, but that didn't seem to matter; she just wanted to play. I guess she just enjoyed the action. Some of my earliest memories are of playing cards with her. My mother is now eighty-nine years young, and I believe her long and healthy life can be attributed to her optimistic outlook and the sacrifices she made along the way. I'm grateful to have had her in my life for so long.

When I visit her now, we will play cards well into the night and enjoy every minute of it. She still never seems to win, and it still doesn't seem to bother her.

Some of my thoughts at night on ambush patrols would be of friends and of people who greatly influenced me over the years, although they were more than likely unaware of it. It seemed like everyone—or just about everyone—I grew up with went to Vietnam; it became a badge of passage for the group of guys I grew up with. It seemed that if you didn't go, there was a good reason you didn't. But I'll tell you this—I feel everyone I was close to as a teenager would have gone without question.

My younger brother Harold went and came home, as did my best friend Bill Wallace. Bill was someone I had looked up to and admired ever since I met him when we were just teenagers hanging around the corner trying to figure out what we were going to do with our young lives. Bill didn't have a father at home either, and I think we kind of played off each other in this respect. He would be the first to go into the service, as a Marine, in (I believe) January of 1965. Bill had just turned seventeen years old. That's right—seventeen years old. How young he was and how scared he must have been to go to Vietnam at such a young age. When he came home after his first tour of duty in Vietnam a couple of years later, he was quite a different young man than when he had left. The change in him has stuck with me ever since.

I have always had the greatest respect and admiration for Bill; he's someone I've always looked up to and trusted, a man that I am proud to say is my friend. I only hope that I've been as good a friend to him as he has been to me over the years. After spending time with him upon his return from Vietnam I knew that I would also be going into the service and from there on to my time in Vietnam. I only hoped that I could make him as proud of me as I was of him. Going into the service and serving our country in Vietnam was the best decision of our lives. The lessons about life we learned there we couldn't have learned anywhere else.

There were also guys I grew up with who went to Vietnam and didn't come home, and my thoughts would be of them on some of those nights I was out on patrol. I would wonder if basically the sights and sounds and smells that I was experiencing were the same ones they had also experienced, and I always said a silent prayer that this night on patrol wouldn't be my last, as one such night had been for them. I would also say a prayer for them and truly hoped that they hadn't suffered as they made the ultimate sacrifice for their buddies who were with them at their last.

We all have people who come in and out of ours lives as we grow up; some of them we can't even remember, and some of them we can't forget. Sometimes as I would sit there in the darkness feeling scared and all alone, out on patrol waiting for something to happen but praying nothing would, my mind would go back to some of these people. I never told them the effect that they had had on my life, so how would they know? Not telling them is something I regret to this very day. Even after I came home, you would think I would have sought these people out and given them thanks for helping me through some of those nights in Vietnam. But I didn't, and I don't really know why.

One of those very special people was Mrs. Ann McEachern, my high school adviser in the tenth grade. There was a glow about her; she was so much in love with life and had so much to give that it was contagious. She wasn't someone I saw every day, but when I had the opportunity to stop by her office I always did, and I always felt much better for having spent time with her. I'm sure I wasn't the only one who felt that way about her.

Mrs. McEachern helped me out in many different ways, ways that I'm sure she never even realized. She was truly the first person outside of my family to give me a sense of self-worth, a sense of meaning to my life. I had never met anyone like her before. During my tour in Vietnam I would sometimes stop for a moment to look for some direction as to what was right or wrong and what course should be taken. I would stop and ask myself, *What would she have done in this situation, if she were here? How would she have handled this situation?* I asked myself those questions over there on many occasions, as I would throughout my life. I thank you, Mrs. McEachern; you have lived a very meaningful life and I am so proud to have known you and called you my friend.

Mr. Harry Allen: now there was an unforgettable teacher. As I look back now on the whole process of my formal education, the one teacher I took with me to Vietnam was Mr. Allen. Some nights on ambush patrol my mind would fade back to senior English, Class of 1966.

Mr. Allen was quite a guy, and a great teacher. He seemed a lot older than we were at the time, but who didn't? In reality he was probably all of ten or twelve years our senior, at most. He had a real feel for education in its purest form. What do I mean by this? For example, on our very first day of senior English class I remember him saying to us that he felt that whatever we were going to learn about the English language he was sure we had already been taught. So what he was going to try to attempt to teach us now was what to expect when we left high school and went out into the real world. Boy, he really got my attention that first day, and I never missed his class my entire senior year.

Mr. Allen had so much to offer us and teach us about life. He taught us the basics of life, things like taking responsibility for our own actions. "Stand up like a man and be counted," he would say. One of Mr. Allen's favorite subjects was the Korean War. He was a Korean War veteran and was very proud of this fact—rightfully so, I might add. War was of great interest to us guys because we all knew that the majority of us would be going off to war, as Mr. Allen had before us. We were very interested in what he had to say, as he had really been there. It was the first and only time in my education that I could really ask a teacher questions about real life and get a true answer from someone who had really been there. It was refreshing to have a teacher that I felt was from the real world, not someone I felt had spent his or her entire life hiding out in academia. I would call back to those days and Mr. Allen's teachings many times in Vietnam. I thank you again, Mr. Allen, and I salute you for your service to your country, as well as to me, one of your very grateful students.

Melanie Sullivan is one other person I would like to mention at this time. Mel's presence in my life had a great influence on me and she was a very special friend during my high school years. She always had an encouraging word for me whenever we would meet and that is one thing that has stayed with me all these years. She was and I'm sure still is the most beautiful person I had ever seen, both on the inside, as well as the outside. My mind would often wander back to her while I was out on those long-range patrols in enemy territory. Thoughts of her would remind me of how simple life really was back in high school. Mel married an old friend of mine named Rob Florio and when they got married I was very happy for them both. I haven't seen her for many years now, but I pray she and Rob are well. Thank-you again Mel and may "God" always be at your side.

I would be untruthful if I were to say that John McGrath never entered my thoughts on those long nights on patrol in the jungles of Southeast Asia. John was a special kind of friend to me. He was someone I felt I had to look out for, as he was always doing something dumb, like getting into trouble over nothing, being in places he shouldn't be, and saying things he shouldn't be saying to people he had no right saying them to. He would always come to me for help or advice—not that he ever took any of it, as far as I know. But as I look back on it now, most of the time I was probably the last person to get advice from.

John was one of those guys who would have been better off if he had served in Vietnam. I would have given anything to have had him by my side during some of those long days and nights on patrol; we could have learned so much together. Jack wanted to go to Vietnam early on, as so many of his friends and relatives had before him, but he was newly married with a beautiful little baby girl, and the government wouldn't take him. By the time all the single guys had been used up in Vietnam and they were starting to take the married guys as well, we had all come home and Jack would have had to go in alone. The time for Vietnam service had come and gone, and Jack didn't want to go any longer, now that everyone had already finished serving.

I could see that—I wouldn't have gone under those circumstances myself, but I feel Jack always regretted not having gone to Vietnam. When we as a group would get together for a few beers after the war and the conversation would turn to war stories, I could always see something in Jack's eyes. Jack was not stupid; he knew he had missed out on the greatest adventure of our generation, and he didn't want to be reminded of it. I would always try to change the subject, if I could, because I knew it hurt Jack and he was my friend and I would have done anything not to have Jack hurt.

John McGrath would leave this world at the age of thirty-nine; I miss him terribly to this very day. Oh, they say it was the alcohol that killed him, but I know it wasn't. I believe it was the fact that all his friends left home and served their country in Vietnam, and he couldn't go because of his married status that really killed him. So in the long run it was Vietnam that indirectly killed Jack. One didn't even have to go to Vietnam to have it kill you; Jack was proof of that. I miss you terribly Jack; rest in peace.

Chapter 6
My First Ambush

We set up our ambush position right outside of a small farming village with the name of Trang Bang. It was very much like all the other farming villages in the area: population approximately five hundred people, with just as many farm animals. The animals helped these people farm this hot and dangerous place they called home. The night was passing very slowly for me. I still hadn't gotten a good night's sleep in-country, and I was exhausted from all the walking we had done this day. But the smells and sounds of this strange land, as well as the hardness of the ground that I was trying to make a bed of, just wouldn't allow me to doze off completely.

It was well after midnight when the sounds of Vietnamese words being spoken off in the distance got our attention. My eyes were wide open, and my ears strained to pick up any kind of directions from my fellow soldiers as to what was going to happen next. What would be expected of me in the next few minutes? I didn't want to make a rookie mistake in this situation and get myself or someone else killed. So as the moments passed I continued to lie there as still as possible and waited to see what was going to happen. I felt like a spectator and I guess I was but I was also part of the situation as well. It was a very stressful position for me to be in, as I waited in the darkness to see what would develop.

Everyone in the platoon was on their highest alert; and we were as quiet and motionless as humanly possible. A couple of machine guns being taken off of safety and clicked over to full automatic were the only sounds that I could hear. However, those sounds were ever so slight that one would have had to been right next to them to hear it being done. Lieutenant Baker was lying right beside me now, having crawled over from his normal ambush position, which was always alongside the captain. He leaned over to me and said, "Rich, hug the ground and stay as low as you possibly can and do not fire your weapon when we blow the "bush" (ambush)". I didn't question this "order" as I was in unfamiliar territory, and he had been here before and knew exactly what he was doing. Lieutenant Baker was a good man, as well as a great officer, the kind of person that you would readily follow into combat, unlike some of the other officers I was to meet over here.

The sounds of voices speaking in Vietnamese were now getting a lot closer to our position, as I strained to hear them I was also trying to figure out how many of them there were. I'm sure that was exactly what Captain Lewis was trying to do also, before he gave the command to open fire and blow the voices in the darkness to oblivion. There were only eight of us in this ambush position, and even though we had the element of surprise on our side we didn't want to bite off more than we could chew. It was two o'clock in the morning in the pitch-dark jungle outside of a village that was not known to be very friendly to U.S. forces, and we would not be in a good position if we blew this ambush on a hundred or so of the enemy.

The voices were very close to us now, yet we still couldn't see them. They seemed to be chatting away as if they didn't have a care in the world; a slight bit of laughter could also be heard in their voices, as they passed right in front of us. It struck me as odd that these soldiers would not have had more discipline than this; after all, they were walking a trail at night in a "Free Fire Zone". It was a well-known fact that this area was a notorious enemy infiltration route and had been so for years. They would have had to figure we would have our ambushes set up all over this entire area, wouldn't they?

As they passed right in front of me I felt I could almost reach out and touch them—they were that close to me now. My eyes strained to bring them into focus but I couldn't quite see them yet, it was so goddamn dark. I was concerned that they would look over our way and see us, but they didn't look our way at all. Through this complete darkness a few figures were coming into focus, and the shadows that I began to make out looked more like small children than enemy soldiers, for they appeared to be so small. So this was the enemy, I thought, as I tried to get a closer look.

As I continued to strain my eyes to get a better look at the enemy, three very loud explosions shook the ground and pierced the soundless night air. It felt like all hell had broken loose. The explosions were right in front of us, and it scared the hell out of me. We had blown the ambush on the silhouetted figures; their cries of pain would stay with me long after the ambush was over. Our machine-gun bullets pierced their flesh and tore through their bodies as if they were rag-dolls full of blood.

The idea of an ambush was to eliminate the enemy long before he had a chance to return fire, and everyone except me had let loose with everything they had. The deafening sounds of machine-gun fire that sent red tracer bullets screaming through the air aimed directly at the unsuspecting enemy right in front of us, took me by surprise. They were so close to us that if we had wanted, we could have reached out and grabbed them. At that exact same moment, three more claymore mines that we had set up earlier in the evening were also detonated. Their lethal power and deadliness was a shock to me. The suddenness of the act, even though I knew it was about to happen, lingers in the back of my mind to this very day. I can still recall it, as if it happened yesterday. It was such a brutal and final act to be a witness to. The killing of these enemy soldiers had only taken a few seconds at most.

The sounds of gunfire and mines going off was now over, all that was left was the smell of the gunpowder, a choking acid residue that would hang in the air long after the shooting had ended. Not a sound was heard from the shadowy figures that only a few moments before had been walking directly in front of us. We had completely annihilated them. It dawned on me that not one shot had been fired back at us; we hadn't given them a chance to return fire at all. Not getting any return fire from the enemy was the mark of a successful ambush, pulled off with perfection, and we were all quite pleased with our night's work.

But now it was time for us to get out of the area. We couldn't really be sure as to how many of the enemies had been on that patrol. We felt we had gotten them all, but we never could be completely sure. So we put our gear back together and prepared to move out with our machineguns at our sides, locked and loaded ready for any surprises. We took one last look around so as not to leave anything behind and moved out quietly and very slowly.

Moving out of an ambush position sounds a lot easier than it really is. First of all, everyone for a mile or so around you knows an ambush has been effected; what they don't know is the outcome of said ambush, and this includes the bad guys as well as the good guys. Our most vulnerable time out at night was when we were moving, for we could get ambushed ourselves by our own troops, not to mention the bad guys. The first thing we had to do was let everyone in our area know who we were and the direction in which we would be moving. This would be the responsibility of the RTO (radio transmission operator). As soon as this was completed it would be safe for us to move out.

We moved along ever so slowly on our hands and knees, trying our best not to make a sound. We didn't really have to travel all that far, maybe a couple of hundred yards or so—just far enough to get out of the area; that's really all we wanted to do. We would then set up another ambush, and who knows; maybe we would get lucky again this night. At first light we would make our way back to the first ambush site to see by the early morning light more clearly what exactly had taken place a few hours earlier.

The rest of that night I would spend sitting up, wide-awake, running the ambush through my mind, over and over again. It seemed so brutally final. That's about the best word I could think of to describe it: so goddamn *final*.

It had been four hours since the ambush, and hardly a word had been spoken about what had just happened a few hours previous. The sun rises off to our east very early each morning in Vietnam, but not early enough for me this morning; it had been quite a night, and I really needed to talk a little about it with the guys I was with. I particularly wanted to speak to Lieutenant Baker and get his feel for what had happened. Was this something that I could expect on a nightly basis, or what? I was still so new—and very scared. I needed to speak to someone about what had just happened.

As the sun began to peek its way over the horizon of the rice fields that we were set up alongside of, the thick fog that lowers itself every night on these fields was also beginning to lift. At this time we began our morning ritual of getting ready for the day's patrol. It was cool and very damp the morning after my first encounter with an enemy patrol, and I was having a tough time getting myself together. I was still very tired from the lack of sleep the night before. The captain came around and said we would be moving out in twenty minutes; that would give us plenty of time to grab a cup of coffee and clean up and be ready to move out. Personally, all I needed was a few minutes to wash up and brush the night from my teeth, and I would be ready to go. A shower would have been nice but a canteen of water to wash up with, would have to do. I looked over to Lt. Baker and caught his eye. He then motioned me over to his position. We would spend the next fifteen minutes going over what had happened last night and talk some more about how he saw the reality of our role in Vietnam.

Lt. Baker was very smart and an interesting officer as well. I was glad he was there to show me the ropes. I believe that if it hadn't been for Lt. Baker guiding me through those first couple of weeks in-country, I wouldn't be alive today to write this story. I will always be grateful to him for those lessons in how to survive in the jungles and rice paddies of Vietnam.

Lt. Baker's perspective on the war was really quite simple: First, he told me not to take the war personally; the enemy soldier didn't really hate me, it's just that he'd been taught to hate what I stood for. If I took his actions personally, I would never be able to put this place behind me. I would always be carrying deep within me the hatred of the enemy; so in essence I would never really leave Vietnam—I would always be fighting the war, wherever I went, for the rest of my days. If I was lucky enough to survive it, that is! Second, the lieutenant told me to trust my instincts as I had never trusted them before, because my senses would never be as sharp as they would be in "combat". He also advised me to trust my fellow soldier, as he would be putting his utmost trust in me. He reminded me that there are no heroes over here; the real heroes of Vietnam are the ones who go home before their tours are up, in body bags. I have never forgotten Lt. Baker's advice that day. Throughout my tour his advice would serve me well.

Lt. Baker and I continued to talk on our way back to the ambush site, and along the way I found out a little more about him. He was twenty-six years old and had joined the ROTC (reserve officers training corp) at the University of Oklahoma. The government would pay for part of his schooling, as long as he went into the army for three years after he graduated, even though by that time he would be married and have a little girl. He thought it was a necessary tradeoff, as he would have been unable to afford school without it. He was neither for the war, nor against it, it was just something he had to do. I kind of felt the same way myself. The lieutenant and I thought a lot alike; maybe that's why we hit it off as well as we did right from the beginning. He was looking forward to seeing his family in a couple of months. The lieutenant had less than sixty days left in-country when I met him and was way past due to rotate back to the Battery, which generally should have occurred after eight or ten weeks in the field. (You may have noticed I keep on referring to this guy as "the Lieutenant" or "Lt. Baker." I'm embarrassed to say that for the life of me I can't remember his first name. I feel bad about that, but it must be a mental block or something; it's just the way it is, and I'm sorry.)

As we approached the site of the ambush, its appearance was very different by the light of day. I thought we had been hiding behind a small stone wall at the site, but this turned out to be a small mound of dirt with a few stones on top of it. In the darkness it had seemed to afford so much more protection and cover than it actually had. It was lucky for us that we didn't receive any return fire during the ambush, as we didn't really have any place to hide. The only thing that hid us was the darkness and the element of surprise; this was to become all too familiar as my tour progressed. Looking around the site, there wasn't a lot to see. This surprised me, for I had expected to see at least three bodies—maybe more—but there were no bodies.

I knew that we had killed some people in this area not five hours earlier, but here we were and not one body was to be found. There was nothing but some scuffmarks in the trail, along with one small black rubber sandal. There were also some splatters of blood and a light blood trail that led off down the trail. As we followed the blood we could make out some footprints in the dirt, and it was clear to us that whoever had lost their lives during the night's ambush had now been carried away. The trail of blood and footprints ended in a small clearing in the thick jungle about one hundred yards from where the ambush had taken place. In this clearing were three mounds of dirt; it was clearly a fresh gravesite but without markers of any kind. I stood there in silence. I wasn't prepared for this, and by the looks on the faces of the guys I was with, they weren't either. *What now?* I thought. Capt. Lewis took the radio handset from his RTO and called into Fire Support Base Chamberlain to get some clarification as to what his next move should be. Clearly he had not run into this situation before and he really didn't have a clue as to what he should do next.

Word came back from Major somebody or other from Division Headquarters that we were to dig up those graves and see if we could find any intelligence material. The brass was always looking for intelligence material to show to their superiors. I mean, think about it. Why would the VC bury material that they thought was of importance? Wouldn't they have taken it along with them? It didn't make much sense to us, and besides that, no one wanted to upset those graves—least of all me. I mean, talk about bad karma! Since no one would volunteer for the job, it was given to Phil and a guy from Seattle named Buzzard. The bodies were only in the ground a few feet and the dirt was soft, so it only took them a few minutes to uncover the bodies by scooping out the dirt with their helmets. What we had in front of us was shocking, even in a war zone where nothing was particularly shocking.

We hadn't ambushed the enemy at all. What we had done was cut to pieces two old farmers and a little girl. That's why they appeared to be so small in the darkness. That's why they lacked the discipline of a soldier, as they made their way down the trail. I remember them just chatting away as if they didn't have a care in the world. All they were was a couple of rice farmers who had stayed out too late and had too much to drink at a fellow farmer's house. It was after midnight when they tried to make their way home; didn't they know about the dusk-till-dawn curfew? Of course they did. Everyone did! The girl was probably their grandchild, who was sent to get them and to make sure they got home safely. Their bodies had been wrapped in white sheets and carefully laid to rest, but we could still see the damage we had brought upon these unfortunate farmers. Hell, we had cut them to pieces—that was evident.

They had been buried by their relatives, I assumed, who must have heard the explosions and machine-gun fire and rightly thought something was terribly wrong and gone out to look for them at first light. It must have been horrible to come upon the site of the ambush and find their loved ones in the condition we had left them in. They must have thought we were animals, to have killed these innocent people and just leave them the way we did. No wonder the villagers hated us so. I would have felt the same way.

We unwrapped their bodies to look for anything that would tell us anything at all, as we were ordered to do. The task wasn't a pleasant one and it wasn't an easy one to watch, never mind perform. I'm sure Phil and Buzzard never forgot it, as anyone who was there that day would never forget it either. After our search was completed we closed the three graves, leaving them pretty much as we found them. We stood there for a few moments after the last scoop of dirt was placed on their grave and as a group we just kind of stared at them in silence. As I look back on it now, I think, How hypocritical was that? Here we were, the soldiers who had just killed these three innocent people a few hours earlier, and now we were having a moment of silence for them at their gravesite. It was just that there was nothing else we could have done for them, it was all we could do. But it felt hypocritical to me then and even more so now, this many years later.

As the morning went on and we made our way through the jungle on our daily patrol looking for the enemy we spoke some more about the previous night's activity, and we started to justify what happened. I guess it was a way of taking ourselves off the hook for being involved in such a hideous act of war.

We said to ourselves that it wasn't our fault; after all, we didn't ask to be over here—South Vietnam had asked us to be here to help them fight communism. Furthermore, we just wanted to survive ourselves and get the hell out of here in one piece. And go home to our girlfriends, wives, children, and loved ones and to our cars and beer, not necessarily in that order. These were the things we missed the most, and these were the things that we were fighting for—not the South Vietnamese government, but our way of life. As shallow as our lives may have seemed at the time, it was all we had, and we wanted it back. Goddamn it, we didn't want to be here anyway, the results of that ambush was not our fault, how were we to know who was walking down that trail in the darkness anyway? Those farmers should have known better than to be out that time of night. Didn't they know that after dark in a "Free Fire Zone" we would shoot anything that moved? We were sure they must have known that. Christ, everyone knew that! These farmers had just taken their chances and stayed out too late, and look what happened to them. It wasn't our fault, it wasn't our fault. Over and over we said this, and to a man we all agreed: It just plain wasn't our fault and that was all there was to it, Period!

The more the day dragged on and the hotter it got, the more miserable we became, sweating our asses off trudging through some of the thickest jungle terrain this country had to offer, the more we were all in agreement. It was just an accident of war and that shit happens in war. It didn't take much longer to convince ourselves that it wasn't our fault and that was it and we didn't speak of it again! It was over, and that was that!

It was my first ambush and I will never forget it. As I'm sure the guys I was with that day will also never forget it.

Chapter 7

Out on Patrol

Good morning, Vietnam. The patrol was just putting itself together after another night's patrol and ambush duty two miles southeast of Tra Cu, a combination small Vietnamese village/Navy outpost along the Vam Co Dong River. It was the day before Thanksgiving 1969, and it was going to be a very hot and humid day as usual. We had been ordered to work our way to this small village/outpost and use it as our base of operations for the next couple of weeks. Tra Cu had approximately fifty or so army personnel attached to it, along with five navy patrol boats that were manned by some "Brown Water Naval" personnel. We would be replacing "Bravo" Company, who had been at this base for the previous two weeks. We figured it would take us the better part of the day to walk there. That is, if we didn't run into anything unexpected along the way—and Vietnam would always be full of the unexpected.

The terrain is very flat and mostly wet in this area of Vietnam. This area is also full of rice paddies that have been planted and replanted for over a thousand years. It was harvest time in Vietnam, and the farmers were getting ready to harvest their rice from the fields. We would pass by these farmers working in their fields on a daily basis. We knew that these people who were farmers by day would trade in their shovels and rakes for rifles at night and would then become our enemy. As we passed them, they would be watching us as closely as we would be watching them. They would note how many of us there were out on patrol, what unit we were from, and in what direction we were headed. The gooks had a bounty out on the "Wolfhounds", so we were always of particular interest to them. We would often double back on our patrol pattern just for this reason. We always wanted to keep them as much off guard as possible, but this would be very difficult; we were playing in their backyard, and they knew all the hiding places.

The area along the river was always wet, and this was the dry season. When the monsoon rains came in the summer, this area would become impossible for us to patrol. As we patrolled along the river, working our way to our destination, we would come upon little shelters that the VC (Viet Cong) would hide out in during the day to rest and stay out of the heat and humidity. These were common in this area, as they were so easy to build. Every time we came across one or more of them, we would treat them as if they were occupied. Sometimes they were, but most of the time they were simply empty—the lookout would have seen us coming a mile away. The only time we would have any contact with the enemy was when we would catch him sleeping or he would ambush us; this would always be done under his terms, and happened all too frequently.

Coming upon these little shelters made of dirt, mud, grass, and branches, we would blow them up in place. We were always trying to take away the enemy's hiding and resting places, to give us a better chance of getting him out in the open where we could engage him. This day we came across a couple of these huts along the river, and after checking them out we wired them up with some of the plastic "C-4" explosive material we all carried with us and blew them apart. C-4 explosive was something the army had developed years before; it was pliable like silly putty, light and one hundred times more powerful than dynamite, which made it perfect for this kind of jungle and rice-paddy warfare we mostly found ourselves fighting in. It was also great to use as a fuel to cook our meals with. We would take a small bit of it and light it with a match, and it would burn very fast and very hot. One had to be very careful with it though, as it sometimes blew up—hell, that's what it was made to do. We'd all heard of accidents happening with C-4 over here, so whenever we used it we were very, very careful.

It was past noon now and with the sun directly over our heads the heat and humidity was becoming unbearable. It was something one never really got used to, but was just one more thing you had to adapt to and deal with on a daily basis. Some of us did it better than others, but you really never got used to it. You learned to respect it though, as heat stroke would come on very quickly and when it did, it could make you deathly sick. One of our daily rituals was the taking of salt tablets along with our malaria pills each morning; we took more salt pills during the day, as we needed them. With the heat and the fact that we were carrying over seventy pounds of gear on us at all times, the body would sweat off a lot of liquid, so those little pills were lifesavers.

Upon reaching the small village of Tra Cu, we stopped to rest and look over the situation. The village was only a few hundred yards from the small fire support base that we were making our way to, so it was decided not to enter the village at this time. We felt that with it being so close to our support base, which we would be going in and out of on a daily basis, we could continue to monitor it as we pleased from the base camp. To a man we weren't in any mood to search another village this day, for we were just plain exhausted from our walk here. We could now see the base camp from where we were standing. It was off to the west and very close to the Cambodian border. It was so small that, even though we knew it was there, it was tough for us to make out. If it weren't for the antennas sticking up in the air from the command bunker, we probably wouldn't have been able to see it at all. I had been expecting a much larger base. Phil and Lt. Baker had been here a few months previously and were glad to be back, because it offered some creature comforts that were impossible for us to get in the field.

As we walked along, Phil explained to me that it wasn't a bad place to be spending the next couple of weeks—if we were lucky enough to do so, that is. For the company was always moving around and we really didn't know where we would be from one week to the next.

The base was a combination Army/Navy patrol base because of its location right on the river. For the next couple of weeks we would be working with the Navy on their small patrol boats, PBR's (patrol boats river). This sounded interesting to me, as I always liked to be around boats back in the world. Patrolling out in the jungle was starting to take its toll on me, as I had just arrived in-country and I was beat from all the walking and the heat. At this base camp, Phil explained to me, we would be taken out by the Navy to our ambush positions at sundown and picked up at sunrise. That sounded good to me, and the fact that the patrol boats were close by at all times for support made me feel a little more at ease. The base also had sandbag hooches where we could get some rest during the day. They also had real cots for us to sleep on, that sure as hell beat sleeping on the ground any day. But Phil saved the best for last: there was a small outdoor movie theater next to the enlisted men's club, where we could have a few cold beers and enjoy a movie on the nights that we were not out on ambush patrol. Cold beer, this place was sounding better to me all the time.

Our small group of wary warriors from Alpha Company had now made their way to the river's edge. The captain who was in charge of Bravo

Company was on the other side of the river, waving us over to his side. We were glad to have made it through the day without contacting the enemy, and we were ready for a little rest and maybe a few of those cold beers Phil had mentioned. The Navy sent one of their patrol boats over for us, as the river was too deep and wide for us to wade across. It was a nice reprieve for us to sit on that boat and take the short crossing to the base. As we walked up the small hill to Tra Cu Base Camp, I was glad to be able to take my radio and backpack off my back for the first time in hours. The straps had left marks along my shoulder blades, and my back was aching from carrying so much weight. It was just so nice to be able to sit down and relax in the relative safety of the base camp. I swear I must have lost ten pounds my first full day out on patrol.

Chapter 8

Thanksgiving at FSB Tra Cu.

T ra-cu base camp was a listening post for any movements of the enemy along the infiltration route coming in from Cambodia. It couldn't have been more than twenty thousand feet square in size. Thirty-five sailors of the Brown Water Navy, as they liked to call themselves, were stationed there. Those guys had it made, as far as we were concerned, what with their bunks and refrigerators and air-conditioning. Hell, all I ever saw them do was go out in their boats during the day and have some beers and a barbecue at night. I'm sure they all went home and told a bunch of war stories, but the truth of the matter was they had some pretty easy duty. After all, they were in the Navy, now weren't they?

The base also had a communication bunker, which had ten to fifteen men manning it. I really didn't know what branch of the service they were in, as they pretty much kept to themselves and didn't wear a uniform. They could have been with the CIA, as Air America helicopters were coming and going all the time. We were told not to take any pictures of these helicopters, but I did anyway. You couldn't miss them they were the only choppers in Vietnam painted an off-white color.

And then there was Alpha Company. We had fifty or so troops there that made up First and Second Platoons, as Third and Fourth Platoons were still pulling ambush duty outside the base. Our mission there was to guard the base camp along with the Navy personnel. Sometimes, we would be out on ambush duty at night, and sometimes, we would be on guard duty within the camp itself.

The place kind of made me nervous though, being the size it was, and so close to the Cambodian border. But what did I know? I was new, just in from the States, remember.

We settled in the first night for a little rest. There would be no ambush patrols this night as all the troops of First Platoon, as well as Second Platoon, were just plain exhausted.

I grabbed a cot for the night, and some guys were picked for guard duty. I thanked heaven I was not one of them and settled in for the first good night's sleep since being in-country. My back and shoulders ached from the radio and the pack I had carried all day. I was not used to that, and I was a little out of shape after the thirty days' leave I had enjoyed before coming over. I fell right off to sleep. The night passed without incident, and I awoke early, as would be my habit throughout out my Vietnam tour.

The sun rises early in Vietnam, and with it our day began. Tra Cu had bathroom facilities along with real showers. They were to be the only ones I would see in a camp this small. We would all take full advantage of them; it was nice to get the grime and reddish dirt washed off our bodies. Here I was along the Cambodian border on Thanksgiving Day 1969, but I was starting to feel a little better about my situation and myself. I'd gotten to know a few of the guys I was with and was feeling more confident about handling myself in a combat situation. Even though I had a lot to learn, at least I had a little action under my belt and felt good about it. This fire support base also had a full kitchen area, and I'll bet you could never guess what they were preparing this day? Yes, you're right: It was going to be turkey with the all the trimmings. We were in a small camp, but we were also with the Navy, and those guys always seemed to have the means to get what they wanted. Those boats they traveled around in all day weren't just for fighting, you know!

By late afternoon we had finished up a great Thanksgiving Day meal, and to a man, we were grateful. But you know, it made us think more of home than ever. In many ways, the more they tried to bring home to us over there the more homesick we became. I'm sure the high command thought they were doing the right thing, but it was tough being so far away from home when all you had were letters to keep you company. And speaking of letters, I had not received any yet, and I was getting a little concerned. Was anyone going to think of me? Were my friends and family going to forget me? Was my girl going to write? Out of sight, out of mind, and all that stuff. I talked to one of my new buddies, Pfc. Bernier—I would get to know him pretty well during my tour. He said it took almost a month for his letters to catch up with him. That made me feel a little better. I had only been in-country for ten days now, so I guessed I would have to wait a while longer.

After a nice, lazy day of good food and looking around the area, Bernier and I took a walk down by the patrol boats and wished we had joined the

Navy. My father had been in the Navy during the Second World War and had tried to steer me in that direction also, but you had to join the Navy for three years and at the time three years seemed like a very long time. So I went into the army for two years instead; if I liked it I could always re-enlist. But after seeing how these Navy guys were living and fighting the war I wished I had gone into the Navy after all. Riding around on those boats all day didn't seem so bad—well, not as tough as humping through the thick jungle all day. At least you had the breeze blowing in your face to help keep you a little cooler while out on patrol, and great food, and—let's not forget—a cot to come back to at night. With what we had to deal with on a daily basis it sounded and looked pretty good to us. Those Navy guys can walk around wearing their black berets like they were the only ones fighting this war, and they can say what they want, but not one would have traded places with a grunt over here; and that's all I'll say on that subject at this time.

We found the Navy patrol boats very interesting indeed. They were thirty-five feet long, with machine guns at both ends. They were made of wood and fiberglass—not very much protection there, but they were extremely fast and maneuverable, so they could get in and out of trouble within a moment's notice. A couple of things they had onboard that were of special interest to us were the twin, electrically fired, fifty-caliber machine guns that were mounted up front. This was an awesome weapon; I pity any enemy soldier that got in the way of that thing. The fifty-caliber machine gun was developed to shoot down airplanes during the Second World War, so that gives you an idea what they would do to the human body. They were just incredible and very lethal in a firefight.

The other piece of weaponry they had on board was a napalm gun. This, I believe, was by far the worst weapon for the enemy to have to endure over here. This thing would shoot out big globs of liquid fire, and shoot it up to a two hundred yards away. It was an exceptionally cruel weapon: not only would it burn everything in its path, but it also couldn't put it out with water! I thought, *who ever heard of not being able to put out a fire with water?* But that's what this stuff was all about. The only way you could put it out was by smothering it with mud to take its air source away or cut it off. It was a horrible way to die, and I always felt bad when that stuff was used against enemy troops. Sometimes when my demons come back to haunt me during the night, they always bring the screams of those soldiers we heard and saw burning to death after being napalmed. As far as I'm concerned, that stuff was invented by the devil himself.

The darkness of night was coming now, and the nighttime was always more dangerous than the daytime for the soldiers in Vietnam. It was Thanksgiving night, and it was very hot and humid. Since we were along the river, we always had mosquitoes to deal with. They were the big ones, not like the ones we had at home. They were huge and very aggressive and carried malaria to boot, so they were always a concern to us. We took our malaria pills every day and prayed we avoided this dreaded disease.

This night started out very quietly. All that was going on was some flares going off in the distance. It was probably just FSB Chamberlain lighting up the sky around its position so the guards could see better. This would happen all night long, and one would get used to it after a while. But this night would be different. It was after 2 A.M. when Pfc. Bernier reached over and poked my arm to wake me and whispered for me to grab my weapon, helmet, and a flak jacket, and follow him outside to where the camp kept the hand grenades. One of our ambush patrols had spotted a large force of enemy soldiers moving in our direction. The patrol hadn't blown the ambush on them because of their size. We grabbed a box of thirty hand grenades and made our way to the wall of sandbags and barbed wire that surrounded the camp, keeping as low a profile as possible. Within a few minutes someone came by and gave out a few more belts of ammo. We waited and watched the field as well as the tree line in front of us. Not a word was spoken as we waited for what was to happen next.

I was just as nervous as the next guy; no one could say what we were up against, because no one seemed to know. We would just have to wait for the enemy to make the first move, and then and only then would we have an idea as to the size of the force that we would be facing. And then we would react accordingly. Even though there were only a hundred or so soldiers protecting this small camp out here in the middle of nowhere, we felt we could do so effectively with the firepower that we had at our disposal.

We didn't have to wait very long for the enemy to show his position. One of the gooks tripped a flare right in front of us, and at that exact same moment another one went off over to our right. That first flare had a claymore mine attached to it, and the explosion got everyone's attention real fast. We set off some flares of our own from within the camp, and the area in front us lit up like daylight. There must have been seventy-five to one hundred of the enemies within two hundred yards of the camp perimeter. Some of them were on their bellies, trying to sneak under the barbed wire that was strung all around the camp; others were crouched low and moving slowly towards our position, trying to get at us.

As soon as the flares lit up the sky the battle was on. Bernier and I immediately took out a sapper who was right in front of us. Everyone was firing with everything they had. Landmines were going off as well as hand-grenades. The enemy was firing back with everything they had also, and the noise was deafening. The ground and sky were full of red tracers and green tracers. I could hear the screams of the enemy every time a grenade went off. The bullets whizzing through the air were coming frighteningly close to our position. Bernier and I were trying to keep our heads down and throw our hand grenades as fast as we could get them out of the box. It only took us a few minutes to empty that first box, and Bernier raced off to get another. By the time he got back to our position only a few minutes had passed, but the firing and the confusion of the attack had died down. Clouds of acid smoke created by the explosions and gunfire hung in the air over us and made the simple task of taking a deep breath difficult.

The assault on our position had lasted only fifteen minutes or so, but it was the most intense fifteen minutes I had ever experienced in my young life. It was quiet now, and all that I could hear was some crying out for the medic on our side and some moaning coming from the area directly to our front. These moans were coming from the dying enemy soldiers right in front of us because they couldn't get to us, nor could they get back to escape with their comrades. We could see out about two hundred yards or so. There were dead and dying enemy soldiers everywhere. We couldn't see very clearly, due to the fact that all we had for illumination was the eerie light that was projected down upon us from the flares that hung in the sky over our position. There was still quite a lot of running around on our side, what with the wounded being taken care of and the re-checking of our weapons just in case the enemy tried another attack. I sure as hell hoped he didn't, as I was still shaking from this one, my first real encounter with him.

I was now starting to come down from the adrenaline high that one gets from such an intense experience, and as I looked around I was thankful that neither Bernier nor myself had been wounded in any way.

This combat experience would bond Pfc. Bernier and myself for the rest of our time in Vietnam, and we probably still share that bond today. It's not something that we speak of or even share with our families and friends, but it's something we have that we can't deny, and I'm sure it will always be there.

The fighting appeared to be over for the night. We would have to wait until dawn to really get a clear look at what had happened, but the aftermath of the firefight showed how lucky we had been. We had only suffered five wounded. Three were serious though and would be flown out on the first medivac chopper that morning. I heard later that one of the soldiers that had been shot up pretty bad that night lost a leg. I felt kind of bad about that, but there was nothing I could have done to help him.

At first light we looked out on the field in front of us, it was not a pretty sight. We counted twelve enemy dead on the battlefield; five of those still had satchel charges strapped to their backs. These were the sappers, who had tried to sneak up on us during the night and blow us all to hell. If it hadn't been for that ambush patrol from Third Platoon and the fact that they warned us of the enemy's approach, which gave us plenty of time to get ready for them, it could have been a hell of a lot worse for us. If we hadn't been warned ahead of time, they might have even been able to overrun the base.

That was probably their intention, but we will never know for certain. There is one thing that we did know for sure though, and that is they left twelve dead soldiers on the field of battle that night, and there must have been five times that many making the assault, maybe more. We had been lucky this Thanksgiving night, and it had been one I'd never forget. In fact, as I look back on it now it was kind of fun; I know that's strange to hear, but I can't deny the fact that that was how I truly felt then and I still feel the same today. We were all very thankful for the warning that Third Platoon's ambush patrol had given us.

In the morning a patrol was sent out to check the enemy to see if any were still alive; they weren't. The enemy bodies were checked and re-checked for any documentation that would help us determine what regiment had attacked us the night before. Any pieces of information that we could get from them would only help us in the future. After this grisly task was completed, we lined up the enemy dead and half covered them over, out along the wood line that was about one hundred yards to our front. We sort of milled around over them for a few minutes, giving these dead enemy soldiers a few last thoughts; after all, they were soldiers just like us, and they had given their lives for a cause that they had believed in. We left their resting-place unmarked, not out of disrespect but because we knew the enemy wasn't that far away, and they would be watching our every move. We would let them take care of their fallen comrades at a later date.

Chapter 9

Ambush Along the River

The morning after the attack on the fire support base came very early for us. We really hadn't slept very well. The thinking was that we might be in for another attack, but that was not to be. Capt. Lewis set our day for us. We were to go out with the Navy personnel and work our way up river. This would bring us closer to the Cambodian border than we had ever been before. Our mission would be to seek out and destroy any remnants of the enemy that had attacked us the night before—if we could find them, that is. We were to have helicopter support this time, though, as well as the support of the Navy boats that would bring us into the enemy's area. The choppers were to flush them out, and then the boats would bring us in. We had to be ready early to load up on the boats, for the sun always rose about 5:00 A.M. in Vietnam. It didn't seem to matter what time of year it was, it was always the same, for there was no daylight-saving time in Vietnam as there was back in the States. Vietnam had only two seasons: wet and dry, and both were hot and humid.

The sun was now starting to rise over the rice paddies that surrounded Tra Cu, and it was time for our day's mission to begin. Three small helicopters had arrived as advertised, and the patrol boats were ready to move out. All that was missing for the operation to begin was Alpha Company, and we were working our way to the shoreline to get on board the patrol boats at this very moment. It sometimes took us a little longer to get our ass in gear, as we would be carrying everything we would need for a week's stay on our backs. Unlike the pilots and Navy personnel, who would be going back to their cozy little bases that night, we would be staying out until our mission was accomplished. This kind of operation was just a day job for them. For us, it could last a day, a week, or even longer; it all depended on what we ran into.

As we moved slowly up river, the morning air took on a kind of coolness. The morning's fog had not quite lifted from the river yet, and hung six to eight feet off the surface of the calm, slow-moving, muddy river—just enough to give us the cover we needed. The cover of early morning fog would allow us to get to our predetermined area without being detected by any potential enemy ambushes waiting for us along its banks.

We passed the little village of Tra Cu, which was also coming to life. The people in the village were always up early to get their washing done in the river and take their morning bath. Whatever else they would be doing at that time of day in the river I could only imagine, and I really didn't want to know. The river was their life's blood; without it they would surely perish. They bathed in it, drank it, and ate the fish they caught from it. The river meant that much to them.

As we slowly made our way past them, they could care less that we were there. They hardly gave us a passing glance. The firefight at our fire support base the night before hadn't fazed them one bit. Half the people in this village were the enemy, and the other half could give a shit if we lived or died. As far as they were concerned, we were just kind of there, until we weren't, I guess. I had thought we were here to help these people or save them or something like that, but I was new and I was naive, and my attitude would change as my tour progressed.

Our patrol boat moved along at approximately ten miles per hour as we made our way to our predetermined drop-off point. We watched the river's edge for any signs of the enemy, signs that would tell us if he was here now or had been here not long ago. The gooks liked the river's edge; they could hear us coming and actually get into the river and use it for cover if they had to. It was a very dangerous way to hide from us though, for if we spotted them—and those guys on the patrol boats were experts at noticing small changes in their area of patrol— it would be all over for them.

The radio was going pretty good now, what with the radio traffic from the boats to the choppers and then on to the fire support base filling the airwaves. We were all on the same frequency so we could talk to one another in case of contact or the spotting of the enemy, which was just about to happen. We hadn't been out for forty-five minutes when one of the choppers located a small group of enemy soldiers between his position and the river. We could see his chopper hovering out about three hundred yards from us. He was pinpointing their location to us by dropping smoke grenades and said he was trying to herd them to us. This he could do by coming in very low; with the door gunners trying to shoot them in the open, they would have no choice but to run towards the river to seek a place to hide. This morning, we would be waiting for them.

The patrol boat we were on moved its bow up to the shoreline, and we managed to jump off—no easy task with all the gear we were carrying. There were seven of us who would set up a position in the high reeds with the river to our backs and wait for the enemy to come to us. Lt. Baker was by my side as I was still too inexperienced to be trusted to call in the artillery if it was needed. I felt a lot more secure with him close by, but to tell the truth, I was becoming more comfortable with my job and felt I could do it alone if I had to and I would have to in the not-too-distant future.

Close by, as we waited in the morning fog and the oppressive heat and humidity, was another friend, Pfc. Bernier. It was always nice to see him nearby, as he was a seasoned veteran of this kind of fighting. We were crouched very low in the tall weeds and grass, waiting for the enemy to come to us. The sweat was rolling down my face and neck, and all the tiny little insects that called this place home were having a feast on my exposed skin. But the enemy was very close now, so I had to ignore the discomfort and prepare myself for what laid ahead. We could hear the gooks sloshing through the high grass, as they ran towards our position. I was nervous, but the adrenaline was pumping so fast now that there wasn't really any time to be scared; what was going to happen was going to happen. We were too deep into the ambush to change anything now.

The sound of the helicopters over our heads was becoming very loud now: they seemed to be right on top of us. One chopper couldn't have been more than twenty-five yards away from us, and it was only about thirty feet off the ground right to our immediate front. We couldn't hear anything else, because the noise of that chopper was so damn loud. Why, I thought, if the enemy was so close to us, hadn't he backed off and let us take it from here? Then a horrible thought raced through my mind: What if he didn't know our position? What if he couldn't see us? I didn't want to get on the radio and tell him that we were almost right under him, for fear that the enemy would hear me trying to contact the chopper and stop and open fire on us. And I really didn't want to poke my head above the reeds we were hiding in either; the door gunner could have mistaken me for the enemy and open fire. I had to speak to that chopper! I had to take the chance and contact him.

Screw it! "Chopper One, this is Two Zero Echo Bravo," I frantically screamed into my handset, "Chopper One, this is Two Zero Echo Bravo, you are right over us, please back the hell off, we can handle the situation from here. "Over". "Chopper One", do you read me? "Over." I continued to yell into my handset.

A long moment passed, and then I heard, "Two Zero Echo Bravo, I read you loud and clear". "Over". "Be advised you have eight to ten Victor Charlies twenty yards to your west". "Over."

"I understand, eight to ten VC twenty yards to my west. Over," I replied. At that moment the chopper pulled off to our west. I breathed a sigh of relief. He had flown so close to us I swear I could see freckles on the door gunner's nose. We would soon have our hands full enough with the enemy, who was running right for us, without the worry of getting shot by our own helicopters. I had been concerned, and rightly so, that they wouldn't have been able to see us; the reed and river grass was so damn thick around us that it would have blocked the helicopter's view of our position.

Now we could hear the enemy running through the grass that was six inches deep in the river's run off, the grass brushing against their bodies with their every move. They sounded like a small herd of elephants, and they were closing in on our position with each and every step that they took. Our problem was that we were also in the thick grass, and we had no open area in front of us for a clear field of fire. What we would have to do was fire at the sounds the men were making as they ran through the wet grass. The seven of us had previously flattened down an area of ten yards or so in a semicircle around us. Thus providing the eye-to-eye contact we needed between us.

Within seconds the first enemy soldier, who was running ahead of the others, was right on top of us. He broke through the small clearing that we had made in the tall grass and surprised the hell out of us. The look on his face was one of utter surprise also—or was it just plain shock? I really don't know, but what difference did it make? Within moments he was dead. He couldn't have been any older than we were. I would estimate that he was about twenty years old. He was dressed in a light brown uniform and a small brown-rimmed helmet with a bright red star on its front. He was also carrying a Chinese-made AK-47 submachine gun that he had been ready to let loose on us if we had given him the chance. But before he could gather his thoughts and figure out what he was going to do, a burst of M60 machine-gun bullets hit him right -square in the chest. The power of the blast lifted him a good three feet in the air backwards, and as his arms flung out to his sides the machine gun he was carrying flew harmlessly into the air. As he hit the ground there was a splash of water that came up around him. It all seemed to happen in slow motion. I'm sure he never knew what hit him—he was probably dead by the time he hit the ground. That soldier never stood a chance.

We then let loose with everything we had at our disposal in the direction that first soldier had come from. The other enemy soldiers couldn't have been more than twenty feet in front of us when the shooting started, yet with the thickness of the reeds and river grass, the only one we actually saw was the first one, who had breached our small perimeter. The shooting lasted for approximately thirty seconds. That may not seem like a long time, but in combat with the constant firing of our weapons in this manner it is a very long time.

Our hearts were pumping and the blood was flowing very rapidly in our veins now. We stopped firing and crouched there, not wanting to make a sound. The sweat was still running down my face and down the back of my neck, but as far as I could tell there was no return fire and not one of us was hit. The grass was now cut down in front of us to a height of about two feet off the ground. We could see approximately thirty yards to our front, and there was no movement at all. We could smell and taste the acrid smoke of the gunpowder that hung in the air and clung to the wet grass surrounding us. It sort of smothered everything it came in contact with, as if it were going to stay there forever as some sort of memorial to the VC soldiers who had died there that day.

Our biggest concern, though, was our own condition. We all looked around at each other, and not one of us had suffered a scratch. It could have just as easily gone the other way: we were just lucky this time. The radio was alive now with the sound of traffic coming from the choppers that were flying all around us, as well as our command base, with the one question we were glad to answer. We had no friendly casualties to report.

We would now sweep up what had just been eight to ten enemy soldiers running for their lives a few minutes before. It was a good early morning's work for us this day.

This was not some movie set where everyone gets up after the director yells, "Cut!" This was real, and today, it was so real it was frightening. The only way I could rationalize the death of those soldiers was by telling myself it was either them or us, and if I had anything to say about it, it was always going to be them. Today, everything had gone our way. There were to be other days when this wouldn't be so. Too many of those days were to follow, but for now this was our day, we were the victors, and we were proud of it.

As we walked amongst the dead VC soldiers, the sight was not a pretty one. They were lying in the most horrible positions one could imagine. Our bullets had cut a couple of them almost in half. Yet another one didn't look like he had been shot at all, until we rolled him over and saw the numerous gaping bullet holes that had ended his life that morning. What we were doing was taking their ammo and weapons and again looking for any documents that they may have had on them in order to get an idea as to what regiment they belonged to. This was important, as it would give "S-1 Intelligence" back in the rear the information they would need to determine who these soldiers were and where they came from. We were always looking for information about the enemy, which most of the time they carried on them.

We didn't get any prisoners this day, so the unpleasant job of dragging the bodies together and placing them in a small pile had to be done by us. This was the second group of dead enemy soldiers I had seen, and it was an awful sight. It was a sight I would never get used to, but as I look back on it now, I have to say it didn't bother me half as much as I had thought it was going too. The situation called for the results. I didn't make the situation—I was just a player. I think this thought process saved me from carrying around a lot of excess mental baggage, both then and now. We were soldiers, and we were just trying to stay alive. No one wanted to be here but we were, and if this was the way it was going to be then we felt we were going to win, and after it was all over we would be the ones going home. The saying in Vietnam was that it was best to make the other guy die for his country, and we tried to do just that every chance we got. And we weren't ashamed of it one bit, either. We were just trying to stay alive and get the hell out of there in one piece.

After we policed up the area of everything we felt that was of importance, we moved over to the boat that had brought us up river to this place, put our gear and ourselves onboard, and made our way down river and back to Tra Cu. There really wasn't much conversation on the way back. I'm sure we were all lost in our own thoughts at this time.

My tour was just beginning and if this was the way it was going to be, then I had no idea how I was going to survive a whole year of this. But this was war, and in order to stay alive, I was going to have to fight it the best way I knew how. But for now, I would make my way back to our fire support base and take stock of myself as I prepared to go back out again that very same night.

The breeze in our faces on the boat ride down river had a cooling and refreshing effect on us. Upon arriving back at Tra Cu Fire Support Base, we would put ourselves back together by cleaning our weapons, etc. Some of us would take a shower, grab some breakfast and try to relax. The captain had given us the rest of the day off—not that we could go anywhere anyway, but it was nice just to hang around and write a letter home. It had been quite a morning, and some time to reflect on it was in order for me at least. I dozed off for a few hours. As my year progressed, this was something I would do as my time permitted. It was my way of leaving this place, if only for a short while.

Alpha Company would have to get itself together for the night's ambush patrol soon enough, but for now, some of us wrote home, some got up a card game and some took naps. We needed this time to wind down from the morning's activity. The nighttime would come soon enough, and we would have to go back out on ambush, as we did every night. The day's event was behind us now. We would leave it there and move on. Sounds kind of cold, but it was the right thing for us to do. Hell, we couldn't carry it with us from day to day- surely we would have all gone mad. I was new to the act of killing, and I think that it bothered me more than it bothered some of the guys I was with. I couldn't get the sight of those dead men out of my mind. Even though there were to be many more to follow, the scene of those dead soldiers has remained with me to this day.

Chapter 10

Just a Normal Night on Ambush

It was just after 6:00 P.M. when Captain Lewis came around and told us to get our gear and ourselves ready to go out for the night's ambush. It doesn't really get dark in Vietnam until around eight o'clock, but we would have to travel by boat to our position, and then we would have to walk another half-mile or so to set up for the night.

It only took us about fifteen minutes to get ourselves together in order to move out. The company would begin to load themselves on the small riverboats for our trip down river to our jump-off point. On the boat the company would break down into squads and start looking at the maps to find the best places for us to set up for the night. This may seem like something that would be easy to do, but in reality it takes coordination and communication between six or seven different groups of soldiers to do it correctly. We would have to be sure where each and every one of our ambushes were, so as not to be in each other's line of fire. When an ambush was activated all hell would break loose; the last thing you wanted was to be in the line of fire of an ambush in the middle of the night.

It takes a little doing just to set up an ambush. We couldn't just go out and lie in wait for the enemy to walk by, even though that's exactly what we would end up doing. My job was to go over the ambush plans with my lieutenant and determine who we would be spending the night with. The captain would spend each night on ambush with a different squad, and the RTO (radio transmission operator) would always be with the captain to call in the artillery. To set ourselves up for the night we would have to know where each ambush was so we could set up our firing points of reference around each position. These points of reference would save many lives in combat; during a firefight things can get very confusing, and with our points already sent back to our FSB (fire support base) we could call in the fire that we needed simply by giving a reference number. The guns back at base would already have them plotted in. A lot of time was saved in this manner, and in combat time saves lives.

Once we were set up in our ambush and our field of fire was established and our claymore mines had been set out all around our position, it just became a waiting game. A sergeant would come around and give out the sleeping hours and the hours we were to be awake. This would include the officers as well; on ambush we would all share in these duties. The last thing I would do is double-check my radio and make sure I had communications with everyone, and most importantly that I had the ability to speak to the Artillery Battery that would be covering us this night. The Battery was usually Battery C (Charlie Battery) for this was my home-base Battery, even though I would rarely see them. I would talk to them every day and every night. Even though my call sign was Two Zero Echo Bravo at this time, they had nicknamed me "Boston" because of my "Boston" accent. The name didn't bother me one bit; in fact it made me feel more part of the team than ever.

Being an RTO had its good points and its really bad points. One of the good points, I came to find out, was the mere fact that whatever was happening in any given situation that the company found itself in, I always had firsthand knowledge of what was going on. Also, being on the radio and having it with me at all times, I could monitor all types of activity, such as what the brass were saying about what we were going to be doing next. And during any combat situation that we found ourselves involved in, I would play an intricate part in what was happening. Calling in the artillery and on occasion speaking to the helicopter and jet pilots and telling them where we needed them to fire their rockets and drop their bombs. Having the radio on my back, as heavy as it was, did have its advantages.

One of the disadvantages of carrying the radio was its weight. It was just so goddamn heavy! And because it was so heavy, that meant I could only carry so much of the stuff I considered important, like water (eight canteens), food (five days worth at all times) and ammo (ten twenty-round clips). The only personal stuff I would allow myself was a small lightweight nylon blanket; two extra pairs of socks; a small towel; a toothbrush and toothpaste; a razor; and a small bar of soap. Oh—and a pen and a pad of paper to write on. Later in my tour I did acquire a 35-mm camera, with which I took as many pictures as I could. I'm proud to say I still have most of those photos. One day back in camp I weighed the radio and the small pack I carried through much of my tour in Vietnam, and it weighed eighty-five pounds. I was always trying to carry less, but I always seemed to be carrying more.

The other big disadvantage of carrying the radio was that I had an eight-foot collapsible antenna sticking off my back at all times, as I worked my way through the rice paddies and jungles of Vietnam. This made me the easiest and most vulnerable target for the enemy soldiers to try to kill first. It would be important for them to take out the Company's communications as soon as they could during a firefight. The first shots in combat were always aimed at the RTO and anyone around him, because they knew that anyone close by was probably an officer and it would be best to eliminate us both if possible. It was said that in a firefight the life expectancy of an RTO was less than seven minutes.

A group of guys in combat without communications and an officer down would be easy pickings for the enemy on most occasions. It was because of these facts alone that during combat, guys would not want to get too close to yours truly. I understood this; and given the same set of rules I wouldn't have wanted to be by my side either. So those were some of the advantages and disadvantages of being an RTO in combat, and if I had it all to do over again I wouldn't have traded the experience for the world. Very few soldiers who went to Vietnam got to experience combat, feel it, smell it, and—yes—even taste it so up close and personal as an RTO. And wasn't combat the reason why I volunteered for Vietnam in the first place? I had gotten what I wanted. I just didn't know what I wanted, when I volunteered for it.

Now that our ambush was established and everyone was in his position and knew his role for the night, it was time to kick back and relax and look up in the sky and watch the night's activities before sleep would slowly overcome me.

Nights in Vietnam were always busy—at least the first part of the night anyway, with all the stars putting on their show. There always seemed to be a shooting star or two or three each and every night. Along with this activity in the skies, flares continuously went off during the night to light up the numerous fire support bases that were located all around us. Big C-130 Gunships flew around firing their lethal brand of greetings (*death from above* they liked to call themselves) at the enemy wherever they could find them or wherever we would ask them to fire. Most of the time they couldn't see shit, but they sure as hell weren't going back to their bases with any of their ammo left either. Whenever these cowboys were in our area I would always make sure they knew exactly where we were, for fear of being mistaken for the enemy by them in the darkness of the night.

What scared us the most on night ambush patrol were the B-52 bombers. To this day I still can't believe that they knew where every ambush in their drop-zone was; I believe more than one American ambush patrol was blown to bits by these guys, and they never even knew it. Why were these planes so scary? Well, to begin with, they flew at 35,000 feet, and you couldn't hear them from the ground. The only way you knew they were around was the horrendously loud and destructive sound of their bombs being dropped in your area. Those bombs would leave craters in the ground that during the rainy season we would swim in—that should give you an idea of how destructive they were. When the explosions were close enough, you would have to cover your ears and open your mouth because of the concussion of the blast. Most of the time we would be a few miles away from the actual drop-zone, and it would still be that loud. I just can't imagine what it must have been like to be directly under a B-52 strike; it must have been hell on earth for the enemy.

On most nights we wouldn't even know the bombers were in our area until we heard the bombs hit the ground with such force that they would actually shake the ground and wake us up. Being around a B-52 strike, even though it may have been a few miles away, was the most frightening experience that I would have during my time in-country. Even though we had a radio with us at all times it would have done us no good once a strike had begun. The damage would have already been done by these high-flying and silent messengers of death.

On most night operations we would have no contact with the enemy. We would all take our turns on guard duty; how long this duty was depended on how many of us were out on patrol. It was usually two hours up and six hours down throughout the night, until dawn broke and the day started all over again with its own special daytime-related problems.

Most mornings in this hot-ass place started out the same. A ground fog two feet off the ground would usually surround us during the night and still be there to greet us in the morning. This fog, which slowly descended upon us during the night, always played havoc on our line of sight during an ambush. The fog would bring with it a clammy, humid kind of coldness that permutated our uniforms and would stay with us each day until the sun was high in the sky; only then would our clothes dry out. Sometimes during our ambushes we could only see the enemy from the waist up, and it was very surreal to shoot at him from this perspective. The low, early-morning fog did provide us with some excellent cover, especially on our patrols along the river. Not being native to such a strange environment, we had to take advantage of everything this country had to offer us in order to stay alive.

Chapter 11
The Sugar Mill Area

My birthday had come and gone on December 10, and it was now December 14, 1969, the date we would leave the river for the last time. Alpha and Bravo company would rotate with Charlie and Delta company and we would now be working out of the Sugar Mill Complex. The area that was know to us as the Sugar Mill was located ten miles east of the river, right in the middle of a large sugar plantation. This area would prove to be the busiest and the most dangerous during my entire tour of Vietnam. The area immediately around the "Mill" was the only thing I ever saw that resembled a factory while I was in-country. Also located in this area was the "Iron Triangle." This area was extremely dangerous for us, as it housed the Cu Chi Tunnel Complex. These tunnels were the most extensive in Vietnam. They could be three and four levels deep and housed upwards of two thousand enemy soldiers. During our time in this area we would try every method at our disposal to kill the enemy soldiers who had taken refuge in these tunnels, but with limited success.

The tunnel entrances were always well camouflaged, but once we located one we would secure the area around it and try to decide how much of a tunnel we had. If we felt it was big enough, we would take the appropriate action to destroy it. Sometimes these tunnels would be small, and sometimes they were just the beginning of a larger tunnel complex. The only way to know for sure was to have someone go in and find out. This most dangerous of jobs always went to the "Tunnel Rats". The soldiers that were known as tunnel rats were a special breed; every company had a few of them assigned to it. They were always small guys, because the openings to these tunnels were so damn small and they were the only guys that could fit in. I personally thought they were suicidal or at best just plain crazy. But the one thing that was very clear after you worked with these guys on a daily basis was that they were some of the bravest men in all of Vietnam.

Tunnel rats were specially trained for their demanding assignments. It took nerves of steel and plenty of guts to go down into a dark tunnel with only a pistol and a flashlight. They would never really know what would await them once they dropped into that hole in the ground, but in they went anyway. These guys took great pride in their jobs, as well as they should have, and they were a very tight knit group of soldiers.

Once they were in the tunnel they could be gone twenty minutes or so, or they could be back out in a few seconds. If it was only a few seconds, you could be sure it would be followed by the explosion of a tripped mine or grenade. Many tunnel rats would lose their lives or be seriously wounded due to the fact that they just hadn't been able to get out fast enough. The tunnel itself was too small to turn around in, so they would have to try to scramble out backwards as quickly as they could. I saw this tragedy more than once while we were working around the Sugar Mill. One quick story that I feel I have to record was of a tunnel rat sergeant that I met my first month in country, I honestly can't recall his name, but I can recall him getting his 3rd Purple Heart as if it were yesterday.

We were working an area that we knew had plenty of tunnels from our previous experiences of being there. Sure enough, we came upon one opening that we thought would be worth a look. Most of the time we would just blow them in place with C-4 explosives and move on, but this tunnel opening looked larger than most, so we secured the area in order to take a better look. The sergeant was called forward to go into the tunnel to give us a better idea of what we had stumbled upon, so we could then make an educated decision on what to do with it. It only took the sergeant a few minutes to get his gear in order to go into the opening. He carried one of those flashlights that had an "L" shape to it. This kind of flashlight was perfect for this type of work. He also carried a .45 caliber handgun. It was the first one I had seen in Vietnam. That weapon must have been damn heavy to carry around all day, but in a small tunnel ten feet underground it was a lot of fire power to have in your hand and I'm sure it made one hell of a hole in whatever it hit.

The sergeant gave us a wink and smile then slid face-first down into the tunnel while we stood there and watched and waited. He had been out of sight for maybe ten seconds when all of a sudden he came scrambling backwards out of that tunnel opening as fast as he could. We were all surprised by how quickly he reappeared and equally surprised by the size of the explosion that followed him. A group of five of us was standing by the tunnel entrance, and I was the only one not wounded by the flying shrapnel from the explosion of this major booby trap.

Everyone else received superficial wounds, but the sergeant received a severe wound to the top of his right shoulder. Even though he was in a great pain, as anyone could tell by the look on his face and the amount of blood that was coming from his wound, he was still laughing. It was his 3rd Purple Heart and the army had an unwritten rule that anyone receiving three or more Purple Hearts in combat was to be taken off-line and given a job back in the rear with the gear. He knew he had seen his last tunnel and lived to tell about it. He was a very lucky man indeed. And after the medivac chopper came and took the sergeant away for treatment, I was never to see him again. A couple weeks later I heard that he had scored a great job in Saigon. I sure hope so—he had earned it.

The medic bandaged up the rest of the wounded, and they went about their duties without ever leaving the field. As for me, I was pretty lucky I guess; the radio on my back took a good-size chunk of shrapnel from the explosion, and it saved my ass from being wounded. This was how it was in the field: Even if you were wounded it still didn't guarantee you a few days off. I was to witness too many guys receive small wounds from shrapnel and be treated right on the spot and never even receive the "Purple Heart Medal" that they had earned. The reasoning behind this was that a Purple Heart medal was something very special, to be awarded only to the most gravely wounded. It was not to be given out for a mere scratch from an exploding bomb—Hell that happened all the time in combat. The lesson I learned that day was not to be too curious. And above all, in the future don't stand so close to a tunnel entrance.

Aside from the obvious problems we had dealing with the tunnels, there were always other elements to deal with on a daily basis while out on patrol. One has to remember that for the regular soldier who fought the Vietnam War there were more ways than one to die. If one takes a look at the number of combat soldiers who were really out in the rice paddies and jungles of Vietnam trying on a daily basis to kill the enemy, the figures can be misleading. There just weren't that many of us. The army's rule of thumb was that out of every ten soldiers in-country, nine of the ten would be giving support to the ones that were actually in a real combat situation. Given the army's number of five hundred thousand guys in-country in 69–

70, that would leave only fifty thousand of us assigned to fight the war on any given day. Of that fifty thousand, ten thousand were either on leave, on sick call, or just back in the rear hanging around. So the true figure of men actually out trying to engage the enemy was closer to forty thousand. That's not to say that the men not out trying to actively engage the enemy weren't in any danger. All I'm saying is that they weren't out beyond the barbed wire and sandbags that surrounded the numerous Fire Support Bases that made up Vietnam, as we were twenty-four hours a day, week after week, month after month, until our tours were finally over.

The dangers we had to deal with every day came from the obvious contacts we had with the enemy, as well as from the country itself. One example of something that could kill you—and did—was malaria. Malaria was always of great concern to us as we patrolled the jungles of South Vietnam. The mosquitoes were everywhere in tremendous numbers, and they were very aggressive to say the least. We remembered to take our malaria pill each and every day, whether it made us sick or not. The water that we drank came for the most part from the wells and streams that we would come across during our daily patrols of the countryside. We put iodine pills into this water to help purify it, and it made the water almost undrinkable. On occasion we would have fresh water dropped to us from a re-supply helicopter, but this didn't happen as often as we would have liked.

The heat and humidity that this country was famous for also presented a problem for the average soldier as well. The temperature was always in the nineties, and the humidity was almost always a hundred percent. Given the fact that I was carrying a pack that weighed upwards of eighty-five pounds, one can see that just getting through the day without getting sick from the weather alone was a feat in itself. Many a new guy would be sent back to the base camp with heat stroke after a short time in the field. It took all of us a while to get used to the heat and humidity of Vietnam.

Due to the fact that our area of operations was the rice paddies and the low country of Vietnam, we were subject to all the snakes, scorpions, and leeches this country had to offer as well. On one occasion in early December1969 I was stung by a Scorpion on the index finger of my right hand. I had reached into a bag to get a fresh pair of socks, when I felt a sharp pain in my finger that caused me to take my hand out of that bag as quickly as possible. I thought I had stuck my finger on a needle, but as I emptied out the bag to my horror out came a large, black Scorpion. The sight of it scared the crap out of me. Everything I had ever heard or read about Scorpions indicated they were deadly. The thought of coming all this way and being in a combat situation and getting killed by a Scorpion seemed to me to be such an unmanly way to die. I can remember being very upset at the thought.

The pain that was pulsating from my finger was now working its way up into my hand; putting pressure around my finger only seemed to make it worse. I stood there for just a few moments and stared at my finger, thinking, *Bullshit, what a way to die.* I yelled out in pain, and our medic came running over to me. When I told him what had just happened, he took a look at my finger and laughed it off and told me to put some ice on it and after a while I would be just fine. What did he mean, put some ice on it and I would be just fine? That was it? That was all the medical treatment I was going to get, just the advice to put some ice on it? I wasn't going to die, I wasn't going to get sick, just put some ice on it and I would be fine? There was only one thing wrong with the doc's advice, and it was the fact that I had been in the field for three and half weeks now and I had yet to see a piece of ice. Then it dawned on me: that's why the doc was laughing his ass off, as he walked away. If I close my eyes now I can still feel the pain of that Scorpion sting, but mostly I can still hear the doc's laughter as he slowly walked away, shaking his head.

Snakes in Vietnam were another matter entirely. There were numerous snakes in our AO (area of operation) and they could be very deadly. On December 19, 1969, I had my first encounter with a "Bamboo Viper". This snake is one of the deadliest in the world. Its venom is said to attack your nervous system, unlike the rattlesnake, which attacks your muscular system. Supposedly a bite from a viper can kill you in a matter of minutes.

Our platoon was on a mission east of the Sugar Mill. We had just sent one squad around to the other side of a village we were about to recon to act as a blocking force before we entered. As we waited for them to get to their location, we positioned ourselves in a thicket of bamboo that was growing out of a slight incline. We had fifteen minutes or so before the other squad would be in position to make its move into the village, so our team thought it would take a small break and have a smoke or whatever. Due to the weight of the radio and my pack, as well as the eight canteens of water that I was carrying, all I ever did when we took a break was try to lean up against something. The incline looked just about right for me to take advantage of. I wouldn't be lying down, but I wouldn't be standing up either; it would be perfect in the event I had to move quickly.

As I settled myself into a comfortable position I heard a strange noise coming from above my head, moving slowly through the underbrush. Instinctively I knew it was a snake. But I had yet to see a snake over here, and I was so damn tired and comfortable; if it wasn't a snake I would have wasted all that energy moving. So I decided to just lie there very still, and whatever it was would just go away. I had been in Vietnam now for over a month, and I really should have known better. Nothing in Vietnam ever just goes away.

I was just drifting off to sleep, for by now I could fall asleep just that fast, when I felt something moving slowly across by chest. For some reason, I can remember it was going from left to right. I opened my eyes and looked down ever so carefully, and to my horror I saw a small green snake with a bright red ring around its neck, lying on my chest. I took a deep breath, and jumped up as fast as my gear would allow me, and let out a scream that scared the shit out of everyone with me. We had a Kit Carson scout with us. (A Kit Carson scout was an ex-enemy soldier who had defected to our side and helped us locate the enemy when we were in the field.) He ran after the snake, took out the large knife that he carried with him at all times, and with one quick motion chopped the head off that goddamn snake. He then brought the snake that was hanging from his knife over for me to see and proceeded to explain to me what it was and what it could have done to me with just one bite. I stood there sweating from every pore in my body, completely out of breath. The thought that with one bite that snake could have killed me still runs chills up and down my spine to this very day.

Chapter 12

Christmas and New Years . . .
and Bob Hope, Too

Alpha Company was working the hedgerow area west of the Sugar Mill, when we received word that the Bob Hope show was going to be playing at the division base camp at Cu Chi. A major from our brigade called out to our company commander and said that half of the company would be airlifted into Cu Chi for the show, if we could be ready to go within thirty minutes. The answer from us was no sweat, we could be ready. But now the question was who was to go and who was to stay behind? I was not in on that decision-making process; all I knew was that I was one of the lucky ones who was picked to go to the Bob Hope show, and that was all I cared about.

The show would be nice but what was more important to me was the chance to get into Cu Chi and go to the PX (Post Exchange). We had just been paid and I had a pocket full of money and wanted to buy a camera in the worst way. There was so much I wanted to take pictures of over here, and a visit to the PX was my chance to pick myself up a good 35-mm camera to do just that. There were a lot of guys shopping this day, due to the fact that I wasn't the only one to have a pocket full of money. The PX was mobbed. I was lucky this day though, as one of the girls who worked at the store came right over to me as I entered the building and asked if she could be of assistance. I told her about my quest for a good camera and she knew exactly what I wanted. I was in and out of that place in less than ten minutes.

With my camera in hand and a few rolls of film, it was time to make my way over to the lunchroom, where I bought a milkshake and a burger. A shake and a burger was a big deal for the men who were in the field for weeks on end. After lunch a few of the guys and myself worked our way over to the Bob Hope show just in time to catch the very end of it from a distance. Seeing Bob Hope in person was kind of nice: I had seen all his shows from World War Two and the Korean War on television at home. I just never thought that I would someday be part of the audience myself.

When we got to the show we were about one hundred yards away from the stage, but we could make out what was going on—just barely, but at least I could say I had been there. The front-row seats were all taken by the men who called Cu Chi Base Camp home for their tour in Vietnam. I guess that was the way it was, but to be honest with you, it did cause some of us to be a little pissed off. We felt that we were the ones doing the fighting and putting our lives on the line day after day, and here they were with the best seats in the house. We were relegated to standing in the back with our packs and weapons, getting ready to go back to where we had come from. It was a clear case of out of sight, out of mind, I guess.

The show would end soon enough, and then it would be time for us to leave also. After the show ended we made our way over to the airfield where the same choppers that had brought us in were waiting to take us back out to where they had picked us up. Within twenty minutes of loading up, we were back in the field with the rest of Alpha Company. I felt kind of guilty when I got back, but after telling everyone about the show and handing out some of the chewing gum and candy bars I had bought, I felt a lot better. I didn't feel so much like the new guy any longer. I felt like I was part of the company now, and that's all I wanted to be all along, just part of the team.

It was getting late in the day now and we would have to put the "Bob Hope Show" behind us and get ready for the night's ambush patrol. Tonight it would be back to the business of killing as usual, but the next day we would be off to the Sugar Mill Complex and some rest.

The Sugar Mill Complex was kind of a cool place to spend the holidays. It sure as hell beat sleeping on the ground in the jungle all night. We set up our command post operation center on the top of the Sugar Mill's tallest building; it was around six stories high. From there we could see for quite a distance and that would come in handy for calling in some artillery on Christmas Eve. The trade-off of having our command position up so high was that the enemy would also know where we were and have a clear shot at us with their RPGs (Rocket Propelled Grenades). But we figured it was a good trade-off and it would prove to be so.

The captain decided to send out a couple of ambush patrols on Christmas Eve, while a couple of platoons would stay behind to cover the area around the Sugar Mill. The command unit itself would be up on top of the Sugar Mill's main tower. After the ambushes were in place for the night and we had plotted their positions on our map, we would all settle in for the night. We then would take turns monitoring the radios for any signs of activity from the patrols we had out. We didn't really expect anything to happen, as it was Christmas Eve, but given the fact that we were right in the middle of the enemy's main infiltration route into Saigon, we had to be on the highest alert at all times, Christmas notwithstanding.

Things were very quiet until 4:30 A.M., when First Platoon blew their ambush on a much larger enemy patrol than they had realized and were calling frantically in to command for as much support as we could get to them, in as short a time as possible. As soon as the call came in to our position for help we sprang into action with a call to Fire Support Base Chamberlain for a fire mission "ASAP". We already had our points of reference plotted on our map and as soon as the call came in we were ready to go. I would say it took all of a three minutes at the most for the first artillery shell to be on its way out to First Platoon's position.

First Platoon's position was approximately one click (one thousand yards) to our northwest. From the window of the Sugar Mill we could now see them engaged in their firefight with the enemy. It was very strange to actually be watching the fight and talking to them from a distance at the same time. It would be the only time that this was to happen during my entire tour of duty in Vietnam, it was like watching a movie from long distance. What we wanted to do was get our gear together and start moving out to their position, but this was impossible during the confusion of an active firefight. We would have to be flown in, but that would have to wait until first light; until then all we could do was wait and watch and give all the help we could from right where we were.

We could see the red tracers coming from their machine guns, as well as the green tracers coming back at them from the gooks' weapons. The sight was as surreal as it was beautiful, with its colorful display of red and green streaks of light piercing the air in all directions. There were also numerous small explosions of a yellowish light that we knew were claymore mines and hand grenades going off. It would have been like watching the Fourth of July fireworks at home, only we were well aware of what was really happening along that river bank and how serious and deadly it was.

After a few minutes of watching this strange show of light and periodically speaking in hurried bursts of words with the platoon leader,

Lt. Flowers, we started to see larger bursts of explosions impact near the platoon's position to the west. We knew these were the artillery rounds that had just been called in by us, as they hit their targets. Lt. Flowers then got on the radio with FSB Chamberlain to adjust the fire-mission himself. We could hear him say, "Add fifty, left one hundred," and then wait a few minutes for the shells to hit. Then he would adjust them again and wait some more. The lieutenant was so calm: It was amazing to hear him in control of such a very dangerous situation. His coolness under fire that night saved many of his men's lives, whether they knew it or not. Lt. Flowers was to receive the Bronze Star Medal with a "V" for valor for his actions that night.

With the artillery fire being handled on the ground by those actually involved in the firefight there wasn't a lot for us to do back at the Sugar Mill. It was during this break in the action that I felt it would be okay for me to grab my new camera and take a few pictures. I went over to my bag to get it and it wasn't there. I couldn't believe it was gone. Either I had lost it on our way to the Mill, or someone had stolen it. But it was gone nevertheless and I just couldn't believe it. That camera had been so hard for me to obtain and I hadn't even taken one picture with it. I would have to buy another one when I got back into Cu Chi, but when that would be I had no idea. I couldn't believe it was gone—I was so pissed off I can still feel the rage I felt that day.

We monitored the fight and called in all the helicopter gun ships we could muster up from nearby Cu Chi Base Camp. Gun ships were always ready for just such a situation and they were always just a call away. Those guys who flew on a moment's notice were the best this war had to offer. Just think about it: getting up in the middle of the night to fly into an active firefight; that must have been one very tough thing to do and these guys did it on a nightly basis.

The firefight was now at least twenty minutes old and twenty minutes was a long firefight in Vietnam. We could still see streaks of red and green tracers coming from the area, as well as continuous artillery shells going off around the ambush patrol's perimeter. The sky now had a fluttering glow to it, as the artillery was also sending in flares to light up the field of fire for our troops to better see the enemy by; of course the gooks now could see them more clearly as well. The decision to call in the overhead flares was always left to the commander in charge at the scene of an ambush, as he knew best whether he needed the light and whether to take the chance that the other side could see him as well. Sometimes we called it in and sometimes we didn't; every circumstance would be different and would dictate our actions.

One of the infantry's most welcomed additions during a firefight, whether it was by day or night, was the sight and sound of the helicopter. The *whomp, whomp, whomp* of those helicopter blades going around and around only meant one thing to the men who were engaged with the enemy and that was that their rescue and safety was now within reach.

We watched as the helicopters started to make their run against the enemy's positions with the able guidance of Lt. Flowers. We could hear everything that was being said between Flowers and the pilots. It was like listening to a radio show and watching it at the same time. As I have said before, it didn't seem real; it is one of those events that has been etched in my mind forever, because it was the first nighttime action of this type that I had been involved in. I say "involved in," because we felt we were, even though we were at a distance.

The sun was now starting to rise above the horizon and it was time for us to saddle up and move out towards the exchange of gunfire that still could be heard sporadically along the river. It would take us about forty-five minutes to get to First Platoon's location. We already had our gear on and were ready to go by the time the sun came up and we couldn't wait to get into the fight ourselves. It's a funny thing about combat: It's not something that one would seek out and want to happen, but once it starts and you are involved, your adrenaline takes over and you seem to want more and more of it. It's like a high from some sort of drug. I can now see how some of the soldiers who had seen a lot of combat over here never could adjust to being back in the States without it. Close combat is like nothing else in this life that you can experience; all of your senses are on full alert. I don't know of another way for this to be achieved, outside of personal involvement in a life-or-death situation. When you personally are in a position of actually trying to take another soldiers life and he yours, the high that you experience cannot really be duplicated in any other way. After we reached First Platoon's position we paused just short of the river-bank area that they were occupying and made contact with Lt. Flowers to let him know that we were a few hundred yards to his east. We were then able to get his assessment of the situation and ask him how we could best be of help to him. All the while the situation right in front of us was changing with each moment, what with sporadic gunfire coming from all directions. It made it very difficult for us to move one way or another.

The lieutenant got back on the radio and informed me that the call for a Medivac chopper had already been made, as they had sustained numerous wounded. The wounded we expected, but the fact that they sustained any casualties was something we never liked to hear. He informed us that he felt the enemy had withdrawn from the battlefield but had left behind a few snipers and for us to move up slowly and watch out for them. We started to move out, on the highest alert for any snipers. Snipers always sucked, because you couldn't see them by the time they saw you. I would experience this firsthand later in my tour when I myself became a sniper. We reached First Platoon's position along the river in about fifteen minutes. It was a bloody mess, what with the number of wounded. I counted at least ten, and then I stopped counting. As we arrived on the scene, a medivac chopper had just set down and was loading up the most seriously wounded. The fact that if you were unlucky enough to be wounded in combat in Vietnam, a chopper would be available to take you out and have you on an operating table in less than fifteen minutes was a miracle in itself. It was one of the things in combat that we all depended upon and those pilots never let us down. Those medivac chopper pilots would fly right into an active firefight to take us out, at great risk to themselves and by so doing saved many a soldier's life.

More helicopters were making their way in now to take out the rest of the wounded and drop off much needed supplies. Some of the men had shrapnel wounds from the grenades that the enemy had thrown; but most had bullet wounds and bullets make one hell of an ugly wound. The caliber of bullets that were used over here was basically the same for both sides. They were very small in size, but when they hit human flesh and bone they would tear through the body with such force that the damage is too graphic to describe. Let me just say that it's a miracle in itself that anyone could survive getting hit by one of those bullets.

After we had positioned ourselves in a perimeter around First Platoon's area and the wounded had been flown out, it was time for us to start to assess the damage that we had brought upon the enemy. After a firefight that causes American casualties the soldiers that survive would be looking for a little payback. In fact, as my time in-country dragged on I can honestly say that payback was something we would be looking for on each and every patrol and ambush. We would always be looking for "Payback"—the more, the better. The feelings of the men that actually fought the "Vietnam War" was that the more of the enemy we could kill, the less of them there would be to kill. I know that thinking sounds kind of weird now, but at the time it made complete sense to us.

Our platoon moved out of its defensive position very slowly and started to search for the enemy, alive or dead. We hadn't gone very far, only twenty yards or so, when we came upon three dead VC (Viet Cong). It must have been a very confusing fire-fight as they still had their weapons lying beside them, this was almost never the case after a battle—their buddies would always take their fallen comrades' guns with them as they withdrew from the battlefield. But they hadn't this time. Well tough shit for them, we thought; they belonged to us now. A few of the guys checked the bodies for documents and such, as was our usual practice and then we moved on, looking for more of the enemy. We continued doing this the entire morning. After we felt we had checked the entire area and located all the enemy that we could find, the total of enemy dead this day would be fourteen. There were a lot of blood trails leading off into the high reeds that ran along the river bank, but this was to be expected as the enemy always tried to drag away its wounded and sometimes even its dead. According to the brass in charge of such things, this had been a good ambush and a good firefight.

As I look back on it now, my feelings aren't any different today than they were then. It wasn't worth it one bit, not with ten or so wounded as our price to pay. I thought it stunk then and I still do today. But once the fighting begins and the adrenaline starts to flow and the willingness to kill and the desire to live kick in, all bets are off. We all took our chances for our country in one way or another and prayed for the best. That's all one could do once a combat situation developed. As my time in-country dragged on and I became more hardened and experienced, I would tune out the possibility that I too could be wounded or killed. I would just go with the flow of the situation. After a while one doesn't really believe he will be making it home anyway. We tried to survive day to day and not worry about what tomorrow may bring—tomorrow was out of our control and was going to take care of itself one way or another. We were all at fate's mercy and there wasn't much we could do about it. For in Vietnam, tomorrow was promised to no one.

Chapter 13
Air Medals for the men of "A" 1/27th

There would now be a change in the way the First Wolfhounds would operate and the area they would be operating in. Our new AO (area of operations) would be north-northeast of Cu Chi Base Camp, between Trang Bang and Dau Tieng. This area had a name: "The Iron Triangle". During the dry season it was all unused rice paddies, rubber plantations and large areas of open fields separated by small jungle areas. Located within these areas were the small villages that fed off the rice paddies and farming areas surrounding them. These villages were famous for hiding the enemy and their weapons during the day, so the VC would have a safe place to rest before they went out at night to attack our FSB's (fire support bases). Our assignment was to surprise the enemy and destroy him and his hiding places. The best way for us to do this effectively was determined to be by quick airborne helicopter assaults. During their time in-country the "Wolfhounds" would make hundreds of such assaults by helicopter; some were very successful and others turn out to be very expensive. The 116th Assault Helicopter Company, better known to us by their nickname, "the Hornets", supplied our helicopters. These guys were the best as far as we were concerned. They where always available to us when we needed them and that was all that mattered to us.

It was the first week of January 1970 and I had been out with Alpha Company for six weeks now. I had seen a great change in how I perceived the war and how I looked at myself since that first day when I was flown into the field to meet the company. Day after day of humping through the rice paddies and jungles of this god-forsaken country will do that to a man after a while. I hadn't been back to the artillery battery that I was assigned to since I left. It seemed like a long time ago and I wondered if I would ever get back. But it really didn't seem to make all that much of a difference, as I was part of the "Wolfhounds" now and it was with them that I would experience Vietnam.

The most profound change to the company was the fact that Lt. Baker was no longer with us, he had moved back to the Battery to serve out the rest of his tour in relative safety. We now would have a new Lieutenant out with us. His name was Lt. White and from the very beginning we didn't hit it off. He made it clear from day one that he was in charge and he wasn't going to be taking any advice from me, a mere Corporal, even though I had more combat experience than him. Hell, he didn't have any at all, but he was the officer and he was going to be in charge and that was the way it was going to be. It was officers who came into the field with that kind of attitude that got guys killed and I knew it, so I would keep an eye on this new guy, officer or not. I wasn't going to let this guy's inexperience get me killed. No way!

After more than seven weeks of seeking-out the enemy during the day and ambushing him by night, the thought of using a different tactic to find him was welcomed by the entire company. The idea of assaulting areas that we knew the enemy would be hiding in by air appealed to each and every one of us. The fact that we wouldn't have to walk everywhere also appealed to us, as it was becoming so damn hot now, with the temperatures in the high nineties day in and day out. My pack, with the radio, extra battery, water, food, and ammo, along with my M16, was weighing in at a good eighty-five pounds or more. As much as I'd try to lighten my load I just couldn't find a way to—I needed everything I was carrying. Anytime that I didn't have to carry it around was fine with me. Flying in a chopper at one or two thousand feet in the air, traveling at a hundred miles an hour, would make for the most refreshing part of my day.

The first day of our new operational tactics began very early in the morning. The sun rises early in Vietnam and the earlier we got going the better. The enemy did most of his traveling during the night and we always liked to surprise him first thing in the morning, as he was settling in for his downtime.

As we waited in a large open area for the choppers to arrive to pick us up, the adrenaline really started to flow in my system. A large group of helicopters flying real low appeared off in the distance. After they landed and were sitting there on the ground right in front of us the *whomp, whomp, whomp* of the chopper blades going around only got us all that more pumped up to get our first combat assault by air underway. The choppers were there right on time at 6:00 A.M. and we were set to board them for our first airborne assault against what we figured would be a small VC base camp. It was a company-size operation, so eleven choppers were assigned to take approximately one hundred of us on a short flight of seven miles or so. Our assignment this day was to fly in and surprise the enemy and attack him before he had a chance to escape.

The plan would be for five of the helicopters to set down about three hundred yards to the west of the target area and set up a blocking line to catch the enemy as he fled. The rest of us would attack the objective from the east. As we approached the suspected enemy base camp the line of choppers would split in two, with one group banking off to the left and the other would fly straight in and land off to the right. We then would start our sweep of the camp area and engage the enemy and drive him towards our blocking force, which would be waiting to our west. The plan looked pretty good on paper, but as with just about all plans something would almost inevitably go wrong; usually the enemy wouldn't cooperate as we had hoped he would. This being our very first helicopter airborne assault, would be one of those times.

The morning sun was now rising higher off the eastern horizon as we flew towards our objective, which was a small farming village off to our west. It would only take us a few minutes to get there. Our choppers would only be flying at a thousand feet on our way to the target area. Flying so close to the ground made us feel as if we were flying even faster than we actually were. It was exactly the way I envisioned what the fighting in Vietnam would be like, but even more exciting.

A couple of miles out, the lift of choppers split in two as planned. As the lead helicopter I was in started to quickly descend from its altitude of a thousand feet and make its assault run into the area that we wanted to attack, the excitement and fear that went through me is very hard to describe. The confusion of a combat assault by helicopter was something that couldn't be taught. For it was truly one of those things in life one had to experience in person. On the one hand I felt that I was here to do a job and I was going to do that job to the best of my ability at all costs, but on the other hand I wondered what the hell I was doing here in the first place. But it didn't matter how I tried to analyze my position, the thrill of what I was participating in was by far the most thrilling thing I had ever done. To be honest about it, the experience was quite an adrenaline rush and I wouldn't have traded it for the world.

As our lift of helicopters started to get closer to the LZ (landing zone) the door gunners opened up with their M60 machine guns from the sides of the choppers to kill anyone or anything that may have made our landing any more dangerous than it would have to be. The helicopters were now firing rockets themselves into the target area. I could feel the chopper shudder as each rocket was fired from the pods that were located right under our feet and with each rocket that was fired my adrenaline flowed even more rapidly. It was like nothing I had ever experienced before. I knew that the longer we were in the air though, the greater chance we had of being shot out of the sky, but I didn't want to stop flying. It was like I had become part of the chopper itself and leaving it would mean leaving the only protection I had. But I knew the sooner we landed the better my chances of survival.

The chopper would fly us into the LZ (landing zone) very fast and then it would pull its nose up as it made its ever-so-brief landing. It would be on the ground just long enough for us to jump out, we then would take a moment to look around before making a run for whatever cover that would be available to us.

As the command team was always in the lead chopper, we would be the first ones on the ground. It was up to us to assess the situation as to its safety for the other choppers to come in and deploy the rest of the company. This would be achieved by the mere fact that if we were not actively engaged in a firefight with the guys that we had come to kill, then it would be relatively safe for the rest of the company to land. We would then pop a smoke grenade. The color of the smoke we would pop had been pre-determined before we left on the operation. The enemy would sometimes pop their own smoke to confuse the choppers on their way in and trick them into putting down at the wrong location, where the enemy could attack them. This was something that we tried to avoid at all costs. Today, green smoke told the chopper pilots and troops on their way in that the landing zone was cold—that is to say, they could get off the choppers in relative safety, as we were not actively engaged with the enemy at that time. If we had popped red smoke, that would have meant the LZ was hot and we were actively engaged in a firefight and the next wave of helicopters and troops coming in to the LZ (landing zone) would need to react accordingly.

The sweep of the suspected enemy area began a few minutes after we landed. After we got everyone on-line, we fanned out and moved forward as a group. The command team was a few yards behind the first line of troops, so as to monitor its advance. But once we got into the thick hedgerow jungle close to the village we would begin to advance on the target area at our own pace, for staying in line would be impossible.

It was early in the morning but the sun had been up for hours now and it was becoming very hot and humid. It doesn't take long for that to happen in Vietnam; it is one of the hottest places on this earth. We started to work our way through the thick underbrush, sometimes stumbling and tripping on the small ground-hugging vines that seem to grow everywhere in this godforsaken land. Off in the distance, about thirty yards or so through the thickness of the foliage, we caught a glimpse of a few small shacks and a couple of bamboo lean-tos. Once we could actually see this potential enemy position right in front of us, we stopped to get a better look.

While we were taking a short break, trying to decide if we wanted to approach this position or to send out a scout-team to check it out, our decision was made for us, for that's when the enemy opened fire. All hell had broken loose on our patrol, with small-arms fire and machine-gun fire as well as a few rocket-propelled grenades coming our way.

It didn't take long for the group of us to hit the ground as one. It was as if we had tripped over the same wire at the exact same moment. We couldn't tell the size of the force that we faced in front of us because we just couldn't see them, but we sprang into action and fired back with everything we had. I could hear, as well as feel the bullets zipping through the low-hung branches of the small jungle trees that we were trying to take cover behind. *Zing, zing, zing,* one could hear the bullets fly by. They say that if you can feel the bullets breaking the air near you, they are as close as three feet. On this day I could feel them breaking the air, as well as see them striking the ground around us. The bullets zipped through the branches of the trees over our heads, causing the leaves to fall all around us; for a moment it kind of looked like green snow falling from the sky.

Lt. White was about ten feet from me when the enemy opened up on us and he was now trying to crawl his way over to me. The gooks had us pretty well pinned down and neither of us dared to move. I proceeded to roll over on my side to take the radio off my back, knowing full well that they could see the antenna sticking up in the air and would be aiming for it. The gooks always tried to take out the radio operator first, as he was the communications link with the outside world and today that soldier was me. I figured that if I got the radio off my back and laid it on the ground a few feet to my left, they would concentrate their fire on it. I was hoping the dumb bastards would figure I still had it on my back and I think they did just that, considering the amount of bullets that continued to hit around that radio.

The radio was now off my back, but I could still reach over and talk through the phone to call in the artillery support we were starting to need so desperately. "Two Zero, this is Two Zero Echo Bravo, fire mission". "Over," I yelled franticly into the phone.

The immediate response was "Two Zero Echo Bravo, this is Two Zero". We hear you loud and clear. What's your situation? "Over."

By this time Lt. White had made his way over to me and had our coordinates (exactly where we were) figured out on his map and was ready to relay them back to the Battery. He was fast and I was grateful for his speed and accuracy. "Two Zero, this is Two Zero Echo," he yelled with breathless excitement into the radiophone. "Do you hear me'? 'Over."

The Battery called back to the affirmative.

He now spoke calmly into the radio. "Give me one round of Willie Peter (white phosphorus) at grid 157263 by 785255." 'Over' with all the gunfire, noise, smoke, and just plain confusion going on all around us, I still can't believe he was as calm as he appeared to be. Hell, I was scared shitless.

Within two minutes we could hear the distinctive sound of an artillery round fly over our heads. And what a welcome sound it was. The lieutenant had only been off by about fifty yards long by fifty yards or so wide. That first call of his was as good as it gets, given the life-and-death situation we found ourselves in.

Throughout the confusion and chaos that was going on along the splintered defensive line that we found ourselves in, the men knew the sound of an incoming artillery round and knew to keep their heads down, because there would be more—lots more—to follow. All up and down the line above all the noise one could hear the phrase "Fire in the hole! Fire in the hole!" being screamed. This meant for everyone to get down and take cover, for the shells were about to come in like rain.

Lt. White called in to adjust fire. "Two Zero, this is Two Zero Echo," give me six rounds of " H.E" (high explosive) as quickly as you can, "Over". All the while bullets were hitting and zooming all around us. I had all I could do just to lift my M16 up over the small mound of earth I found myself taking cover behind to get off a couple of bursts of fire at the enemy. I couldn't see them, but they seemed to be able to see me just fine, judging by how close the gunfire was getting to my radio. That damn radio always drew a lot of fire. That's why I had it sitting up about six feet from my actual location. The lieutenant yelled into the phone, "Drop fifty, Right fifty and Fire for Effect, Fire for Effect. 'Over.'"

The FDC (fire direction control) came back and repeated what he had just said as a safety factor.

The lieutenant and I were lying on our sides rolled up in a ball with our hands holding our helmets on, waiting for that first shell of high explosives to land momentarily. We would occasionally lift our guns up to get off a few rounds as we waited for what seemed like an eternity for the artillery to arrive. I'm sure it only took a few minutes but it seemed like a lot longer to us.

When we heard the screeching sounds of the full six shells coming over our heads and then exploding about fifty yards to our immediate front, we both looked at each other and knew those bombs were on target. The sounds of those rounds going off, one right after another, was music to our ears. We could feel the concussions from our position. I sure as hell wouldn't have wanted them to be dropping down on top of me.

The lieutenant called back into the Battery to adjust fire once again. He moved the incoming shells by telling the Fire Direction Control center to move the shells to the right another twenty-five yards. That would bring those exploding shells even closer to our position, but it would also drop the lethal explosions right down on top of the enemy. I peaked over at Lt. White from under my helmet and gave him a faint smile; even though we knew what we wanted, we were so dependent on the guys at the fire control center to get their jobs done right and right the first time. It was kind of scary being so dependent on someone who wasn't even there with you. But this day they were right on and we were very grateful.

The 105-mm artillery rounds came flying in and landed right where we wanted them to, over and over again. Those shells found their targets with such accuracy, it still amazes me to this day and I know how it's done. I can't imagine not knowing how it's done and seeing it done—that alone must be pretty impressive. After fifteen minutes or so, I figured at least one hundred rounds must have landed on the enemy's position.

After we called into the FDC to stop the fire mission we could hardly hear each other speak. Being that close to exploding bombs does a number on one's hearing. After I grabbed my radio, Lt. White and I scrambled along the ground until we came up to the captain, who was only twenty yards from us.. When we got to his position he didn't say a word to us, he just gave us thumbs up and that was good enough for us.

All sounds of combat had now ceased and it was eerily quiet as we looked around to determine what we could expect next. The first sound that we heard after the artillery barrage had lifted was the sound that we didn't want to hear and that was men yelling for a medic. The call for a medic was coming from three different directions. The small group of us made our way over to the first soldier who had yelled for a medic. We found Pvt. Jones about twenty yards from our position. He was half covered by the dense underbrush we were in and it was sticking to his uniform as he tried moving his body to help control the pain that he was obviously experiencing. When we got there the medic was right behind us. He pushed us aside to get to Jones, who had a bullet wound to his upper right leg that was bleeding profusely, from what I could see. I knew he was in a lot of pain; he wasn't screaming out or anything like that, but I could tell by the contorted look on his face the amount of pain that damn enemy bullet must have been putting him through.

The medic ripped open the private's pant leg to expose the wound and we could see a good-sized hole about the size of a quarter in the front of his leg. But it was the back of the leg that got my attention; it had a huge gaping hole in it. The medic proceeded to put a tourniquet above the hole and this seemed to slow down the bleeding. The medic then grabbed one of the guys that was with us by the shirt and told him to hold the tourniquet tight, but not to tight. The medic then gave Jones a shot of morphine, this seemed to calm him down immediately. All the while this was going on, a few more frantic calls of "Medic, Medic" rang out. The "Doc" was going to have himself one busy morning, by the looks of things. I couldn't tell how many more casualties we had taken this morning, but as far as I was concerned one was too many.

At this time the captain had his RTO on the horn calling for a Medivac helicopter to take out the wounded as quickly as possible. As I was listening to him make the call, my only thoughts were, please "Lord" only wounded, no killed in action this day. I had already been exposed to American soldiers being killed in combat. The sight of a KIA (killed in action) stays with you forever.

There was still plenty of confusion going on all around us when the first medivac chopper came into sight. The captain ordered a smoke grenade set off to let the chopper pilot know exactly where to set down.. Upon the medivac choppers landing, three wounded soldiers of Alpha Company were hurriedly put on board and within a few minutes they were gone, back to Cu Chi to the Twenty-fifth Medivac Hospital for treatment. We took for granted the promise of a quick flight out of this mess if we were to be wounded and knowing that such a thing was only a call away was of great comfort to us. How many men those medivac helicopters saved would be tough to calculate, but I'm sure it was in the tens of thousands. With the wounded stabilized and flown out and all the shooting stopped, it was time to take stock of what we had accomplished and what would lie ahead of us for the rest of the day. The first thing we had to do to complete our mission was to take a quick head count to make sure we were all accounted for. With all the confusion of a firefight it would be very easy to lose someone and we would never want that to happen. There were now forty-eight of us left to start our sweep into the village area. This was the same village that we had just destroyed with our artillery barrage an hour before. We were curious as to how many of the enemy was dead or wounded. We again started our move into the village, this time with a lot more confidence; for we couldn't imagine anyone surviving the number of bombs that had just been dropped on such a small area.

We cautiously made our way into the heart of the village, all the time being on our highest alert for any enemy soldiers that may have survived the artillery barrage. We also had our eye out for any booby traps that could blow our legs off, or worse. A couple of the small Hooch's were still partly standing and on fire, but beyond that it was deathly silent. The smell of black powder from the exploded artillery shells hung in the air so much so that we had to cover our mouths to avoid choking. Looking around the area, we counted all of seven enemy bodies and numerous body parts, so the count of enemy dead was officially put at twenty-six. We always upped the body-count, as it seemed to make a big difference to the Generals safely back in the rear sipping their drinks by the pool. But to the grunts that were in the jungles of Vietnam creating that body-count, it didn't seemed to matter all that much. In fact, it didn't matter at all. All that really mattered to us was that we were all still alive and one day closer to going home. And we were always glad that the fighting had ended, at least for now anyway. The men of Alpha Company checked every nook and cranny of the destroyed village looking for any enemy soldiers that may have been hiding and also for any documents on the dead soldiers. Picking around the bodies of men that an hour earlier were living human beings not unlike ourselves was not something anyone I knew wanted to do, but it had to be done. After we had cleared the village of all the information we could find and after we had put the bodies of the enemy soldiers in a pile, we were ordered to torch what was left of the village and get ready to move out. It had been over two hours since we'd called in the artillery strike that destroyed the village.

It was still early in the day and it was now time for us to link up with the rest of the company, which was waiting for us off to our west. They had held their ground to our west waiting for any of the enemy to try to escape, but none did. It only took us about twenty minutes of walking to locate them and they were just as glad to see us as we were to see them. There were approximately ninety of us together now to carry on with our mission. No matter where one was in Vietnam or what he was doing, it was always nice to have the numbers on your side and ninety soldiers sure as hell beat forty-eight soldiers any day.

We spread ourselves out and made a perimeter for defense as we always did and just kind of laid back and took a break. It had been quite a morning. I thought of the three guys that had been wounded and wondered if they were okay. Calls were made back to Alpha Company's headquarters for someone to go over to Twenty-fifth Medivac Hospital to find out for us, but it would take a while for the word to get back out to us. In the meantime we would take a break for the rest of the day before we got our shit together for the night's ambush patrol.

That's how it was, some combat in the morning and a village or two destroyed before lunch and that gave us a feeling that we had had a very productive day. Yes, a break was in order for Alpha Company. Hell, we felt for the most part that we were out here all alone anyway, left to fend for ourselves. We weren't complaining though, for we wouldn't have wanted it any other way. We knew where we stood and how expendable we were to the Generals who controlled this war, but what they were missing was the camaraderie that we all felt for one another. That was something that they wouldn't be taking home from Vietnam and it was something they couldn't take away from us. Most of us felt that we had two enemies to fight over here: the gooks and our own Generals. The feeling amongst the men that I served with, was that for us not to turn into animals would be a victory in itself.

We thought we had done respectably for our first combat assault by helicopter. If it weren't for the wounded we had suffered it would have been a great day. But a pretty good day would have to do for now. We would get a lot better at it, for there would be many more air combat assaults for Alpha Company in the coming months.

Before I had a chance to doze off, word came back from Cu Chi that the three wounded men were doing fine and would survive their wounds. All three of them would never return to Alpha Company though. Pvt. Jones who had the bad leg wound would be sent off to a hospital in Japan and then he would be going home. The Vietnam War would be over for him, but at a stiff cost. The other two guys were re-assigned to non-combat jobs in the rear, I never did find out where. There were only three ways out of the field in Vietnam: (1) receive a bad enough wound, (2) get killed, or (3) serve out your time. Those were the only three options the grunts that fought the Vietnam War had. All they could do was take each and every day as it came and pray for the best.

Chapter 14

My Return to Fire Support Base Chamberlain

The next morning would start out like any other morning in the field, but something that had never happened before was about to. Alpha Company would get the word to make its way back to FSB Chamberlain to take over perimeter duty for the base. This was something that took place every six or seven weeks or so, depending on what was going on with operations in the field. I had been in country for seven weeks now and for six of those weeks I had been out with Alpha Company patrolling the jungles and rice paddies west of Saigon.

The men that I was serving with were pretty excited about going back to Chamberlain, as the duty would get us out of the jungle and back to some semblance of civilization. Being back at base camp would offer us some hot meals and hot showers and what we all looked forward to: a chance to get a nights sleep not being out on ambush. I was to find out also that we would be getting the chance to get back into Cu Chi to go shopping at the PX. A shopping trip back at Cu Chi was such a rare occurrence that it took on a special meaning all of its own. I was really looking forward to buying another camera to replace the one I had lost earlier and I really wanted a thick chocolate milkshake in the worst way.

Our position was about five clicks (five thousand yards) west of Chamberlain, so the decision was made to walk our way into the base camp. The walk would take us the better part of the morning, but we didn't mind—we had a destination we were looking forward to.

We finally made our way out of the thick jungle about three hundred yards north of Chamberlain. As we made our way towards the front gate of the FSB, I got my first look at the base I had left six weeks earlier.

The base hadn't changed much, but the change in me was significant. I was no longer the new guy, that only a month and a half ago caught a chopper and flew west out of Chamberlain to join the war. We walked with our heads held high through the front gate and made our way around to the other side of the camp. For we knew deep down inside that we were the only soldiers in that camp who were really fighting the war, so up close and personal on a daily basis.

The guys that made up Alpha Company 1/27 Wolfhounds would settle down in an area that earlier Bravo Company had occupied. They were now in the field taking our place. Lt. White came over to me and showed me where I was to stay. It was a small one-man bunker set up right outside of the FDC (fire direction control center). My own little bunker that had its own fold-up canvas cot—boy, I thought I was in heaven.

The first thing I did was to take off all the gear I had on and place it inside the bunker. Then I stripped off everything I was wearing and threw it away. I then made my way naked over to the makeshift showers and tried to wash six weeks' worth of sweat and ground-in dirt from my body. I think I got most of it, but even if I didn't, that shower was the most refreshing thing I had experienced since being in-country. I found some used (previously worn) clothes and put them on. After making myself presentable I would then have to report to that same big bad First Sergeant that had sent me out to Alpha Company, when I first arrived in the Battery.

I made my way over to the TOC (tactical operations center) to report in, but to my utter surprise I was informed that the First Sergeant was no longer in charge of the Battery, but had rotated home while I was out. To tell you the truth, I was glad he was gone. I just knew that we weren't going to get along anyway. The new First Sergeant had just taken command of the Battery and all he knew about me was that I was the RTO attached to Alpha Company. We started out on the right foot and we got along just fine from then on; in fact, we would become kind of close as my tour progressed.

After reporting in I walked over to the FDC; that was the place I was really looking forward to seeing. It was these guys that ran the center that I had been speaking with on a daily basis for over six weeks now. The FDC bunker was a fairly big bunker, probably twenty-five by twenty-five feet. It was manned by a group of six enlisted men, along with an officer. The enlisted men worked and slept in the bunker. They worked seven days a week, eight hours on and eight hours off, around the clock. I found out after I got off-line and got myself a job in the FDC bunker how tough that job was. I poked my head down into the bunker and walked in and introduced myself. The greeting I got really made me feel like part of the FDC team. There were handshakes all around, with a couple of pats on the back. They were truly glad to see whom "Two Zero Echo Bravo" was and what he looked like. After all, they had been speaking with me every day for awhile now and it was nice to put a face with the name. As I worked my way around the room and greeted everyone, it was nice to be able to put that same name and face combo together myself.

It was just about lunchtime now, so I worked my way over to the chow line with a couple of the guys from FDC, to see what was for lunch. This felt very strange because it was the first time I had been in a chow line since I got in-country. What we ate in the field was always what we carried on our backs and that was always out of a can. If I remember correctly, lunch was just some juice and a ham-and-cheese sandwich, but it was good. And we actually had some ice cream for dessert. Boy, I thought these guys were living pretty well back here at Chamberlain.

After lunch I walked over to the small bunker I would call home for the next ten days. It was nice to lie down on a cot after sleeping on the ground for the last six weeks or so. I managed to get some letters written home, but I was starting to wonder why I was even writing, as I had not received one piece of mail yet. I was really looking forward to something from home. It was late afternoon now and I was starting to fall off to sleep. No one had been around to tell me what my guard-duty time was going to be for the night, so I figured I wouldn't say anything myself. I'd try to stay off the radar screen for this first night anyway. It didn't take me long to fall off to sleep; I was bone tired.

I must have been more tired than I had thought, as I slept right through the night for the first time since I had arrived in-country. I woke up around 5:30 A.M., and just for an instant I didn't know where I was. It must have been the strange place I was in; here I was inside a one-man bunker lying on a canvas cot—which had never happened before. I had gotten kind of used to the ground and my back hurt from the softness of the cot. I went outside and found some water to wash up, brush my teeth and shave with. After getting cleaned up a little I walked around the perimeter of the base and found the men of Alpha Company. Some of them were sleeping in and some had guard duty. Being at Chamberlain was just another place to them, for they still had to protect the Battery; after all that's what we came in for, wasn't it?

My duties would be different back in the Battery. If I wasn't out with Alpha Company on patrol, I really didn't have a job now did I? That's how

I looked at it and from then on I tried to make myself as scarce as possible. That way I would have some time to get into Cu Chi to buy another 35-mm camera, along with some film.

The next morning I would have a chance to go into Cu Chi on a re-supply convoy. The only catch was I would have to ride shotgun on one of the big trucks, but that was all right with me; I was going to Cu Chi and that was all that mattered. Hell, Cu Chi seemed so far back in the rear that it was almost like going home.

Chapter 15

Back To Cu Chi

The re-supply convoy began loading up early the next morning inside the gate at FSB Chamberlain for its ten-mile ride down to Cu Chi. I grabbed my M16, a couple of bandoleers of ammo, a flak-jacket and then took a seat in the first truck that was in line. The driver was a guy named Gus. He said he was from California and had been in-country for seven months. All he did was drive this truck down to Cu Chi three times a week. He also mentioned that he went up-country to Tay Ninh once a week. He liked his job as it got him out of the Battery and when he was on the road he was pretty much on his own. The job did have its dangerous side though, with the ever-present chance of getting ambushed on the road. But Gus hadn't seen any trouble so far, and I was praying that his luck would hold up with me on board this day also.

Cu Chi was over ten miles away, and the drive down took us over an hour to complete. Making up the convoy this day were eight trucks and two jeeps, and we had to go real slow in order to stay together for our own safety. The base camp of Cu Chi was a very large base camp as base camps go in Vietnam. Cu Chi was the home of the Twenty-fifth Infantry Division and numerous support outfits, along with the Twenty-fifth Medical Evacuation Hospital. If one was unlucky enough to get wounded in the field, this is where he would be flown. The convoy rode right past this hospital and I took a good look at it, knowing damn well that was all I ever wanted to see of it.

I could go on and on about how big Cu Chi Base Camp was, but I'll just say one more thing: if I had been stationed there during the war, I don't believe I would have worried about getting home one bit.

The trucks pulled into the warehouse area to pick up some supplies, and I asked Gus how long would it take to pick up everything he needed. He said they would be there for at least a couple of hours. That's all I had to hear; off I went to find the PX and get my hands on that replacement camera I wanted so much.

One really had to be there to experience the true size of Cu Chi Base Camp. The base seemed to have everything one would need to enjoy a very comfortable tour. Some of the things that were in place on the base were swimming pools, clubs for enlisted men and non-commissioned officers, and of course the officer's clubs. In addition to the watering holes, there was a Chase Manhattan Bank set up in a trailer. A massage parlor employed local Vietnamese girls whom the GIs would pay for their services. (I think you can read between the lines.)

Along with the non-military stuff, there were also plenty of troop areas for the new soldiers arriving in-country, and another area for soldiers who were leaving to stay while this process was completed. The helicopter units we used on a daily basis for close air support had their own area out at the airport. There were areas for everything from food and clothes to weapons and bullets and bombs. Cu Chi was one pretty damn big place. It was so big and so Americanized that for those of us whose jobs were with the infantry in the field, Cu Chi was impossible to relate to—our Vietnam was just so different and so much more dangerous.

After a twenty-minute walk from the warehouse, another soldier from the Wolfhounds and I found ourselves walking in the door of the building we had come to find. We had a list of stuff to get for the guys' back at Chamberlain. I know I'm making the PX sound like heaven itself; it wasn't heaven, but it seemed pretty damn close to the two of us who had been out for over six weeks now.

Inside the PX were all kinds of stuff for us to buy—stuff that we couldn't get anywhere else. We had just gotten paid, so we were more than ready to spend some of our hard-earned money. With our pockets full of money, we felt like a couple of little kids in a candy store. The first move I made was to the camera section. I picked myself out a Cannon 35-mm camera with lots of film to go with it. This camera was smaller than my last one and I prayed I would be able to hang on to it a little while longer this time; as it worked out, I would eventually take it home with me. If I remember right, the camera and film cost me approximately $50—not cheap for someone only making $350 per month, but not all that expensive either. I was so happy to get my hands on a real good camera; there was just so much to take pictures of and I didn't want to miss a thing. I was in one very strange country, doing some very bizarre things and I wanted a record of it, whether I made it home or not.

Our shopping completed, we stopped by the snack bar on the way out and got a cheeseburger and that thick chocolate milkshake I had been looking forward to for so long. After lunch we worked our way back to the re-supply area to catch the convoy back to Chamberlain. It had been a pretty productive day visiting the headquarters of the Twenty-fifth Division and seeing how the other half lived. I couldn't help but feel envious of the men that called Cu Chi base camp home for their tour of duty in Vietnam. As I rode out through the gates of Cu Chi, I didn't know it then, but it would be another five weeks before I would get back for our first stand-down (a three-day, four-night mini-vacation in a protected area inside Cu Chi Base Camp that was set up just for the infantry). The stand-downs were something everyone really looked forward to, for it gave us all a chance to unwind and put the fighting behind us, if only for a short while.

Chapter 16

Ten Days at FSB Chamberlain

Back at FSB Chamberlain, life was good for the Wolfhounds. All Alpha Company's 120 men had to do was pull guard duty at night and relax all day. What was my job while we were at Chamberlain? It was anything I wanted it to be, because I really didn't have a job description while I was back at Chamberlain. What I did do while I was in camp was go around and get to know the guys on the guns and tell them how much I appreciated them for getting the shells out to me and on target whenever I asked them too, day or night. During the day I would also spend some time over at the fire direction control center. Those were the guys I would really get to know, as I would be speaking with them every day from the field. But I had an ulterior motive: when I was re-assigned off-line I would need a job and I wanted that job to be in the FDC bunker. After all, I really didn't want to spend my entire year on-line, now did I?

I also had my new camera to get to know. When I bought it I had never even seen a 35-mm camera, never mind own and use one. There was so much to take pictures of in this very strange land; everywhere I looked there was a new and interesting opportunity to shoot a picture that would help me tell the story of my time in Vietnam. Once I got to know how to use the camera and had taken photos of the base and the guys assigned there, I started taking pictures of the countryside that surrounded the FSB. Every day a patrol would go out of the base to check the defensive perimeter and the trip flares and landmines that we had set up all around us. I would always go out with this patrol, in order to get to know the country as well as look for interesting camera shots to take.

On my second day out, after we checked the perimeter the patrol was assigned to look into the local village for any enemy activity. The village was only about a quarter of a mile from our base. I thought that was a little close, but what did I know? I was new, remember? We made our way into the village from the east, just to look around—not to clean it out or anything like that. Which was our usual operational procedure when we were out on patrol. This village was close enough to us that the Generals back at Division figured we had it under our control at all times, and there hadn't been any trouble coming out of this village for as long as FSB Chamberlain had been there.

As we walked through this village, which had a population of probably a couple of hundred farmers, small little shops, etc., we were not expecting anything out of the ordinary to happen. All of a sudden a grenade was tossed out of a small grass hooch. Someone yelled, "Grenade!" and we all hit the ground as fast as we could—all of us, that is, except Pvt. Burke from New York. The grenade had landed right at his feet. He kind of looked down at it, and I guess he froze, with a look of combined surprise and fear on his face. When you're in a combat situation and your guard is down, because everything is going smoothly and you aren't really expecting anything to happen, that's when you are at your most vulnerable. When something does happen, it takes you so utterly by surprise that you kind of stop and look out of curiosity. I guess by the time you can react, which is only a second or two later, you're either dead or wounded. In this case, Pvt. Burke was badly wounded. His screams of pain were chilling to hear. And who could blame him? His right leg was bloody and torn up. The pain he was enduring from the hot metal that had just moments before seared through his leg must have been unbearable.

After the surprise of this sudden and unprovoked attack on our patrol we opened up with our machineguns, shooting into the hooch that the grenade had come from. Within moments we had put over a hundred bullets through the grass sides of that poorly made excuse of a building and set it ablaze. There were fourteen of us on this patrol, with Lt. Abernathy in charge. He was from the Third Platoon, and this was the first time I had been out with him. I was normally out with the captain when we were on patrol, but this wasn't a real patrol—at least that's what I thought going into it. In fact, I had been looking forward to it, because I had been told one could always buy a cold Pepsi in this village, and I was looking forward to that Pepsi. With the surprise attack on our patrol, that had all changed. We had not come under any small-arms fire, as would be expected in this kind of ambush; only the one grenade had been thrown, and that had wounded one of us badly. Our patrol immediately spread out and set up a small defensive perimeter around Pvt. Burke. We waited on our knees for a moment or two while the medic stabilized Burke and then dragged him off to the side of the road that served as the village's main street. From this position we could pretty much see the entire village. We were now viewing the people who inhabited this village through different eyes. They were the potential enemy, and it would serve us well never to forget that and never to let our guard down again. The village had gone deadly quite. I guess they were all pretty much afraid that if they showed themselves they would have been blown away, and you know what, they would have been right. We were in no mood for talking or taking prisoners for that matter.

The radio was alive with a request for a medivac chopper to come in for Pvt. Burke ASAP. I was to find out later he had only been in-country for a couple of weeks. There was a saying in Vietnam that if you were going to get wounded; it was best to do so early in your tour. I can see the reasoning behind that, but I don't know if I agreed with it. Personally, if I had to get wounded, I would like it to happen about halfway through my tour, as I would like to have experienced Vietnam and have a reason to show for why I got wounded.

The lieutenant was on the radio with the captain, who was back at Chamberlain, and was asking for another squad or two to help us properly sweep the village and the entire area around it. The captain said he would get back to us in a few minutes. We kind of looked at each other in silence and disbelief. I was kneeling there taking it all in; I didn't know what to make of such a simple request not being granted immediately, and for that matter no one else did either. We had been put on hold for some other requests in the past, like an air strike to level a village or an artillery barrage to do the same, but never for just some more men to search a village. The captain came back on the radio a few minutes later and ordered the lieutenant to pull out of the village and return to the fire support base "ASAP". To a man we were in shock to hear the captain give us that order. What we wanted to do was level the village and burn it to the ground with everyone in it. We wanted to extract our pound of flesh for what happened to Pvt. Burke. We had just been attacked, and there was no doubt where the attack had come from, unlike other times when the attacks had come out of the jungle and we couldn't be quite as positive as to where they had came from. This time it was a no brainer; all we were asking for was permission to search and then destroy a village that had just attacked us. Hell, this was something we did all the time. The lieutenant confirmed the captain's order; we would not get our revenge this day on this village. There would be other days and other villages to get as much revenge as it would take to satisfy our need for payback. Was this what my tour was developing into, one big need for payback? I was beginning to wonder.

The lieutenant looked at us and told us to keep the area we had set up secure while we waited for the medivac chopper to come in for Burke, so that is just what we did. Burke was now stabilized with the help of the medic and a shot of morphine. We were all very thankful for morphine: That stuff did wonders on wounded soldiers over here. Burke was cut up pretty bad from what I could see, but I was told he was going to make it and probably not lose his leg, and that was real good to hear.

We waited for what seemed like a half-hour, although the chopper actually arrived in less than ten minutes. While we waited for the chopper to come in, a couple of us, along with the lieutenant, made our way over to the burned-out shell of hooch that the grenade had been thrown from. We worked our way up the same side of the road that the hooch was on, keeping as low as we could to avoid any snipers. When we got right in front of the smoldering hooch, the body of the enemy soldier we had expected to see wasn't there. We couldn't believe it; we had leveled that building in a matter of moments from the time that grenade went off. No one could have survived the number of bullets that we had put through that hooch—nobody—but there it was, burned to the ground, and there was no one inside.

We started to poke around a little inside of the area where twenty minutes earlier the small but well-kept hooch had stood. One of the guys took a step and stopped very suddenly. We all followed his lead and stopped in our tracks. He was standing on the lid of a trap-door in the floor. He slowly backed off the door as we all fell in behind him. With one quick motion, something he had done numerous times in the past, he bent down and slid open the door and dropped a grenade of his own down the hole. As he did so, he yelled, "Fire in the hole!" and we all hit the ground as one. The grenade went off about five feet under the ground. We could feel it, but the thickness of the ground kept us shielded from its lethal blast of shrapnel. Well, at least we had found out the reason that gook had gotten away: there was an escape tunnel dug under the hooch. As soon as he had tossed his grenade, he had jumped down into it and made his way out the other side. This was the first use of a tunnel for escape after an ambush I had experienced, but it wouldn't be my last. As my tour progressed I would see the enemy's use of these tunnels to ambush us become almost a daily occurrence.

This gook was long gone, and we knew it. On an ordinary patrol we would have sent in a tunnel rat to look for him, but all we would do this day was put a few pounds of C-4 explosive down into that hole and blow the tunnel's opening closed. The medivac chopper was now on its way in. We loaded Burke up and gave him the thumps up as he lifted off, and he gave it back to us. For whatever reason, it made us feel better; I hoped it did the same for him. I would never see Burke again. We were told that he didn't lose his leg, and we were grateful for that.

After more than an hour of walking in the hot noonday sun, we arrived back at Chamberlain and walked through the main gate. It was just another day on the job for us, but you know it really wasn't just another day on the job now was it? It certainly wasn't for Pvt. Burke from New York and not for me either. It was the first time that I would really see the politics of Vietnam up close and personal and how it could and did directly affect me and the soldiers I was fighting this war with. That goddamn village was not to be destroyed because someone was making a buck somehow from it—so much for being such a safe village and all that crap. What I found out that day late January 1970 was that no place was safe in Vietnam and that some villages, no matter what happened, were not to be leveled. As my tour progressed we would find ways around what happened that day outside of Fire Support Base Chamberlain, and we would burn a lot of deserving villages to the ground before politics and the generals back in the rear had a chance to stop us. We were the ones that were putting our lives on the line day in and day out and we were going to survive, despite the politics of war. Oh ya, I never did get that Pepsi I was so looking forward to.

Chapter 17

Back to the War

Our ten days off-line back at Chamberlain were now over and it was time for Alpha Company to get back into the war. A ten-helicopter assault lift was planned for the next day that would take the entire company a few clicks west of Tra Cu. This would be the closest the company had been to the Cambodian border since I joined them in November.

It was the first week of February now and after our rest at Chamberlain we were ready to get back into action—ready, but not all that eager. It was a funny thing about combat: once you were actively involved in it, you wanted out, but once you were out, you wanted back in. Strange.

We would line ourselves up in a long row right outside of Chamberlain on a bright and cloudless, hot and humid morning and wait for the choppers to fly in and pick us up for our first operation after our ten-day mini-vacation. The day before we'd been briefed on what our mission would consist of, and from what we heard none of us liked the plan one bit. We were to fly over the Vam Co Dong River west of us. The choppers would then put us down as close to the Cambodian border as possible without actually crossing over the line into Cambodia. The only problem with the plan was that out west of the Vam Co Dong River there were no border markings, only what seemed like an endless track of thick jungle with more enemy soldiers calling it home than we cared to meet up with. It was referred to as "triple-canopy cover"; once inside it, one couldn't even see the sky above. Our thoughts at the time were "Oh, boy. Here we go". "The Battalion is just using Alpha Company for bait to get the enemy out in the open again." We had had this feeling before when we were camped out at the small FSB (fire support base) named Tra Cu and as if that weren't dangerous enough, now they were going to put us right in front of the enemy along the Cambodian border. It was like putting a bone right in front of a dog and then telling him not to eat it. I don't think so.

After hearing the basics of the plan, we all knew we had a problem; but what the hell were we going to do about it? Nothing, that's what we were going to do about it. We were going to make the best of it and do the job and try to survive. Lt. White came over to me and told me not to worry, but I did anyway. I was really scared this time, but I didn't want to let him know just how scared I was. He said to make sure my radio was in great working order and to take along a couple of extra batteries and some extra ammo. For he had no idea of when we would be getting re-supplied. I was way ahead of him though, as I had already taken care of that the night before.

It was daybreak now and after a sleepless night a few of us were packing up our stuff. When I was done with that, I went looking for my morning's cup of coffee. I never ate breakfast the morning before a big mission; coffee was all I ever wanted. Along the way I found the base post office and mailed home the letter I had written the night before. This letter to my parents was short and sweet—the usual stuff, how much I missed them and how much I wished I was with them at that moment and not to worry about me, for I was all right and God-willing I would be home soon. I never wanted them to worry about me. It was kind of a tough position for me to be in: On the one hand I wanted them to know exactly what I was going through and to care and feel kind of sorry for me, but on the other hand I didn't want my mom to worry. So I chose not to tell her everything I was doing in my letters home.

The distinctive sound of chopper blades off in the distance coming our way was now becoming very clear. It's a sound that we usually liked to hear, but on this morning they were coming to take us someplace we definitely did not want to go. We stood there and watched them land right in front of us. Our new Captain and his RTO, along with Lt. White and myself would be boarding the lead chopper this morning. Along with us would be five other soldiers from First Squad, so that would make a total of nine of us on board the lead chopper. As we all ran to load up that first chopper I could feel the additional weight on my back that the extra batteries and ammo had added to my load. It only took a few minutes for Alpha Company to fill up those choppers and once that was accomplished we were off. Off on a mission that had us all apprehensive, to say the least.

For me, flying high above Vietnam was the best. It was times like this when I wished I had taken the army up on their offer to learn to fly one of these miraculous machines. The countryside of Vietnam as seen from the air at three thousand feet was so green and beautiful, if one didn't know there was a war going on below, one would think he was in a tropical paradise. The air was cool to the face at this altitude and that was always a nice feeling; it was the only way for the grunts of this war to cool off.

Our group looked around at what was going on as we made our way towards the Cambodian border. Little eye contact would be made on these trips; we all knew what each of us was thinking, and only the guys who have made this kind of trip really know what it feels like and what thoughts go through one's mind. On this particular flight I was thinking of the 2.5 million guys who had served in Vietnam; of that total only approximately seventy-five thousand had ever made a combat assault by helicopter. That only comes out to approximately 3% of Vietnam veterans who can say they served their country in this manner. Seventy-five thousand men: that's about the number of people who attend the Superbowl each year. I just thought I would throw that figure out there: it's something to think about the next time you consider the men who really did the vast majority of the fighting and dying during the Vietnam War.

We were now approaching the base camp of Tra Cu; we had come down a little from the three thousand-foot altitudes we had been flying at and we could clearly make it out now, off to our right. Our flight was almost a half-hour old now and we knew it couldn't last much longer as Tra Cu was only a short distance from the border. We could feel the chopper power back now and start its descent; the terrain in which we were about to land was now starting to appear to our front. As our chopper was about to pull its nose up upon landing we were already standing on its skids in anticipation of its ever-so-brief stop to let us off. The shooting would soon start and we knew that when that happened there would be no turning back. The area we were going to be landing in had been prepped (the artillery had bombed the hell out of the area for over an hour before we got here this morning). As far as I was concerned they could have prepped our LZ (landing zone) for a few more hours; they never seemed to prep it enough for the troops that had to make the assault.

We could see the area of our landing coming up to our front now; this was one of the advantages of standing out on the skids upon landing—it gave us a great field of vision, as well as allowing for a quick exit from the chopper itself. The LZ (landing zone) was a big flat grassy area about the size of three football fields, plenty big enough for the entire eleven-chopper lift to land all at the same time. The noise of the chopper blades became louder and louder the closer to the ground we got. As usual, the machine-gun fire that was being put out by the door gunners aimed at the tree lines on both sides of us was deafening and confusing. We couldn't tell if they saw something we didn't, or they were just prepping the area around us. The choppers would be on the ground only for a moment, just long enough for us to jump out and take our positions on the ground and then they would be off. I always looked up at those choppers leaving and waved to the door gunner and he always waved back or gave me the thumps up. I always wanted to be on that chopper leaving, but it was never to be: my job was to keep the communication link between the Company and the Battery as strong and clear as possible—when we needed artillery support, we really needed it.

I felt my job with the company was an important one, but everyone that was out on these types of operations had their own vital job to do. We all depended on one another to get the job done—and done right—in order to give us the best chance at survival. Every mission was different, but they all shared the same thing: it was one more mission that had to be accomplished before we would be allowed to go home and put this nightmare behind us.

Alpha Company was on the ground now, ready to move out to its objective: a suspected enemy base camp just over two clicks (two thousand yards) from our present location. The choppers had put us down as close to the area as we could have possibly hoped, considering the thickness of the jungle around us. This operation didn't have a name that I was aware of. It was just like any other recon mission. We called them RIFs, which stood for "Recon in Force"; this meant that the whole company of approximately one hundred twenty men would be out on this operation. We only went on a few RIFs while I was with Alpha Company. Mostly we would be out on much smaller operations, fifteen to twenty-five man recon patrols.

We started to make our way west of the LZ (landing zone), and after about ten minutes of walking came to the edge of the thick jungle wood line that we would now have to enter on our way to locate what we had come for. What I was to hear from the captain as we cut our own trail through the trip-vine, bug-infested, hot and humid jungle, was that the enemy we came to destroy was the same group of enemy soldiers who had made the midnight probe on Tra Cu, my first week in-country. Intelligence felt that there was a company or more of the enemy that were using this area close enough to the Cambodian border to actually be in Cambodia to stage their attacks on our Fire Support Bases.

A good example of their method of operation was the attack on Fire Support Base Tra Cu. It was felt that they would come out during the night for their ambushes and raids on our positions and then make their way back to what they felt was a safe and secure area to rest and get re-supplied for the next night's activities. Our mission was to eliminate these soldiers and the threat of future attacks on our positions, at least for the short term. After hearing the reason for the mission I personally felt better about what we were about to engage in. What we all wanted—and it seemed to be the same thing we always wanted—was to get in and get out as quickly as possible, but at the same time we wanted the mission to have a purpose.

I can't begin to describe what it is like trying to make your way through the thickest jungle you can imagine, all the while carrying a pack on your back that pulled at you with each and every step you made. The jungles over here became sort of surreal, like someone must have made them up—they couldn't exist for real, now could they? The jungle in which we basically lived was also home to the strangest array of bugs, snakes and animals one could ever imagine. During the day we would hardly ever see these creatures, but at night they all came out to hunt for food and such. Along with the ever-present mosquitoes that attacked us constantly all night long, we would encounter numerous snakes, rats and lizards. On occasion, off in the distance, we would hear the loud screaming noises that big cats make. Our nights would be composed of taking short naps at best, while staying alert to these creatures coming into our ambush positions to scare the hell out of us. It was no wonder we were all on the verge of exhaustion, all the time. No one I ever served with in Vietnam ever got used to living in the jungle, day in and day out for long periods of time. Even more than the sporadic firefights with the enemy, it would be the constant beating the jungles of Vietnam gave us that in the long run would take its toll.

As we worked our way towards our objective, the morning heat and the thickness of the jungle were starting to beat us up pretty good. The jungle was the thickest that I had ever encountered; we couldn't even see the bright blue sky that we had left behind once we entered its true heart. This type of jungle—"triple-canopy cover"—was the worst kind of terrain for us to be in. Not only was it tough to walk through, but the enemy would be able to hear and see us long before we could sense his presence. This made it extremely dangerous for us and we knew it. But one of our worst fears was the reality that if we were to be wounded, the medivac choppers couldn't even land and take us out. We would have to be lifted out by harness to a chopper hovering overhead, which would put us in an even more dangerous position of being a sitting duck for the enemy to take us out on the way up. As we entered the thickest part of the area that we had to go through to get to our objective, this patrol was starting to look pretty bad from every angle.

The area that we wanted to investigate now started to appear in front of us. In fact, we were in it before we even knew it. We could tell that we had arrived by the mere fact that all the trees in this particular area were broken in half from the artillery barrage that had preceded our arrival. Once we were deep into the area we could see the damage the bombs had brought on this section of jungle. The trees were all damaged in one way or another, with most of them being split in half or stripped of their bark. There were also holes all around the area; we would have to watch our step. The hundreds of artillery shells that had landed in this area had really done a number on it, and I couldn't see how anyone could have survived that kind of shelling.

Once it became apparent that we were in the heart of the area we had come to check out and destroy, the company spread out into platoons and then into squads in order to cover the target area thoroughly. As always, I was with the captain and the lead element of the patrol. Being up front on patrol did have some advantages—at least I always knew firsthand what the hell was going on with the patrol. But to be honest about it, I would have been much better off back in the rear of the patrol formation. Whenever we did run into an ambush it was always the guys up front who took the brunt of the enemy's bullets, land mines and booby traps.

The sweat ran down from under my helmet and over my forehead and stung my eyes, so much so, that I was constantly wiping it away with a small dark green towel that I kept hung around my neck. In the field that towel became my best friend.

My thoughts began to wander. I had to work to keep them in check and concentrate on where I was and what I was doing at all times. It really hadn't sunk in all the way yet that I was in the middle of a killing zone and the only way out for me was to kill the enemy before he took the opportunity to kill me first. Out on patrol one's mind had a tendency to play tricks; after all, what we were doing was so foreign to the majority of us. Being on high alert and constantly walking through some of the thickest jungle this earth of ours has to offer and always being at the point of exhaustion took some getting used to. The soldiers that fought in the jungles of Vietnam would have to carry at least six to eight canteens of water on them at all times. We would always be stopping to take a drink from these, as the typical soldier would be expected to sweat off ten to fifteen pounds per mission. I felt so new to this jungle fighting that it was becoming in my mind at least a foregone conclusion that I would not be making it home after all. But as my tour progressed, I would give it everything I had to make my getting home a reality.

After all of us had completed our individual patrol assignments and made our way back to the point where we had started we were all exhausted. It had also become quite clear that the intelligence that we received before we left Chamberlain that this would be an enemy base-camp, was pure "Bullshit". As so many of the so-called "Intelligence Reports" that we had to follow up on turned out to be. All we had to show for our efforts was a bombed-out section of jungle out in the middle of nowhere. What was the use of beating the hell out of ourselves flying in here and walking all this way to get to an area that was void of any enemy activity? But the more I thought about it, the better it looked to me. At this point in my "tour of duty" I didn't really want to engage the enemy anyway. As far as I was concerned it was just another day that I had survived, another day of preparation to take on the "VC"(Viet Cong) in his own backyard. What I needed was more time and experience in dealing with the jungle that I would be calling home and today's dry run was another day under my belt, another day of learning how to survive the jungles of Southeast Asia.

It was decided next that we would make our way to Tra Cu. The small fire support-base that we flew over on the way in and served as home to a small Navy patrol boat squadron along the Vam Cong Dong River. That made its contribution to the war effort by shuttling Twenty-fifth Infantry Division troops to their ambush positions along the rivers that made up the great Mekong Delta. That's not to say that was all they did; I'd like to think that they set up their own ambushes, but I doubt it. The only contact that I had with them was for rides to and from our ambush patrols.

We were glad that the decision was made to make our way there, as it would give us a night out of the damp, wet jungle that constituted the vast majority of the area around this particular base camp. One of the best things about staying at Tra Cu was the fact that this FSB had its own little barroom run by the Navy boys. We could buy a few cold ten-cent beers and pass the early evening hours away listening to some good old rock-and-roll and letting loose a little steam. Along with some well-earned beers I would be remiss not to mention that the Navy always had a big barbecue each night and everyone on base was always welcomed. We didn't know where they got those great steaks they fired up each evening, nor did we ask but we were grateful for the time we spent at Tra Cu Base Camp and the perks that came with it.

As my time in-country passed I had the opportunity to see how others were putting their time in fighting this war. It became quite apparent that there was the Infantry and then there was everyone else. Sometimes our living conditions were so bad that the only thing we had to hang onto was each other and that alone would bind us together like brothers for the rest of our lives.

It was almost noon now and it was time to saddle up and start our long walk towards Tra Cu. Looking at my map I figured it would take us at least four or five hours to get there. There really wasn't any trail nearby for us to make our way down, so we would have to carve our own way out of this triple canopy jungle one yard at a time and that would be no easy task. The jungle was so dense that we hadn't moved the company more than a few hundred yards before it was time to stop and take a rest. After taking another look at his map, the captain announced we would have to change direction 180 degrees and move due west in order to pick up a trail that was on his map. We stood there in exhausted silence and stared at him like he was crazy. We had just wasted over two hours of exhausting work to get this far and now he wanted us to go back? And march in the opposite direction of Tra Cu, Boy were we pissed. I'm sure we all had the same thought going through our minds: This asshole can't even read a map and he wants us to follow him into combat? We were beginning to have our doubts about this new captain, and in the following weeks our doubts about him would evolve into a nightmare.

We turned ourselves around—all one hundred and twenty of us, and that was no easy feat—and headed back through the jungle that we had just fought our way through. After listening to the captain tell us what he had in mind to get us over to Tra Cu, I took out my map and took a guess that it would now take us at least another hour to make it to the tiny little trail that was on the map—that is, assuming it even existed. Besides all the extra time that would be lost working our way out of the thickness of the jungle we were in, one also had to think that the more time we took, the more vulnerable we became to an enemy ambush. Suffering an ambush in this terrain would have been a disaster for us. I was having a tough time just seeing the guy in front of me; if we were to be hit it would be all over for the company.

We had been working our way out of this mess for over three hours now and we didn't seem to have much to show for our efforts. If we didn't show significant progress in making our way to our objective (Tra Cu), I was sure the captain would have us set up our ambush positions for the night right here and guess what that would mean? No cold beers and steaks for Alpha Company this night.

The company was now reduced to a slow meandering string of exhausted men who didn't appear to have a clue as to where they were or where they were going. When to my utter surprise, out of nowhere, working his way down through the line of men came my buddy Phil, who had been assigned point-man duty unbeknownst to me. He had some great news: He had found the trail and it was only fifty yards to our front. Thank god for Phil! That's all I had to say. We found our way onto the trail and spread out in scattered groups of five and ten soldiers to take a well-earned break. We were all grateful for the fresh air and the ever so slight breeze that being on the trail gave us. Just getting out of that hot and humid oven of a jungle was like something sent from heaven itself.

The maps we used in Vietnam were large picture maps. What was on the ground was on the map, so if you had a large tree in front of you, a picture of it would be on the map you carried. I can't recall what these maps were called, but I can't imagine getting around this country without one. After consulting my map, I could see to my amazement that we were only a couple of clicks from our objective, Tra Cu Base Camp. It looked like we were going to make it there by sundown after all. The captain had been right—or was he just lucky? A little of both I figured, but what the hell? It was going to be beer and steaks for Alpha Company tonight and that's all we cared about.

After another hour and a half of walking the flat mushy grasslands that lead up to Tra Cu, the river finally came into view, followed by the base camp itself. By this time Alpha company was truly one large group of exhausted soldiers. The sight of the base camp was a beautiful one. After we walked through the gate into the camp we learned that it was Bravo Company's turn to guard Tra Cu, but most of them were already out on river ambushes, so except for a few Bravo Company soldiers, the only soldiers in the camp would be us.

It was an unexpected treat to be the only soldiers in camp for the night. Most of us found a place for our gear and headed first to the bar for a few cold beers; then it would be off to take a shower and after that a visit to the barbecue area would be in order. Tra Cu would become a very special place for me as my tour progressed. It was the first place I had experienced the enemy trying to over-run a base camp and now it had become like an oasis in the desert, with its cold beer and relative safety on a night when I really needed it.

Cambodia, May, 1970

Re-supply Chopper Bear Cat

Flying over Tra Cu March, 1970

Medivac Chopper Landing, January, 1970

River Crossing South of Cu Chi November 1969

Taking a lunch break Outside of Tra Cu November 1969

Captured VC West of Cu Chi December 1969

Taking a break south of Black Virgin Mountain Dec.1969

Sniper Duty April 1970

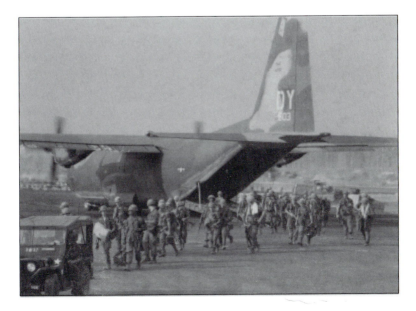

Wolfhounds arriving at Tay Ninh on the way to Cambodia,1970

On patrol outside of Tra Cu November 1969

Patrolling with the Navy outside of Tra Cu December 1969

Patrolling along the Vam Co Dong river December 1969

One buddy helping another south of Bear Cat Feb.1970

APC's inside of Cambodia May,1970

South of the "Iron Triangle" December 1969

Sitting inside of my personnel bunker at FSB   Chamberlain,1969

Artillery fire mission Bao Trai December 1969

Village of Hiep Hoa on the Van Co Dong River February 1970

Resuply mission outside of Cu Chi January 1970

Taking a bath in stream Bao Trai February 1970

Bob Hope USO Show Cu Chi December 1969

Getting fresh water from well in village February 1970

Catholic services in Cambodia May 1970

Wounded helicopter pilot Cambodia May 1970

Down time while out on patrol January 1970

Outside the wire N. Dakota March 1970

Fire Support Base N. Dakota April 1970

175 inch Howitzer fire mission Cambodia May 1970

Chapter 18

The Company Splits up Again and a Letter from Home.

The sun always comes up early in Vietnam, but this morning after all the beer that we consumed the night before, it came up a little too early. It was time to get our gear in order and prepare to move out to an area about two thousand yards from Tra Cu. It was at this time the company would split up, with each platoon going its own separate way, to give us a better chance at finding the enemy. I would miss this combination Army-Navy base, and as my time in-country passed I would miss it more and more. I didn't know it then, but it would be the last time I would enjoy its relative safety and comfort.

The company was now ready to move out to our split-up point, so off we went—not with a great amount of enthusiasm, but we moved out nevertheless. It would take us the better part of the morning to reach an area that would afford enough space for the helicopters to land and pick us up. The land within a thousand yards of Tra Cu was too wet and marshy, so we had to walk to another area in order to be lifted out.

The walk to our pick-up area was as I had expected—long and hot. We made it in three hours and settled in to wait for the choppers to come and pick us up for our next mission. The drills were always the same in this hurry-up-and-wait situation; we would set out our perimeter for security and then settle in and wait. Some of the guys would lie back and take a nap, some would write home, and still others would break out the C-rations and have some lunch. Everyone approached their individual time in Vietnam differently. It was kind of interesting if one were to take an interest and really look, but most didn't; I sure didn't pay much attention to what others were doing with their time. Like most of the men I served with, I had my head full of my own thoughts—mostly of home at first, but as time went on I thought less and less of home and more of just staying alive until the next day. I would let the possibility of going home take care of itself.

Our wait for the Helicopter lift to come in and pick us up didn't take very long, maybe forty-five minutes or so. We got the heads-up that it was on its way, and we lined up to board the choppers as soon as they landed. The choppers made a great target for the gooks, so the pilots always wanted us up and ready to go as soon as they arrived; it was safer for everyone that way. With the choppers now on the ground, we all ran towards the chopper that was designated to be ours. It was easy for me to remember which chopper was mine, as I was always assigned to the lead chopper. Once we were on board the chopper lifted off. Today, the whole process couldn't have taken thirty seconds. We were getting better and quicker at loading up; I guess practice makes perfect.

The company was now split in two, with the command team going out with the First and Second Platoons. Being up in the air on our way to our next drop-off point was just as exciting as it always was, with the air rushing through our hair and the scenery as bright and brilliant as usual. Flying at two thousand feet over the countryside of Vietnam was always a rush for me. Looking at the view from the air, it was hard to imagine that the beautiful countryside we were flying over could be so deadly upon our landing. Our lift consisted of seven choppers, with seven or eight soldiers in each. Along with me in the command chopper there was also the captain, Lt. White, the captain's radioman Sammy and a recon sergeant named Bill. (We called him Wild Bill—he was quite a character.) Usually that was the extent of the command team, but on this trip we also had a sniper named Bowers and a Kit Carson scout named Tran, assigned to our team.. I had a great deal of respect for Tran, who as a North Vietnamese defector took his life in his hands day in and day out to help us find the enemy. It was not only his life that was at stake, for if he were to be caught his wife and children would have been killed also—that I thought was quite a price to pay to be working for us. I don't think under the same set of circumstances that I would have done it. These guys had a name and it was Chu Hoi's, I always believed that they should have received much more recognition than they did for the help that they gave us, at great personal risk and sacrifice, I might add.

Tran would work with us for a couple of months, I can honestly say that during that time through his knowledge of the countryside he helped us avoid at least ten ambushes. That alone saved many of us the real prospect of becoming a casualty of the war. Tran would also play a big part in helping me avoid a deadly situation in the coming weeks.

So in the lead chopper there were seven of us that were ready for combat. Behind us there were six more choppers with seven or eight soldiers in each, which would make approximately forty-eight the total of guys who would make this assault, not counting us. By the time we hit the ground there would be fifty-six of us looking for the enemy this day; not a bad number, I thought. I had been out with a hell of a lot less; the more of us out on patrol, the better I liked it.

The radios were making a lot of noise now that we had the LZ (landing zone) in sight. "Chopper 142, this is chopper 658. We have the landing zone in sight, approximately one-half mile to our front". "Over," our chopper pilot spoke into his headset. "Chopper 658, this is 142. I read you load and clear. We will follow your lead, just take us on in, and let's get the hell out of here". "Over." The landing zone we had in mind was about fifty yards wide by two hundred yards long, set between a rice paddy and a large group of thick brush and some large trees. We could have picked a larger landing area; I felt we were too close to the tree line, and we didn't know what would be waiting for us in those trees. It wasn't my call to make, but I was starting to get the gist of what it would take to make as safe a combat assault by chopper as possible; you might say I was becoming a veteran at combat assaults.

The choppers all landed at the same time. It was a tight fit, but the more choppers that could land at a time the safer it would be for us; we wanted as many men with as much firepower on the ground at the same time as possible. We hit the ground running and made our way over to the cover of the thick brush that was off to our right. Between the time we landed and the time we hit the thick underbrush surrounding the trees that we were running to, the helicopters had lifted off and were gone.

After a few minutes of waiting for something to happen, it was determined that the LZ (landing zone) was cold. It would take a few minutes longer for us to get our maps out and get our bearings in order to get ourselves ready to move out of the area.

The sweep of the area would start out like all the other sweeps that we had done in this area. I would call them low and slow; that is to say, it would take us all day to get to our objective and we would keep as low a profile in doing so as possible.

This day on point would be none other than my favorite point-man, Phil. I always liked to see him out on point, as I felt a lot more at ease with him there. Our two platoons would be moving in a semi-straight line as we crossed the rice paddies that stood between us and the small village we wanted to take a closer look at this morning. Moving in such a line was always a calculated risk for us, as the enemy would have a great line of fire to engage us from a distance, and it made us feel exceptionally vulnerable to them. I personally hated to approach any of our objectives in this manner. All we could do was keep an extra sharp eye out for any movements along the tree line and hope for the best as we moved towards our objective. As we crossed the rice field it struck me as strange that the people who lived in a village that we were headed for would never even give us a look; they would just go about their business of tending their rice. After over an hour of walking we finally reached the outskirts of this small village that made its living from the rice fields that we had just trampled on our way in.

Upon entering the village everything seemed to be as normal as possible. With all the able-bodied grown-ups out in the fields, only the old people and the kids remained in the village. The fewer people there were in a village as we checked them out for any signs of enemy activity, the better for us. Nothing of importance was found in this particular village, but that didn't mean that the village was clean; all it really meant was that we hadn't found anything this time. Some of these villages we would come back to over and over again, and sometimes we would find what we were looking for and sometimes we wouldn't. After we got to the other side of the village it was decided it was time to take a break and relax for a few hours. The sun was high in the sky now and it had to be over one hundred degrees; a break was in order before we all passed out from heat exhaustion.

Once we were settled in I took a few minutes and re-checked my map to see exactly where we were and called our position into the Battery. For our own safety this was always done when we stopped for any period of time. To let the Battery know where we were and to give them an opportunity to plot us on their maps just made good sense; that way they could give us the artillery cover that we needed in case of trouble. We wanted to be under an umbrella of artillery support at all times.

A few minutes into our long break, Sammy got a call on his radio that a re-supply chopper was in-bound to our location. Sammy needed to get ready to pop some smoke to let the pilot know exactly where we were so he could land and re-supply us, with the least exposure to his helicopter as possible. Within a short time we could hear the unmistakable sound of chopper blades in the sky close by. Sammy went out and popped some smoke and guided the chopper down to the ground as close to us as he dared. A few guys ran out to the chopper and took some ammo boxes off, along with a large bag of new uniforms and the always-welcomed red bag, which carried our mail.

That red bag was what everyone was looking for. If we were being re-supplied and that red bag wasn't on board, it would be a tremendous letdown. Mail was the only link we had with the outside world, and it was very important to us. I had been in-country for over ten weeks now and I hadn't received my first letter—or anything else—from home yet. I was dealing with it, but it wasn't getting any easier. But this day's mail call would finally be different: I would get my first letters from home and what a glorious and memorable day this would be. That's how important mail is to the soldier far from home.

For the first time since being in-country I heard my name called out at mail-call. What a great feeling! All kinds of thoughts were whirling through my head. Here I sat, with twenty-three letters and a large package sitting on my lap. I wanted to cry (but I didn't). It had taken a while for my mail to catch up with me, but it finally had, and I was the happiest guy in the platoon. I didn't know where to start; I was like a little kid at Christmas with so many presents to open that I didn't know where to begin. I started by looking at who had written first, but I also had my eyes open for one return address in particular. The letter I wanted to see the most was from the girl I had left behind when I went off to Vietnam. This was the girl I had spent all my time with while I was on leave and she was the one I would be going home to once my time here was up. It was her picture that I carried with me at all times and she was the one I missed the most. I scanned each and every envelope for the return address I was looking for and finally there it was.

As I handled this precious envelope ever so gently in my hands as if it would somehow disappear and return whence it came, I couldn't help but notice how thick it was. A nice long letter, I thought. Boy, I would be reading this letter all day and my thoughts would be more of home and much happier times than the hell I was experiencing at this moment. Before I opened this most important letter from the one I loved who was so far away, I brought it up to my nose in the hopes of smelling the sweet perfume of the most important person I had left behind. I then proceeded to open the letter ever so slowly not wanting to disturb even one word that awaited these eyes that had been waiting so long for the reassurance of the love that was so far away.

As my eyes began to scan the first line of this much-anticipated correspondence, my heart sank in utter disbelief. It was like someone had punched me right in the stomach and knocked the wind out of me. My heart was beating faster than it had ever beaten before, and I found it hard to catch my breath. I couldn't believe the words I was reading. "Dear Richard, I'm sorry, but by the time you get this letter I will have gotten married."

Total shock overcame me, and tears began to well in my eyes. I couldn't believe what I was reading, but most of all I couldn't believe where I was reading it. This was your classic "Dear John letter", and it was addressed to me. I just couldn't believe it, I was in total shock. I wanted to get up and run —to where I didn't know or care, but I was having such a hard time just sitting still, I didn't know what else to do.

A moment passed, and then minutes, finally over twenty minutes had passed. I had gotten my senses back, and I was angry, real angry. How could she get married? Why couldn't she have waited for me? Didn't she know what I was going through? Didn't she care even a little bit; after all we had been through and shared together? The more I thought about those words "I'm getting married," the more anger I felt towards her and the situation I was in. I tried to tell myself that if I weren't in Vietnam she wouldn't have done what she had already done; but I knew that wasn't true, she would have done it anyway. I wasn't the one she truly wanted and loved, or she would have waited for me, as I would have waited for her.

A long time would pass that day before I finally got my head back on straight and reminded myself of where I was and what I was doing. If I hadn't done so right away I'm sure I would have ended up going home in a body bag and that was not going to happen to me. I now had one more reason to make it home and I would, if only to confront this person and explain to her what her letter had done to me, at my most vulnerable of times. My life would go on here in Vietnam, what other choice did I have? But it would be different for me now. Not much would matter. I would take chances I previously wouldn't have taken, but my overriding desire was to make it home and confront this girl. In reality she probably did me a favor in the long run, because the image of her face and what I would say to her when next we met helped get me home.

I must have been sitting by myself for over twenty minutes or so when Bernier came over to see what was in the package that I had received from home this day. Here was this good-sized package sitting next to me, and somehow I had forgotten all about it. My thoughts had been so far away and my mind so absorbed by the "Letter" that nothing else seemed to matter. But now it was time to get back to reality after my short break of feeling sorry for myself.

So here was Bernier sitting next to me, waiting for me to open that all-important package from home. It kind of reminded me of when I was kid and my brother Harry would be beside me, waiting with bated breath for me to open a birthday present. This package was far more important than any birthday present that I had ever received, for it truly represented to me who cared and who didn't and helped me get back to the reality of my position.

Packages from home were something we all shared over here. Packages from home were unlike letters; a package from home usually contained stuff that could be shared with the guys who were close to you in the field.

This package was special as it was my first, and it contained stuff that I had asked my mother to send, things that I couldn't get over here in Vietnam. With some anticipation the box was finally opened and to my surprise, the first thing I beheld was a large envelope that contained a long and loving letter from my mother, my father and my older brother Larry. I would read that letter over and over again for weeks to come; hell, I think I finally just wore it out.

This special package also contained cans of tuna fish and crabmeat. These things were impossible to get here and would make for a pleasant break from the C-rations that were the usual, mostly uneatable fare that we had to look forward to each day. Along with a few home-town newspapers to help keep me abreast of what was happening back home, my package contained a couple of special surprises. The first was two dozen homemade brownies that had made it all the way here and were still edible. I would hand them around to all the guys and they were very grateful for this unexpected treat from home. Handing out all of those brownies helped me become much more a part of the team and for this alone I felt grateful. I was still fairly new in-country, but after sharing my gifts from home I finally became an accepted part of the "Wolfhounds". It felt great.

The last thing I took from the package was wrapped separately and was the best gift in the box. Here in my hands I held one hell of a great gift:

"two small blow-up beach pillows". Now you might ask, What would a soldier in the jungles of Vietnam want with such a thing? The soldier in the field spent each and every night sleeping on the ground, and the only thing he had to rest his head on was his green towel, folded up in the shape of a pillow. This was the same towel that he used to wipe away the sweat from his face all day, and by the end of the day it was pretty ripe. A folded towel just wasn't made to double as a pillow, but a plastic blow-up pillow—that was another thing all together, and it worked just fine.

From that day on, I became the envy of every soldier that I pulled an ambush patrol with. I guarded those pillows with my life, until the day I left the field and gave them to another soldier, who I'm sure guarded them with as much zeal as I had. Those silly little pillows became the best present I ever received in Vietnam. They were something one just couldn't buy over here—I know, because I always had an eye out for them whenever I had the chance to get back to the rear and go shopping at the PX (post exchange). I never did see those pillows or anything like them again while I was in-country, which just showed me how special and hard to get they were.

Our short break was now over. With the rest of my letters safely tucked into my backpack to be read at a later time, I reluctantly joined Alpha Company as it moved out once again in search of the enemy.

Chapter 19

Phil Gets to Go Home

It was the middle of February now, and we were still out on patrol. The only thing that had changed was that we were now re-conning the area just southeast of Tay Ninh, the area know to us as the "Iron Triangle". Gone for a while at least would be the rice paddies and farming villages that we had been patrolling for the last two months. They would be replaced with small, thickly jungled areas that the enemy called home, it would become our biggest nightmare. This particular area of Vietnam was very difficult for us to work, as it had been the enemy's home base for many years. The American soldier would find making a friend in this area of the country, just about impossible. It was a kill or be killed situation for us every time we patrolled this extremely difficult and very dangerous part of our AO (area of operation). Now that our area had changed, so would our tactics in finding and engaging an increasingly elusive enemy.

First of all, our chopper lifts, which had been occurring two or three times a day, would now only happen two or three times a week. That meant we would have to carry more on our backs, as we would no longer have the choppers to carry our stuff for us. It had been real nice working with them on a daily basis. As with all things in the army, we knew it wouldn't last; we just wanted it to last a little while longer that's all.

The jungle that we were patrolling in this day at the base of Nui Ba Din (The Black Virgin Mountain) was the thickest I had ever been in. It was just like I had envisioned Vietnam, hot and humid and every bit as scary as the instructors' back in training had forewarned us of. Even though the training we had received back in the States was some of the best in the world, it still hadn't come close to duplicating the real thing. Surviving this new AO was going to be tough, and I knew it. My one and only thought would have to be to concentrate on where I was and what I was doing at all times, in order to stay alive to fight another day. My Dear John letter would have to be cleared from my mind if I was going to make it through my tour of duty. That fact had become crystal clear to me, now that we had started working this new and very dangerous AO. The enemy would help to make this easy with what they had in store for me, as well as the rest of the guys of Alpha Company, as we worked the area south of Tay Ninh.

This morning started out like every morning does during the dry season in Vietnam, hot and humid. That was the one thing about this place that was predictable—the weather. Everything else about it was unpredictable and every day was a learning experience; that is if you survived.

Phil would have the point once again. I swear he was out there more than all the other guys combined, but he didn't seem to mind it and that was fine with me. He was the best and I had complete trust in his instincts.

The sound of a muffled explosion came from the front of the column, just as we started our first recon of the day. It didn't sound all that large, but it did get our attention. The call came back for a medic to come forward. Doc, our medic ran by us on his way to the front not knowing what to expect. Doc was a good man and a good medic; he knew his job, and if you were unlucky enough to be wounded out here you would have wanted him to be the one who came running to your side.

We took a knee and waited to hear what was up, as no other sounds of explosions or small-arms fire were heard after that one small explosion. We all knew the sound that we had heard was a booby-trapped mine, as it turned out it was a lone booby-trap and not the beginning of an ambush. After a few minutes of intense silence holding our breath in anticipation of a possible ambush, we came to realization that it was a small land mine that had been tripped, and that there was no enemy in the area. What a relief, I thought. One less ambush was all right with me. We looked up and running down the line towards us was Corporal Jackson, a tall black soldier from down south somewhere with the word that a medivac chopper was needed and needed ASAP (As Soon As Possible). It was Phil, our point-man who had set off the land mine and he was wounded pretty badly. I couldn't believe the name I had just heard, Phil was wounded, that was impossible. He was the best that we had and now he was wounded, Jesus Christ, I thought to myself, if Phil couldn't avoid these lousy land mines, how the hell was I going to avoid them?

The captain's RTO called in for a medivac chopper, for we had one down and Alpha Company was possibly engaged with the enemy and at this time. He called in the request and got the message that a chopper would be en-route to our location and we were to pop smoke when we heard the chopper get close. We then made our way up front to Phil's location and went into our SOP (standard operating procedure) of setting up a perimeter and securing the surrounding area while we waited for the chopper to arrive. We got the area secured in no time; we didn't want any surprises from the VC (Viet Cong) as we prepared to fly our wounded back to the Twenty-fifth Medivac Hospital at Cu Chi.

The command team reached Phil within a couple of minutes and what we found will stay with me for the rest of my life. Through the dark smoke and the dirty red dust that the explosion had put into the air, we could see Phil lying on his back with the "Doc" holding a large compress to his stomach area that was quickly turning red with Phil's blood. Poor Phil was in such obvious pain that at first I had to look away to compose myself. He was breathing very hard and erratically while he waited for the morphine that Doc had just administered to take effect. I got up right next to him and knelt by his side. He had a real scared look on his face. I grabbed his hand and looked him straight in the face and told him he was going to be all right, that the "Dust-Off "was on its way in and would be here in a few minutes and for him to hang in there. I didn't know what else to say to him. Part of me wanted to go out and find the gook that had set up that mine and a part of me wanted to stay and give comfort to my friend. As I knelt there at Phil's side waiting for that damn chopper to get to us, it was difficult for me to see my friend in so much pain. What was taking that chopper so long? Didn't they realize that this soldier could die right here in front of us while we waited for them to arrive? Didn't they know it was Phil lying there in so much pain and that he was the first guy who had befriended me my first day in the company? Of course they didn't know that, and if they had it wouldn't have made any difference—they were flying as fast as they could to get him the hell out of there, just as they always did.

I could see that it wasn't just the gaping wound in his side that was the problem; as he had numerous wounds throughout his entire body, especially his legs. There was so much blood everywhere and so many wounds to treat; I didn't know where the doc would begin. One wound in his right thigh was oozing blood at an alarming rate, so I took my PCB (personal compress bandage), put it over the wound, and pressed down ever so firmly to help stop the bleeding. The bandage that I used on his leg was the one each of us carried for our own personal use; it was not to be used on another soldier, per Army regulations, but I figured at that time Phil needed it a lot more than I did. Hell, I had seen so many soldiers leave the jungle without ever having to use their bandages, what difference would it make? Screw the army and their bullshit regulations—this guy needed my bandage more than I did and that was all there was to it. Phil was quiet now. I guess the morphine was doing its job. He was breathing a lot easier and he wasn't moaning from the pain that had been inflicted upon him by that one lousy booby-trapped hand grenade. It had been attached to a small tree at waist-high elevation, so it could do the most damage.

Through the noisy confusion and controlled effort of stabilizing Phil a faint sound off in the distance could be heard. Slowly but steadily, the distinctive sound of the medivac chopper (Dust-Off) was coming into focus. Over the radio one could hear the voice of the pilot asking us to pop some smoke so he could get an exact fix on our location. The captain's RTO grabbed a smoke grenade off the back of my radio and ran out to the clearing to let it's yellow smoke guide this life-saving miracle of a flying machine to us. I don't have a figure on how many men were saved by those medivac dust-offs, but I'm sure it must have been in tens of thousands.

The distinct *whomp, whomp, whomp* of helicopter blades cutting their way through the air was a welcome sound. It's tough to explain to anyone who wasn't there what it felt like to hear that unmistakable sound. Sometimes it could mean fresh water and food, or mail from home, but on this day it meant life. We ever so gently lifted Phil up and put him on one of the dark green waterproof ponchos we all carried to keep ourselves dry during the monsoon season. These ponchos came in handy to carry our wounded and our dead to waiting choppers.

Phil was feeling no pain as we carried him out to the clearing that the chopper had landed in, about thirty yards from where he had tripped that goddamn booby-trapped hand grenade only minutes earlier. As we rushed Phil along, trying not to brush him against the ground, he was looking straight up at me. Or was he just looking up? To this day I really don't know, but I like to think he was looking right at me and trying to reassure me that he was going to be okay. We loaded him as gently as we could onto the waiting chopper and off he went. And just like that, Phil's time in the jungles of South Vietnam was over. I was kind of envious of him for a moment as his chopper disappeared in the distance, but that feeling would soon pass; the price Phil had just paid to get the hell out of here was just too high. What was I thinking? Was I really fantasizing about getting wounded just to get out of this place? I thought I had better get my head screwed back on straight—and in a hurry—because as much as I would miss Phil, I certainly wouldn't have changed places with him just to get out of the dangerous situation that I currently found myself in.

Our patrol would go on that day and we would settle in for the night's ambush without hearing word on Phil's condition. We called in a few times during the day, but he was still in surgery every time we checked. We would have to call again in the morning to find out how this very important member of Alpha Company was doing. Our prayers that night would be for him, and we would be ever so alert this night in the hopes of getting a little payback for the hurt the enemy had inflicted upon us this day. It might be said that the enemy had won today's match, but tomorrow would be another day. There would be many more days that we would win and win big, because we were Alpha Company 1/27 Wolfhounds, Twenty-fifth Infantry Division, and we considered ourselves to be quite a fighting force. I would learn during my tour of duty that the enemy had a bounty out on us, because we had caused him so many casualties. Perhaps the fact that we always stuck one of our "Wolfhound" pins in the foreheads of the gooks we killed in combat had something to do with that. I'm sure that kind of pissed them off a little. Screw them!!!

The next morning couldn't have come early enough for me. I was on the radio with the Wolfhounds rear base first thing to get the word on Phil's condition. Phil had spent the better part of the previous day in surgery to remove shrapnel from numerous locations throughout his body. By the time the doctors were done sewing him up, he would have over two hundred stitches throughout his body to remember this day by, but he was alive and was expected to recover. Boy, that was great, great news. If he had been wounded the way he was in a previous war or if he hadn't had the immediate care of such a skilled medic and then the chopper ride out of the bush within fifteen minutes of being wounded, he might not have survived his wounds at all.

Phil would spend the next few days in the hospital at Cu Chi Base Camp and then would be flown to Japan for a few more surgeries to lessen the scarring such wounds can leave. And then he would be going back to the States. Phil had put his time in and I was glad that he was going home. I only wished he wasn't carrying around so many scars to remind him of his one and only missed step over her—one small mistake after making so many right choices throughout his tour. But that's the way it was in Vietnam, one missed step here or one missed step there, and you were dead or seriously wounded. The damn place was just so unforgiving. There would be more than a few occasions to come when I would wish Phil were by my side. I would never see Phil again after that fateful day south of Tay Ninh, but not a day went by that I didn't think of him. I was grateful to him for taking his time to show me, the new guy in-country, some tricks that I'm sure helped to get me home in one piece.

Chapter 20

Lead Chopper Takes Enemy Fire

It had been over three weeks since Phil left us, and it was now early March. We were still in the field looking for the enemy every-day and setting up our ambushes every-night. We hadn't had any contact with the VC for over three weeks now, but we continued to patrol and kept looking for them nevertheless. This day would start out like any other day but would end up quite differently for me, as well as the rest of the men of Alpha Company.

The company had gotten itself together and was getting ready to move out on patrol when word came from division headquarters for us to make our way to a stand-down area and to meet up with some armored personnel carriers (APCs) and tanks of the Fifth Mechanized. It was about time. The company had been out for almost a month now without a day off and we needed one badly. We thought we would be going into Cu Chi Base Camp, but that was not to be, so any safe area for a few days off would have to do. Our stand-down area was about five clicks (five thousand yards) away. The walk would be an easy one, for it was all even terrain; after the thickness of the area we had been working in, it would be a like a stroll in the park. At the end of our walk to the stand-down location, we would have the opportunity to take it easy for a few days, take a shower, have some hot meals, read our mail, and just rest and catch up on our sleep without worrying about the enemy as much. Alpha Company had earned this rest and we were looking forward to it a lot.

Then a call came over the radio from division headquarters. Some Green Berets had gotten themselves into some trouble a few miles from us and they wanted to know if we wanted the assignment. Division was asking us if we wanted it; I'd never heard that before. They weren't telling us we had to take it. They were asking. There were plenty of others in the area that would have taken it—and gladly I might add. But Alpha Company had just gotten itself a new captain a few weeks earlier. He was new and untested in the field and we could see his face light up with the chance to prove himself to the rest of the lifers back at division.

There was only one problem with these guys proving themselves and that was it was always at our expense. The company had been moving to the stand-down area light; that is to say, we hadn't been packing any food or water because we expected to have plenty of that when we got there. Anytime we didn't have to carry extra stuff with us, we would take advantage of that situation, because it just didn't happen all that often. The captain had made his decision. We would change our direction and wait for the choppers to come in and pick us up.

It's funny how the army works: when *they* want to do something they can move pretty quickly, but if *you* want something from the army it takes forever. We had barely gotten to the landing zone, when off in the distance we could see a lift of ten choppers flying in to take us into—what? We had no idea, and I was concerned. On previous combat assaults we would first have a briefing and that would give us a relatively good idea of what we would be up against, but on this assault we had no idea whatsoever and no time to formulate a plan of action. Some Green Berets had gotten themselves into some shit and had called for help; that's all we knew about the mission that awaited us. And the Green Berets very rarely called for help, so this was going to be one very interesting assignment for Alpha Company.

Here we were, not really prepared for a mission, standing on each side of a small field waiting for the choppers to land. We had been through this drill so many times before it truly had become second nature to us. That's not to say that an assault by helicopter was anything to be taken lightly; it was just familiar to us, that's all. Every one of the choppers landed at the same time and it only took us seconds to load up and get airborne and on our way to an unknown place and an unknown situation.

I was in the lead chopper as usual and could hear the radios of the choppers, as well as the captain's RTO going pretty good now with the voices of the guys on the ground that we had come to help. Their voices spoke in short sentences and they sounded out of breath, as if they were running and would only stop and speak to us for short moments at a time. The Green Berets had tried to recon a small suspected enemy stronghold about seven miles to our west and ran into a lot more of the enemy than they had expected —a lot more.

The Berets were a tough bunch of guys over here and very proud of it. If they were calling for help then they must have really be in a hell of a lot of trouble. The decision was made to have the Green Berets find some cover, because we were going to prep the LZ (landing zone) with a few hundred rounds of artillery fire from FSB Chamberlain before we would attempt our landing.

The choppers found a safe place to land just a short distance from our LZ and put down so we could wait for the shelling to end. After we landed and set up our security perimeter, all we could do was wait for the shells to come flying over us on their way to the LZ. The Green Berets at the landing zone would call the artillery in and adjust it accordingly. All we could do was wait for the shelling to end. In a few minutes the sound of six 105-mm artillery shells came screaming right over our heads and found their targets up to our front. There is a funny thing about the sound of artillery rounds going over your head: they sound great because you know where they are going and that after they make their landing and do their job, your life will be safer because of them.

After the barrage had lifted, it was our turn to fly in. We were now ready to load up the still-running choppers and make our way to the target area. The choppers lifted off and we were on our way into a situation that I hadn't felt right about from the very beginning. My feelings were about to be proven correct.

Off to our left front we could see smoke rising out of the jungle area we had just lit up with our favorite weapon, a few hundred rounds of high explosive 105 artillery rounds. We always felt safer making our assault after we bombed the hell out of the LZ (landing zone) first; the more bombs the better I always thought. Our radios were crackling now with the voices of the men on the ground, informing us of their location and telling us to come in, but to be on our highest alert for enemy troops, because they were everywhere. They feared the bombing hadn't taken care of them all and that the LZ (landing zone) was sure to be, "Hot".

The spot that we had picked out for our landing appeared just to our front now, and the adrenaline was really starting to flow. To a man we were just plain scared, not knowing what the jungle clearing ahead had waiting for us, just a few short minutes of flight away. The choppers were all in line now; the flight pattern was very tight, for we all wanted to land at the same time if possible. But that wasn't to be. The lead chopper, which was the one

I was flying in started to take some hits from the enemy gunners below. We had taken hits from the enemy's machine guns upon landing before, but I could tell this was different from the very first shot, because the holes that were now starting appear in the roof of the chopper were much larger than I had ever seen before. We were so close to putting down and so close to the ground that we made one hell of a large target for the enemy's guns. The chopper just hovered there, like it was on the end of a string. It was a massacre just waiting to happen, and I was in the middle of it.

Our door gunners were firing with their M60 machine guns at anything and everything that they could see on the ground on each side of us. We were also firing our own guns at anything we saw—anything to help suppress the enemy's fire, so we could get on the ground safely. Once on the ground we would have a better chance of engaging the enemy. All of a sudden time just seemed to stand still. Our chopper started to shake and shudder, as I had never felt before. It went back and forth and up and down, all in the same motion. We were now starting to take some hits from what seemed like a larger-caliber weapon for sure, as above my head and also off to the right side of the chopper I began to see larger holes appear in its fuselage. *Oh shit,* I thought. *This chopper's going down.* I looked to my right, and sitting there—thinking the same thoughts I'm sure—was Corporal Downs from Texas. He was from Second Platoon, and I had only just met him a couple hours earlier on our way to the stand-down area; now here we were getting shot out of the sky together.

As I turned my head to look over my left shoulder, the chopper with a shuttering violent motion lurched to its left also and just that fast the three of us closest to the door were thrown out. For a moment I was kind of glad that I was out of that chopper, as I didn't want to be in it when it crashed. The drop was probably only about fifteen feet or so, but it seemed to take me forever to hit the ground. During the fall the weight of the radio on my back turned me around slightly, just enough for me to land on my back. I could feel my head snap back in a violent manner, so much so that my helmet strap broke and my helmet went flying as I hit the ground, even though I had had it strapped on securely before we took off.

The landing knocked the breath out of me, as I'm sure it did to the other two guys who had fallen with me. There was still plenty of shooting going on all around us as we looked up to see the line of choppers lift and bank off to their right, to get the hell out of there. I couldn't believe my eyes. They were leaving us on the ground! For Christ's sakes, hadn't they seen us just get thrown out?

The thunderous sounds of all the shooting and the thumping sound of the chopper blades going around and around were becoming fainter and fainter now as the choppers disappeared off in the distance. The three of us were on our own now in the LZ (landing zone), our only cover being the four-foot-high Elephant grass that we were crouched down in. My biggest fear of fighting in Vietnam was coming into focus now, and that was being captured by the enemy. When we went out on these types of operations the chance of being captured was always there, but deep down inside I thought it was never going to happen to me. Yet here I was, in an obviously enemy-held area, and the enemy was all around us looking for the three soldiers that they had just seen tumble out of that chopper's door. Downs and I were right next to each other, and another soldier from Second Platoon was only a few feet away. We moved closer together, so that if the enemy were to find us we would have all our firepower concentrated in that one small area and we would have a fighting chance. At least that was our plan anyway.

The jungle was deathly quiet now as we strained our ears to hear any sounds at all. We hoped that if the enemy had seen us go out of that chopper's door, then maybe, just maybe the Green Berets we had come to rescue had seen us also. There were small clouds of choking residue left over from all the gunfire that had just taken place all around us, making our breathing more difficult than it normally would have been. It was hard to kneel there and breathe that stuff, with the sweat running down our bodies, without making a sound to give our location away to the enemy. We were now starting to hear the enemy only a short distance away, methodically combing through the grass looking for us. We kept as motionless as humanly possible, with our fingers on the triggers of our machine-guns; we could hear the gooks talking to one another as they came closer and closer to our position. I snuck a peek over at Downs, hoping to get his attention. I knew full well that if the enemy were to get any closer to our hiding place a decision was going to have to be made, to either open fire or surrender. I never did ask the other guys what they would have done, but my mind had been made up from the moment I hit that ground. I was not going to be taken prisoner, if I could help it.

The enemy couldn't have been more than ten feet from us when the sound of the choppers returning to make their second attempt at a landing could be heard off in the distance. The sound of those chopper blades going around and around couldn't have come at a better time. The gooks that were looking for us were almost on top of us, and if we had been spotted I'm sure it would have been all over for us—as well as for them. A few moments passed, and the "Eagle Flight" that had brought us in was back and right on top of us. And getting ready to make its ever-so-brief landing to let the rest of the company off to engage the enemy that only moments before had been but a few feet from us.

Before the choppers landed they prepped the landing zone pretty good this time, with rockets as well as machine-gun fire. All we could do was roll up into as small a target as possible, so we wouldn't become a casualty of our own men as they fired their machine-guns at random into the jungle right beneath them. The difference this time around was that there was no return fire as the choppers made their landing. The three of us had considered firing into the sides of the LZ at the fleeing enemy as our company flew in, but we thought twice about it and decided to just lie there and not move. Any flashes of gunfire from the ground would only serve to catch the attention of the door gunners in a moving chopper during its landing in a Hot LZ.

The helicopters landed right in the exact same location that we had planned to the first time around. The only difference this time was that the three of us were already on the ground waiting to greet them. That was the first and only time during my tour of duty that I was to have the opportunity to see what it was like through the eyes of the enemy to have an "Eagle Flight of Wolfhounds" come right down on top of you. It was a very scary and impressive sight to behold.

After the choppers had landed and unloaded the men of Alpha Company into the LZ, the three of us made our way over to the men who only fifteen minutes earlier had left us on the ground in order to circle around and make another attempt at a landing. One might think we would have been pissed off, but we weren't. What we were was forever grateful that it hadn't taken them one minute longer to get back to us. If they had taken any longer, those gooks would have been right on top of us. And who knows what the outcome of the ensuing exchange of gunfire would have been? The mission that we came to perform could now begin. Corporal Downs and that other soldier from second Platoon and I looked at each other and kind of smiled. For we knew that we had just shared something that very few soldiers get to share and live to tell about. As my tour progressed I would have other encounters with the enemy with Corporal Downs at my side. But I was never to see that other soldier again after that day, but I do know one thing, and this I'm sure of: that it was one day in Vietnam that has stayed with him for the rest of his life.

Chapter 21

An Enemy Base Camp Is Uncovered

The area around the suspected VC (Viet Cong) base camp was some of the thickest jungle we were to face in Vietnam. The tall trees that kept the sun from the jungle floor and all the trip vines to catch our legs as we walked along was going to make our mission of rescuing the Green Berets all that much more difficult. Alpha Company was now dispersed in a line to sweep the area that we had taken fire from upon our landing. We moved out ever so slowly, due to the fact we couldn't see ten yards in front of us. We knew the enemy could be behind each and every tree or bush that lay between us and the base camp, which we felt was right in front of us, even though we had yet to see it. All the shooting had stopped since we made our landing, but we expected it to start up at any moment.

We made our way along trying not to trip and stumble on the vines that clung to the jungle floor that on occasion reached up and grabbed us, bringing us to our knees. We were moving slower than normal, as we had flown into this situation on a moment's notice and were carrying less water and ammo than we would have liked. With other combat assaults we would have been loaded down with everything we would need long before the choppers ever left the ground. After moving for about fifteen minutes through this most inhospitable of terrain, it was time to take a break and recalculate our position; even allowing for the thickness of the jungle, we should have engaged the enemy by now. After all, we had taken some vicious ground fire on the way in; he couldn't have disappeared totally, could he?

During our short break we took out our maps to see were the hell we were and grab a smoke and a couple of long drinks of fresh water from our canteens. Up above us we noticed a helicopter circling around to get a good look at what was happening below. At that moment the Captain's radio came to life. "One Zero Bravo, this is "Zero One". "Over." I had never heard that call sign before—in fact, I had never heard one that low before. I grabbed my call sign book from my breast pocket and quickly looked up the call sign "Zero One". It turned out that "Zero One" was none other than the General of the Twenty-fifth Division himself. So that's who was flying overhead for the last twenty minutes or so, observing the operation. Boy, I thought to get a general out of his air-conditioned office back at Cu Chi, this must be a very important mission after all. And let me tell you, that call sign got the captain's attention real fast. The captain was a West Point graduate and what we called a "Lifer", and there wasn't anything he wouldn't have done to make himself look good in front of the "boss". The only trouble with that was that most of the time making himself look good, could and did cost soldiers their lives.

The general wanted to know how our mission was progressing and was there anything that we needed? The captain reacted to that question with a quick answer of "No sir, we have everything we need to accomplish our mission." "Over"

Here we were, kneeling and sitting down in the thickest jungle we had ever seen, the enemy potentially all around us, with no food and very little water and the captain was acting like everything was just fine, making himself look good at our expense. What an asshole. Maybe the captain didn't realize it that day, but he lost us right then and there. We could see that this commanding officer was just out for himself, and we as his troops were only there to help him further his career. This captain would come to find out the hard way as his tour progressed, that we weren't going to play his game and be used to further his rise up the corporate ladder.

Our short break was over now and it was time for us to move out again; this time we wouldn't stop until we found what we had come for. We had only been on our feet for a couple of minutes when automatic weapons fire echoed through the hot and humid jungle we were trying to carve a path through. Our point-man had come upon a large clearing in the jungle and had let loose with a couple of short bursts from his machine-gun at five or six enemy soldiers, whom he had surprised right in front of him. As much as we were fighting in the enemy's back yard, he too would make some mistakes that would cost him. He wasn't as smart as everyone always made him out to be. Sometimes he was dumb, sometimes he was careless and sometimes he was slow to react; this was one of those times and now three enemy soldiers were lying dead right in front of us.

The command group made their way to the front as quickly as they possibly could to assess the situation. When we got there we couldn't believe our eyes. We had stumbled right into the enemy base-camp that we had been looking for—talk about dumb luck. It was the biggest camp I had ever seen. In fact it was the first real enemy base camp I had ever seen. As we made our way carefully into the camp itself, I glanced over at the dead enemy soldiers who this day had given their lives for a cause that they believed in. What a waste it was for these three soldiers to have died this way, for nothing, as I saw it. But as the exploration of the camp continued I realized there was plenty here for them to have defended.

The enemy camp was located just off a small dirt path that we had spotted from the air coming in. The camp was composed primarily of a group of bamboo lean-tos with grass roofs, and was so cleverly camouflaged that we hadn't been able to see it, even though we had flown right over it. In the middle of the camp was a larger, much better built shelter with a long bamboo table and a wooden floor. This area seemed to serve as the camp's main meeting place, as well as its mess-hall (cafeteria) area. Off to the right of this location a campfire was still burning; they must have beaten a hasty retreat after we had landed. We explored the camp cautiously, always on the lookout for mines and booby traps. It was becoming more and more apparent to us that we had come upon something of great importance, given the size of the place and all the equipment the enemy had left behind. We would spend all day at this location just sorting through the stuff.

From the very first moment we entered the site we could see all kinds of things lying around, some up against the lean-tos and some underneath them. It's a funny thing that once the gunfire stops, the area becomes deathly quiet. The only sounds that could be heard were those coming from us, as we yelled back and forth to one another. Some of the troops were looking under the jungle brush that was everywhere, and some were looking inside of the hooches themselves. We searched for anything of importance. The enemy fled in such a hurry that they had left behind their cooking pots and clothes hanging out to dry, along with a few weapons and ammo. But what we really wanted to find was anything written or any maps or other documents.

We'd only been in the camp for ten minutes or so when out of the brush at the far end of the clearing came three Green Berets and seven or eight South Vietnamese soldiers, looking pretty beat and very glad to see us. When the artillery shelling started to come down on the area, they had taken cover a few hundred yards off to the west and waited there for it to end. Some of the enemy had tried doing the same thing but had run straight into the Green Berets, who had set up their position so they would have a clear shot at any gooks trying to escape. They said they had killed a half dozen or so, but I didn't go out to see them. I was seeing dead enemy soldiers almost every day now and a few more one way or the other, didn't mean shit.

They thanked us for coming in and getting them out of some serious trouble. They told us they had gotten word from some locals that there was an enemy base camp located in the area. And being Green Berets, they thought they could just waltz in along with a few South Vietnamese soldiers and take care of the situation without anyone else getting involved. Well on this day they were wrong—the small enemy camp turned out to be a large enemy camp. If we hadn't been so close by they would have all been killed for sure. I would like to think that they learned a lesson on this one, but I'm sure they hadn't. The Green Berets were quite full of themselves over here. Sometimes they won and sometimes they lost and on occasion they were just plain lucky; this was one of those occasions.

We'd been on the ground for over two hours now and guess what? We had run out of water—what a surprise. We hadn't brought enough water with us to engage in a combat mission, only enough to get us to the stand-down area. The captain whose command we were now under was starting to worry about completing the mission. We as a group were starting to feel the brutal heat and humidity that comes with "triple canopy jungle". Some of the guys were starting to refuse to move, the heat and the lack of water had gotten that bad. When you are in a jungle this thick, there is no air movement. It's almost like being in an oven, and it becomes hard to even breathe—never mind search the area for booby traps and enemy documents. If we didn't get the water we so desperately needed and get it fast, the possibility of lost lives would become very real. We were in trouble without water and we knew it, even if the captain didn't—or didn't want to admit it. The fact was he had made a terrible mistake by telling the general that we didn't need anything and that we were just fine. It looked like the captain was now going to have to admit his mistake and make that call into headquarters to ask for a re-supply of food, ammo and especially fresh water. And it was going to have to be airlifted out to us ASAP, or our mission couldn't continue.

The captain took a look around at us and noticed that Cpl. Mason, (who was acting as a recon sergeant for the artillery), was taking a long drink of water from his canteen. He walked over to Mason and asked him for a drink. Cpl. Mason looked him straight in the eye and said "No". Boy, was I in shock at that response to the captain's request. I can still see the look of embarrassment and anger on the captain's face to this day. The captain really couldn't order Cpl. Mason to give him a drink, now could he? He looked around at the rest of us sheepishly and gave the order for his RTO (radio transmission operator) to get headquarters on the horn so he could get us the food and water that we so desperately needed. Lack of water in the jungles of Vietnam would bring on heat stroke before you knew it, and heat stroke could be deadly. The captain had made a major mistake that day by putting his career in front of his men's safety and comfort, and it was going to cost him dearly in the near future. As for Cpl. Mason, I never saw or heard of any payback from the captain for his actions that day. It took guts to say no to the captain, but in doing so he got us the re-supply that we should have had from the beginning of the mission.

With our re-supply called in, we could now get on with the business of re-conning the entire area to really see what we had gotten ourselves into. The men were a little weak as they waited for that chopper to come in with the water, food, and some more ammo, it was beginning to look like this "half- day" mission was going to take a lot longer than that to finish up. There was a lot of yelling going on throughout the camp as the men of Alpha Company found items hidden all over the place. It was like Christmas or an old-fashioned Easter egg hunt back home. It seemed like everywhere we looked something of interest was being discovered. But it was Pvt. Jenkins of Second Platoon who was to find the jackpot. He located the first of many escape hatches in the area that led to an underground complex of bunkers, the size of which we had never seen before. We had with us some very experienced tunnel rats and they were more than eager to go down and take a look at just what we had stumbled upon.

These underground bunkers were nothing that I would have an interest in during my tour. Thankfully, we had some guys who were more than willing to take their chances and go down into them. The thought of sliding down into a dark hole in the ground not knowing what kind of booby traps the enemy had waiting for me was not something that appealed to me in the least.

More escape hatches were being found all over the place, once Pvt. Jenkins discovered that first one. Now it was time to go down and take a look at what we were standing on top of. The whole Cu Chi area was riddled with these complexes of tunnels and underground bunkers. We all knew that, because we would take fire from the enemy and all of a sudden he would be gone. He would use them to ambush us at any given moment and just disappear, leaving us with our dead and wounded and no way of getting back at him. So we would ambush him at night to get back at him for ambushing us during the day. That was how the whole war was being fought, just like a boxing match: he would hit us and we would hit him back.

Uncovering so many tunnels coming together in one central location like this was quite a find, and destroying them would ultimately save numerous American lives. Now the only question that we faced was how big a tunnel complex did we find? We didn't have to wait very long for the answer to that question, because one of our tunnel rats was about to emerge from that first tunnel entrance, that we had uncovered an hour earlier.

He came out of the ground all sweaty, exhausted and out of breath. If it was ninety degrees- plus up here, it had to be over a hundred degrees down in those tunnels. This was the first tunnel that was more than one level that he had ever been down in. He estimated that it might be three or four levels deep. The look on his face was one of sheer excitement; he couldn't wait to get back down and see what else he could turn up, but first he had to get some water and another flashlight.

While the rats were busy checking out the tunnels underground the rest of us spent our time looking for more tunnel openings. It seemed like every time we turned around someone was uncovering something. The biggest tunnel opening that we found was located directly under the camps meeting table, it was almost big enough to walk down into. It was becoming clearer and clearer that what we had stumbled upon and was right under our feet was the largest enemy underground base-camp the company had ever seen. We would need to call in some engineers to help us destroy it. A call was made into Twenty-fifth Division Headquarters back at Cu Chi; we were told to secure the area and that the engineers would be on their way to our location, ASAP (As Soon As Possible). We would also need a Vietnamese translator to help us talk out any of the enemy that may still be hiding in this huge bunker complex, before we blew it and then set the entire area on fire. Now all we could do was wait for the engineers to get here with enough C-4 explosive to do the job.

It had been over an hour since we'd called in for our re-supply of water, food, and ammo, and the more time that passed the more we needed it. Soon we could hear a chopper off in the distance and assumed it was the one we were waiting for—and sure enough, it was. Sergeant Jones ran out with a couple of other guys to pop some smoke so the chopper pilot would know exactly where we wanted him to put down and unload the fresh water we all needed so DESPERATELY, for all our water was now gone. The rest of us took up a perimeter position around the LZ (landing zone) in case there were any enemy soldiers around, even though we hadn't seen any since we had landed, over three hours ago. The chopper landed, and the first thing off was a huge, dark gray rubber bladder full of the fresh water we had been waiting for. Next came a dozen or so boxes of C-rations, as well as numerous boxes of M16 ammo and C-4 explosives. Everything was just kind of kicked out of that chopper's door, as the pilot didn't want to be on the ground in this area any longer than he had to. Who could blame him? Hell, I didn't want to be here either.

We carried the stuff that was left by the chopper into the wood-line and each of us got what we needed to help put ourselves back together and finish this damn mission. Ammo belts were filled with ammo and canteens with fresh water. Fresh water was a treat for us out here in the jungle. Most of the time we filled our canteens with water from a stream or a well in a village somewhere and had to add iodine tablets to help purify it. The iodine made the water almost undrinkable, so a fresh water supply was always welcomed. We broke opened the C-ration boxes and picked through them as well, taking what we wanted and leaving the rest to be destroyed.

Off in the distance we could hear the sounds of the Half-Track's (Armored Personal Carriers) that were bringing in the Engineers. We hoped that they had brought enough explosives with them to take care of this huge bunker complex. If they hadn't we would have to stay until more was brought in, and that could've take all day. To a man, we felt the sooner they got here and blew this place to hell, the better it would be for everyone. Everyone except the enemy, for we had them cornered and they knew it.

These guys in the Half-Track's were a bunch of cowboys. We thought they had it made—the mere fact that they didn't have to carry anything on their backs made their lives a lot easier than ours. All the stuff they needed was carried on their vehicle and I envied them that.

They never seemed to ride on the trails either. We all realized the reason for that—land mines—but they seemed to take great pride in the fact that everywhere they went they just rode over things. They thought it was great fun and maybe it was. I wouldn't know, as I always walked around things, never through them. You can say what you want about everyone's role in this war, but I don't think anyone would argue the fact that the "Infantryman's" job in Vietnam was by far the most dangerous and the toughest. I never saw anyone volunteer to go out with us on any of our missions.

We hadn't had any contact with the enemy now for quite a while; we figured he was down in those bunkers waiting for us to make the next move. If he was down there hiding then he had better give himself up real soon, as the engineers were starting to wire the whole complex with hundreds of pounds of C-4 explosives. They were doing a great job, but the site was so spread out they were beginning to wonder if they had brought enough explosives with them to get the job done and done right. We sure hoped so. One of the engineers came over for a drink and mentioned that he had never seen a bunker complex this huge before.

After a couple of hours of stringing together enough C-4 explosives to get the job done. It was time now for the South Vietnamese soldiers that the engineers had brought with them to crawl down in the bunker openings, get on the bullhorn and ask the enemy to come out. They did this over and over again, sticking their heads down in hole after hole, but they got no response. We kept looking at each other with disbelief. The fact that they weren't getting any response from their pleadings for the enemy soldiers to come out and surrender, was just amazing to us. The translators were telling them they wouldn't be hurt and to think of their families and stuff like that, but still there was no response. We knew that they couldn't help but hear the translators—hell, we could hear them plain as day and we were fifty yards away.

What were those enemy soldiers thinking of anyway? At least if they came out now they would be alive and would probably live to see another day. After all this war wasn't going to last forever. But not a single person responded to the South Vietnamese soldiers' pleas for them to surrender. They must have thought that their bunkers were so well built that they could withstand what we had in store for them, but they would be wrong. The thought also ran through my mind that maybe, just maybe, there wasn't anyone down in those bunkers after all. But that was just wishful thinking on my part and I knew it. Hell, a lot of wishful thinking went on over here. In fact, the place was just plain full of it.

Well, our hands were tied now. We had given anyone who may have been hiding down in those bunkers ample opportunity to come out and surrender. Their choice was clear and what we had to do was just as clear. I really wanted someone to come out of those bunkers, but no one did.

Our captain was in charge of this whole operation, and on his order the complex would be blown. He was just standing by waiting for the engineers to complete their job. I was glad the decision was his and not mine. Even though under the same set of circumstances I would have done exactly the same thing, I just wouldn't have wanted to carry that moment of decision around with me for the rest of my life.

The first order given was for all the troops to get back at least another one hundred yards or so, placing us over one hundred and fifty yards from the blast site. The last ones out of the immediate area were a couple of engineers and one South Vietnamese soldier, who had given the gooks one last chance to surrender. Nothing had changed and no one had come out. They ran to our position and waited with the rest of us for the order to be given to blow up the entire area.

We had been here the better part of the day now and we were anxious to get this over with and move on to our stand-down area, if that was still an option. The captain looked around one last time to make sure all his men, as well as the engineers were clear of the blast area. Once he was sure everyone was safe, he gave the order to blow the place to hell.

The sound of the explosion and the trembling of the earth beneath our feet was really something; I had never seen or felt anything like it before, nor have I since. The ground in an area the size of a football field very slowly rose up, almost as if in slow motion. Every twenty feet or so the surface broke open with such explosive force that it blew trees upwards of thirty feet into the air. The trees that were blown into the air came right back down where they had been uprooted. Earth and small chunks of dirt and rock cascaded in all directions. Even though we were a good distance from the explosion we still had to take cover from all the flying debris that came our way. There must have been over a dozen or so trapdoors that led to the bunker complex and each and every one of them was either destroyed outright or remained intact with smoke and flames issuing from them.

After the massive explosion the earth settled back down, leaving a huge depression of at least an acre in size. There was still a large area that was burning as we moved out to see if there were any bodies. As we got closer and closer to ground zero it didn't take us very long to confirm the fact that yes, there had been gooks down in those tunnels. It was evident by the numerous body parts on the ground, as well as in the few trees that had been left standing after the explosion. The sight of such devastation was overwhelming to me, as I'm sure it was to the other soldiers I was with, most of whom had been in-country longer than I had.

We walked all through the area looking for . . . what? I really don't know. I guess we were just looking. I wanted to get the hell out of there; it really felt creepy. It was quite plain to me at least, that there was more than one gook who just a few minutes before had been alive and well, and now was blown to bits. And it just didn't feel right walking around on top of this gravesite. I wanted to get as far away from this gruesome place as possible. But I couldn't—it was part of me now, etched in my memory forever.

The engineers were now starting to spray the place with a film of diesel fuel. The smell was making me gag. I took my towel from around my neck, and soaked it in water, and wrapped it around my head so I would be breathing through the towel. Some of the engineers thought this was quite funny, but my idea caught on and soon half the company was doing the exact same thing.

Once the entire area was saturated with diesel fuel it was time to torch this place and get the hell out of here, once and for all. The order was given to throw a few Willie Peter (White Phosphorus) grenades into the area and move out. The whole area was soon burning with that dark black smoke that only diesel fuel provides and I was sure it would burn for quite a while.

We got onto the small trail that led from the bunker complex and slowly made our way out of the area. When we got to a large clearing that was close by, the engineers and their Half-Track's went one way and we went the other. We were all feeling pretty good about our day's work. Not only had the three of us survived our fall from a helicopter of twenty feet or so, and not been captured. But the company had also uncovered the largest bunker complex to date and utterly destroyed it. Yes, there had been some loss of life—but none of it was American and that in the long run was really all that mattered. We became so hard over here that as long as we all made back alive, we considered our mission a success.

It took us over three hours to get to our original stand-down destination. Every time we looked back we could see the bunker complex still burning off in the distance, in fact the glow from its flames would be seen throughout the night.

Chapter 22

Finally, Back to Cu Chi Base Camp

On our way back to our stand-down area the captain's RTO received a message from division headquarters. Alpha Company had done such a great job on this particular operation that they felt a few days at the Waikiki East stand-down area back at Cu Chi was in order. News like that was very tough to come by and boy, it sounded great. Cu Chi, just the sound of that name made us all sit up and take notice. Cu Chi was the Twenty-fifth Infantry Division Headquarters and it was where all the action was for those of us who would spend ninety percent of our time in the rice paddies and jungles of Vietnam.

And there was more good news: We were going to be flown into Cu Chi, which was rare; most of the time we walked into FSB Chamberlain and were then trucked in to Cu Chi. It was beginning to look like destroying that bunker complex was going to pay off big time for us, after all. We set up our perimeter and waited for the choppers to arrive. We felt kind of special that morning and that feeling was rare indeed.

Soon, off in the distance, we could see them heading our way—a fifteen-chopper lift and just think of it: it wasn't going to be taking us into combat, but away from it. That in itself was something to savor.

We landed at the airport at Cu Chi in less than forty-five minutes. Waiting for us was a representative of the commander of the division. Alpha Company had never been met before; this whole stand-down was going to be different from the very beginning. As it worked out, that bunker complex had been bigger than we realized. It may have been the headquarters of the North Vietnamese Ninth Division in the "Iron Triangle" area. But if it was, then they must have all been on vacation, what did I care. If it made the generals happy thinking it was, than so be it. We could have cared less, but if it made the lifers happy and they were going to give out a few perks, then we were going to take them—and take them we did, with vigor.

As always, the first thing some of us did upon our arrival at Waikiki East was head straight for the cold beer and then on to the shower area, where we took off our clothes and promptly threw them away. Everything that is, except our boots; we had broken them in just the way we wanted them. I always hated to see a pair of boots go, but by the time my tour in Vietnam came to an end, I had gone through three pairs. After a long hot shower it was time to check out the girls in the area. These girls officially were cleaning girls, but for the right price they were available for other activities. Some of the guys took advantage of what these girls had to offer and some didn't; I personally didn't.

Stand-downs were always a lot of fun and a great time for us to let off some steam. This one was set up right in the middle of the base camp, and what was so great about it was the fact that it was for us and us alone; no one but the guys in the company were allowed in the area. They always tried to make it as comfortable and entertaining for us as they possibly could, under the circumstances. We had all the steaks and burgers we could eat, along with the girls and the beer. What more could we have wanted? There were live shows at night and we had twenty-four-hour access to our own Olympic-size swimming pool. It was great.

This stand-down was turning out to be a little different. We had been in for two days now and we had just about worn ourselves out by the end of the second day. When word came down that the General of the Twenty-fifth Division himself would be stopping by to give out the combat medals that the men of Alpha Company had earned since the last time we were in. Most of the guys didn't even know who the general was, never mind have the opportunity to meet him. I was kind of looking forward to it though, as corny as that might sound. But I really was.

It was the morning of our third day in, and we were getting ourselves together to move out and back to fighting the war, when word came down that the general was on his way over to meet us and present us with our hard earned medals. It was typical army bullshit. Here we were, to a man hung over from the night before and we had already drawn our combat gear and weapons. And now he was on his way over?

The company must have been a sight. We must have smelled terrible from all the boozing the night before and we had already changed into our jungle clothes and fighting gear. But what could we do about it? Nothing. I would be standing in front of the general in my worn and somewhat ragged jungle fatigues, with the smell of stale beer on my breath. Oh great, I thought, I was to represent the "Wolfhounds" and myself looking and smelling like an old drunk.

I would be one of ten guys to get a medal this day, for the combat that we had been involved in the previous six weeks or so. As I looked down the line at my fellow soldiers, it came over me that the way we looked was the way we always looked. We always seemed to be coming in from a mission or going out on one, so for us to stand at attention with a clean new uniform on would have been kind of hypocritical. The way everyone was dressed was a much clearer representation of who we really were and we were very proud of who we were. Let the " Base Camp Warriors" get their "Bullshit" medals all dressed up with their boots shined. I was proud to represent the "Wolfhounds" by looking the exact same way I did each and every day in the jungles and rice paddies of South Vietnam.

On this day I was to receive my third "Air-Medal" for twenty combat assaults by air against a hostile force, as well as my first "Army Commendation Medal". I was proud of the fact that I had made it through another twenty assaults. But as I looked around at the men that I was now serving with in Alpha Company, it struck me that some of the guys I had been with not all that long ago, were no longer here. Some of them had rotated home, having served their time; some had gotten jobs in the rear; some had received wounds severe enough to be sent to the States for treatment; and yes, others had been killed. Here it was the first week in March. I had been out since the end of November, and I was becoming an old-timer. It had only been a little over a hundred days and I was now a veteran. It felt kind of strange—I just didn't believe I had made it through the first few days, never mind a hundred. I guess I'd been lucky and for that luck I am forever grateful.

The general had presented us with our medals and was now headed back to his air-conditioned office, to fight his war. And it was now time for us to get back to fighting ours. For they were two entirely different wars, to say the least. We'd all been rewarded for doing our jobs and staying alive. As a group we were a proud bunch, but most of all we were very proud of each other. For we really weren't fighting for the army, per se, as much as we were fighting to keep each other alive and this had been accomplished to the best of our ability. But that was then and this was now; it was time for us to move back out to FSB Chamberlain and what the division had in-store for us from there, we had no idea. We had heard rumors that our AO (area of operations) was going to undergo a dramatic change, but we wouldn't get the final word on that until we got back to Chamberlain. It wouldn't surprise me one bit, for whole units of the Twenty-fifth Infantry Division were going home and the units that were left behind would just have to cover more ground.

Chapter 23

Bear Cat: Our New AO

It looked like the rumors were true: a part of the Twenty-fifth Infantry Division would be leaving Vietnam and going back to Hawaii. It seemed that if you were part of a unit that was being re-assigned back to the Twenty-fifth Division's home base of Hawaii and you had over nine months in-country, then you would be going with them. If you had less time in-country, then you were going to be re-assigned to another unit within the division. I'd only been here for four and a half months, so it looked like I'd be re-assigned to another artillery battery. The reality of my situation was that I would just be staying out with the "hounds" for a while longer. That's all I wanted in the first place, so the fact that part of the division was packing up and going home didn't impact my life in the slightest.

What would change for me and the rest of the guys I served with was that FSB Chamberlain would be given over to the South Vietnamese Army in a few weeks and we would no longer be returning to it for our off-line rest time. What would happen to the First Wolfhounds is that its area of operations would be shifted to the Bear Cat area, east of Saigon. As soon as this change was announced, we all received new maps of this location. It was all jungle and rubber plantations—there wasn't one rice paddy in the entire area. The Wolfhounds had been fighting in the rice paddies of South Vietnam since arriving in-country three years earlier, so this new AO was going to represent quite a change for the six-hundred soldiers in the battalion. I wasn't really sure how the change would affect me, but what I did know was that the terrain east of Saigon was a hell of a lot thicker and thus a lot more dangerous for us to work in. Just when we were getting to know the villages and rice paddies around Chamberlain, the army suddenly changed things on us. Oh well, there wasn't anything I could do about it, but go along with the program and learn everything I could about this new area as fast as I could, in order to stay alive.

Alpha Company spent the next couple of days at Chamberlain getting itself ready for the move. My time was spent going over the new maps and memorizing all the new radio call signs, so I would be as ready as I could for this extreme change. My time was also utilized reading some of the letters from home that I hadn't had the chance to read before. I also had plenty of time to answer them at this time. I know it sounds like we were so busy over here that there was no time to write home, but that wasn't really the case at all. It was that most of the time if I did get a break I was so exhausted that I would use that time to get a few hours of sleep.

I hadn't really gotten over my "Dear John" letter yet, but I had put it behind me for my own well being, to be dealt with later. I hoped that by the time I got back to it, it wouldn't mean as much to me.

I also spent time with some of the guys I had gotten to know in the Battery, who were now going home. I really didn't know them all that well, but I had spoken to most of them on the radio on many occasions. I had only gotten back into Chamberlain a few times during my first four months out in the field, so my face-to-face time with these guys was limited. But a bond had been formed over the radio. On more than one occasion my life was in their hands and they never let me down. It was a strong enough bond that I hated to see it broken. I should have been happy that some of them were able to go home a little early, but in fact I was a little bit jealous. We had worked well together as a team and now I was going to have to re-establish that same bond all over again with a bunch of new guys; that fact alone had me more than a little concerned.

After a couple of days of preparation, it was time for us to move out. Bear Cat Base Camp was located about twenty miles east of Saigon, and it would take the better part of the day for our convoy to get there. The whole area that was assigned to us was well known for its unforgivable terrain. The jungle itself was almost complete triple canopy. Even on a sunny day one could not see the sky from the floor of the jungle. This always presented a problem for the troops who had to work this type of terrain, for if we were to get into a firefight and suffered any wounded we would have a tough time getting them out. And this was to happen on more than one occasion in the following months.

Bear Cat itself was home to a large Korean Army force that had been there for a few years. The Koreans seemed to think the "Wolfhounds" were there to take the place over, but nothing could have been further from our minds—the base camp was one filthy mess and we felt that the less time we spent there the better. Compared to Cu Chi, this place was just plain awful. Its perimeter was falling apart The living quarters were filthy, with rats running around as they pleased. We felt that this place was just too dangerous for us to spend any time at. The fact that we would rather spend our time out in the jungle, summed it up.

The Battalion pulled its trucks into Bear Cat Base Camp, found its designated area and proceeded to unload all its gear. It looked like we were going to be here for a while. Alpha Company got squared away in its own company area and left a few guys there to set up a company rear operation center, while the rest of us marched out the front gate to get our first search and destroy mission in under way. It was the first and only time I felt bad for the guys' back in the rear. The men of Alpha Company considered Base Camp Bear Cat a much more dangerous place to spend the night than out on ambush.

Chapter 24
Ambush Outside FSB South Dakota

We'd been patrolling the area around Bear Cat for three days now and as much as I had always hated being in the field, it was the lesser of two evils. The jungle was a hell of a lot more treacherous than I had anticipated, though. Alpha Company had split into platoon-size patrols, as had been our operating procedure back in our previous AO (area of operations), Cu Chi Province. I for one always liked to patrol in a platoon-size element, as opposed to a company-size patrol; I felt it gave us a better chance at surprising the enemy. All the platoons were with in a half-mile of each other at all times anyway, so if there was any contact with the enemy we could get the company back to full strength in no time at all.

Most days we were exhausted by noontime, as we tried to make our way through some of the densest jungle one could ever imagine. The temperature and humidity hadn't abated one bit, and being in such thick vegetation all day was even more draining on us. We were taking more breaks, and for longer periods of time, which gave us all an opportunity to catch up on our lost sleep from the previous night's ambush. Water was an ongoing problem for us though, as it would continue to be throughout my tour of duty in Vietnam. I never got used to the awful taste of iodine in the stream water I filled my canteens with.

April 2, 1970 started out just like the day before. This day was to be different however. Not only was it my brother Harold's birthday back in the world, but it would also be the first time in our new AO (area of operations) that we would come in contact with the enemy. The terrain we found ourselves out on patrol in just northeast of Fire Support Base South Dakota was by far the toughest for us to work—it was so damn thick and had plenty of those tangle vines on the ground reaching up, grabbing our legs and tripping us every other step we took. It made just walking along difficult and dangerous. Out on patrol I often felt that if the gooks weren't going to get you, then the jungle would.

We were just about to cross a small, fast-moving river. It was just one of many that we had crossed that day and everything seemed normal—normal that is by Vietnam standards. Then just like that, our morning on patrol changed. That's the way it was here: Change could come in an instant, and it was never a change for the good. We had walked straight into our first ambush, just south of Bear Cat. We were almost close enough to FSB South Dakota to see it off in the distance; in fact, we probably could have seen it if the jungle hadn't been in the way.

It was a perfect ambush from the enemy's point of view, not unlike many ambushes that I would be part of from the other side of the gun-barrel while serving with the Wolfhounds. Three soldiers had passed through the river and were waiting on the other side for the rest of the platoon to cross, four were in the river making the crossing, and the rest of us were waiting to cross, when the shooting started. I was third in line making my way down a small but slippery incline, when all hell broke loose.

First came an explosion that sounded like a claymore mine. Then the distinctive sound of an AK-47 machine-gun could clearly be heard firing its lethal clip of bullets right into our patrol. One, two, three soldiers went down in a flash, while the rest of us scrambled to find whatever cover we could. Those of us on the far side of the river had just one problem though, that was the fact that we had been inching our way down that damn slippery slope when the firing started and getting back up it was impossible. All we could do was dive to each side of the trail and take cover in the tall grass growing along side of it. Well let me just say that tall grass offers no protection against machine-gun bullets. We knew this, and as soon as we hit the ground, each and every one of us crawled away on our hands and knees as fast as he could, seeking some sort of shelter from all the lead that was flying around us. Bullets were zinging their way through the grass trying to find us; but thank God, the guys on the other side of the triggers of those machine guns were terrible shots. Or were we just plain lucky? In any case, none of the fifteen or so men on my side of the river were killed or wounded.

The lieutenant and I, along with a couple of other guys, found a large, dead tree that had fallen years earlier and took cover behind it. I immediately got on the radio to FSB South Dakota to alert them to our situation, so they could get ready for a fire mission. To my surprise, the fire mission had already been put into motion; we were so close to them that the base's personnel were able to monitor the situation from the base perimeter. Even though they couldn't see us from their position, they sure as hell could hear what was going on.

Most of the men of Alpha Company were now in a position to return fire in the direction they felt the enemy fire was coming from. We were lying on the ground trying to find whatever cover we could, so where to return fire was an educated guess at best. But it's a funny thing about being in these situations; after a while one's guesses usually turn out to be pretty accurate. Only a few minutes had passed, when all the shooting stopped just as suddenly as it had begun.

This was the way it was over here. We would spend day after day, night after night trying to find the enemy, really not wanting to, but looking just the same. Sometimes we would find him and sometimes he would find us. This day the bastards found us.

The men who had taken refuge with me behind that fallen tree were now making their way very carefully forward to the stream area that had been so deadly just five minutes before. There was plenty of smoke still in the air as we approached the river's edge. The air was so humid that smoke would hang around longer than it would have in a more arid part of the world. When we got to the place where we had waited to cross the river just a few minutes earlier, the medic was already treating one of the guys who had been hit by the initial explosion. It was just as I had thought: the enemy had started its ambush with a U.S. claymore mine. The gooks were forever using our own mines to try to kill us. Who knows where they got them? It was just one more thing we had to deal with on a daily basis.

On the other side of the river, seven or eight Alpha Company soldiers surrounded the three soldiers who had been unlucky enough to be the first to cross the river. The claymore mine had really done a number on them and I didn't know if they were going to make it or not. The lieutenant and I wadded across the river and took our position a few feet away from where these men were lying in great pain but dealing with it the best they could. The medic had already administered shots of morphine and was now starting to treat the wounds the best he could. This type of mine can inflict numerous ugly wounds if it hits you just right; in fact it was designed to take down as many soldiers at as great a distance as possible—not kill them necessarily, just take them out of action.

The rest of the company was now fanning out to find the enemy that had just put such a hurting on us. They were probably long gone by now but we had to go and look for them nevertheless, for that was our job, and under these circumstances it was something we wanted to do. We wanted to find those bastards and lay a hurting on them as payback for what had just taken place.

FSB South Dakota was now on the radio asking for a status report on what they had heard and just about witnessed a few minutes earlier. The lieutenant filled them in on our situation and our plans to move west of their position. The patrol was so close to the base that we felt they might open fire on us, thinking we were the fleeing enemy soldiers.

The captain had already been on the radio letting the base know what had just happened and to stand-down while we were in the area, for we didn't want to be mistaken for the enemy by our own troops and be fired upon. One thing that I was always concerned with during my tour was being mistaken for the enemy by my own side. During a firefight things could become very confusing and being mistaken for the enemy happened on more than one occasion. When I was in a firefight I always liked it to be out away from any base camps and for it to be over quickly. The quicker it was over, the less chance some scared trigger-happy new guy just in from the world had of blowing me away by mistake.

The ambush was over, and the enemy had escaped. There was nothing new about that. The side that fires the first shots during an ambush usually won. Sometimes it was the gooks and sometimes it was us. Today it just happened to be their turn.

The medivac chopper was just landing and our wounded were being put onboard as we arrived back at the ambush site. The count was five wounded, three seriously and one of those was not expected to make it back to the Twenty-fifth Medivac Hospital at Cu Chi. The hospital that we all wanted to be taken to if we were unlucky enough to be wounded, would always be the Twenty-fifth Med back at Cu Chi, for it was "state of the art" and gave us the best chance of surviving. Even though we were now working in the Bear Cat area and Cu Chi was farther away, it was always the first choice of the helicopter pilots who came to pick us up.

After the helicopter left and we put our guards out on the perimeter we took a break and had some lunch, just as though no ambush had taken place at all. It was a surreal experience this Vietnam—only an hour and a half ago we had been taking cover behind a fallen tree and were fighting for our very lives. Now here we were setting up a small secure area and taking a break to have a bite to eat.

At this time a few of us went over the ambush that had just taken place. We came to the conclusion that the only way we could have been so lucky as to have suffered the few casualties that we had, was for the enemy to have been VC (Vietcong) and not the NVA (North Vietnamese Army) regulars whom we had been fighting in the Cu Chi area. The sloppiness of the ambush itself and the fact that they had disappeared so quickly after blowing it led us to believe that they lived in the area and that there were only a few of them. The NVA would have had a much larger force, would have set up a better ambush, and would not have broken off the engagement as quickly. I'm sure this ambush was not planned, but came about because the enemy just happened to be traveling in the same area at the same time as we were and just decided to take advantage of the situation.

We also suspected that they lived in the area and that we would be seeing them again—the only difference being that next time we would be doing the ambushing and we wouldn't be breaking it off as quickly. In fact, we wouldn't be breaking it off at all, until we got each and every one of the gooks who had ambushed us this day. At least now after our first encounter with the enemy in this area, we had a better idea of what we would be up against and could plan our moves accordingly. It was an expensive lesson to learn, but what lesson in war isn't? Someone told me a long time ago that every lesson in life has a price tag on it, and the lessons we had to learn over here on a daily basis only reinforced that fact in my mind.

Chapter 25

A Night in Bear Cat

After a few more days of patrolling the area around FSB South Dakota, word came out to us that it was our turn to come inside the base and perform guard duty. This was always good duty, as it gave us a few days to catch up on our mail and take a shower and possibly get a chance to get into the PX at Cu Chi to pick up stuff that we couldn't get in the field, like film for our cameras. Every month our paycheck—all $350.00 of it—was automatically deposited in the Chase Manhattan Bank located at Cu Chi, so to have any money to walk around with we had to somehow make our way back to Cu Chi and get it. Money in Vietnam was something we really didn't need much of, as we rarely had a chance to spend it. We used the money we carried around with us primarily to buy sodas, beers and gamble with and once and a while we spent a few bucks on the girls that worked the cathouses, that were located right outside of each base. During my tour of duty I very rarely visited those cathouses. (Not that I wouldn't have, it was just that I was rarely in from the field.) On occasion they would bring the girls out to us in the field on the backs of scooters, if you can imagine that.

If there was a way to make a buck, the Vietnamese people would always find it, whether it was hawking stolen sodas and sandwiches or selling girls. I had to admire them for that, and that was the only thing that I did admire about them. As my tour progressed my disdain for these people would only grow. On the whole they were small, ugly, dirty people who would sell their grandmothers for a buck. I'm sure they weren't all like that, but the people I was in contact with on a day-to-day basis were, so what other conclusion could I come to? The vast majority of the gooks I saw during the day were the same ones who were trying to kill me at night. I could never turn my back on one, day or night. Maybe that had a lot to do with my feelings.

After we had arrived back at the base I would have to report to the captain in charge of the Battery. Even though I was spending all of my time out with the Wolfhounds I was officially part of the Battery, and the captain of the Battery always wanted whoever was under his command to report in every time they were back in his area. It was no big deal, but I always found myself in between places. I did all of my fighting with Alpha Company, but it was the Battery that paid me; it was a difficult position for me to be in, but I made the best of it. It was kind of weird, considering I didn't know a soul at the Battery, nor did they know me. To them I was just a voice on the radio and a name on the official Battery roster.

Upon my arrival at the Battery it would be first things first - for me that meant getting a five-gallon can of water and putting it in a shower bag that hung over a makeshift shower. Off came all of my clothes, and under the shower I went, to try to wash the dirt and grime off my body. I hadn't had a shower in over two weeks and it felt great.

Next I got all new clothes and made a visit to the FDC (Fire Direction Control) bunker to introduce myself as the voice of Alpha Company. As soon as I opened my mouth they all knew who I was, because my Boston accent gave me away once again. They treated me as something of a lost soul who just happened to be out with the Infantry. Most RTOs and Recon-Sergeants stayed out for at least six months during their tours and then came back to the Battery and took a job at the FDC center for their last six months. As much as I cared for the guys I was serving with, I was looking forward to my time off-line and a new job back with the artillery. The guys at FDC had a lot of questions to ask me about life out with the grunts. What was it like always out on ambush and basically living off the land for weeks on end? And what was it really like during a firefight? But I really had no answers for them; I guess it was something you had to experience for yourself.

Twenty minutes or so later I left the FDC bunker and made my way over to Alpha Company's location to see what kind of trouble they had planned. We had the rest of the day to ourselves and we desperately wanted to find a ride into Cu Chi. Corporal Bernier, Buzzard and I started asking around about a re-supply run or a mail-run or anything that might be heading for Cu Chi. But the best we could come up with was a ride in the back of a truck into Bear Cat. We looked at each other and without a word being spoken, hopped on board. What the hell, we figured it was better than spending the day at the FSB (Fire Support Base).

Bear Cat did have a PX. We could scare up a few beers and there was a "Cathouse" to help us take our minds off the war, for a short while at least.

So we would make the best of it, as we always did—to tell you the truth we'd gotten pretty good at that.

It was a little after noon when we arrived inside the gate at Bear Cat. We jumped off the back of the truck as soon as it came to a stop. Trying to find our way to our company area that was located here wasn't too difficult, for the base just wasn't that big. We made our way over and reported in, just in case someone decided to look for us. We had already made up our minds to miss the last truck back to the base and explore Bear Cat's nightlife, if that's what you wanted to call it. All we knew was that it had to be better than Fire Base South Dakota's and a hell of a lot better than what we had just been through the last few weeks outside the wire.

Our first stop was the PX so we could load up what we wanted and what we thought some of the guys might want back at the company: things like film and toothbrushes and toothpaste. It was now after 3:00 P.M. and we had dropped our stuff off back at the company's bunker. We would now head over to the enlisted men's club to grab a few beers.

The club was down the road a few hundred yards; we walked over with our M16s on our backs, as was our custom while in-country. We hadn't gone fifty yards or so when the MPs. (Military Police) stopped us. It seemed that being armed in Bear Cat was a no-no. It was our first time in, so how were we to know? So we had to turn around, leave our guns at Alpha Company's headquarters and start out all over again. This was the first time in-country that I didn't have my M16 with me and it felt strange; I kind of felt naked without it. Something was definitely missing. If those were the rules, then they were the rules—but we didn't like being un-armed one bit.

"Welcome to the Bear Cat EM Club: Home of the Manchus," the sign out front read. Oh great, it appeared we would be the only "Wolfhounds" in the club. Fortunately, the club was almost empty—everyone was out on patrol looking to kill some gooks. We just about had the place to ourselves. The place was kind of small, but the music was loud. The place had slot machines, something I'd never seen before, so I grabbed a beer and made my way over to one. It was a nickel machine. I promptly lost ten bucks, so that was it for me.

It was after 6:00 P.M NOW and the three of us were feeling no pain. We decided to check out the whorehouse, which just happened to be located right next door. It was my first time in such a place. Buzzard and Bernier had visited the ones outside of Cu Chi, so they knew what to expect. As drunk as I was, these girls were still just plain ugly and they were so damn young. I felt very uncomfortable just being there. As soon as we walked in a couple of the girls grabbed our arms and led us to the bar. With the camp being pretty empty, I'm sure they were even happier to see us then they normally would have been. They could hardly speak English and my Vietnamese wasn't very good either, but we managed to communicate. After a few more expensive beers, Buzzard disappeared into the back room. Not long after that, Bernier disappeared as well, leaving me sitting there surrounded by five or six bargirls. A short while later I hooked up with what I thought was a cute little working Vietnamese girl and went into the back room with her. It's funny the things one will do with ten or twelve beers under his belt. Rather than get into what happened in the backroom, let's just say it wasn't all that bad and leave it at that.

An hour or so passed and it was time to grab a few beers to go, make our way back to Alpha Company's area and report back in. Just as we had figured the last truck back to the base camp had long since left. That left us in Bear Cat for the night, which was exactly what we had planned. We sat around for a few more hours and had a few more beers and a few laughs. We watched the flares and tracer bullets going off in the distance and were grateful for our unexpected time off-line and our belly full of beer. It had been an interesting day away from fighting the war and we had enjoyed ourselves. Tomorrow would come soon enough and we would be back at it all over again, but for tonight we would just sit there and watch the war from a distance.

Chapter 26
Sniper Duty

We got back to FSB South Dakota on the first truck out, hung over but feeling the day and night spent in Bear Cat was well worth it. Upon our arrival, the other guys from the company for whom we had gifts from the PX greeted us. A package of 35-mm film was saved for the captain, as we figured he would be pissed off at us for missing the last truck out the night before. He was pleased that we hadn't forgotten him and was grateful for the film. Surprisingly, he wasn't upset with us at all. He wasn't born yesterday, and he knew what we were up to; in fact I thought he was a little envious of us. Lt. White, who was my immediate boss in the field and could have made my life miserable, got some film for his camera as well, and even though we really didn't like one another I felt it was the right thing to do.

Our few days in camp passed all too quickly, and soon it was time to get our gear together and get back to the business of hunting down the enemy around FSB South Dakota. The next morning we got going early. The sun had barely come over the horizon when we found ourselves walking out the front gate of the base. We didn't realize it at that time, but there would be big changes in store for Alpha Company in the coming weeks. As it turned out this was to be the one and only time I was to visit FSB South Dakota. Walking out of a FSB (Fire Support Base) was always strange. It felt like we were leaving something or someone behind to go out and fight the war on our own. When we were in the field we felt like we were alone out there—Alpha Company against whatever enemy we could find. Now and then an occasional chopper would pay us a visit with a re-supply of food, ammo and our mail, but that was just about it. The only real contact we would have with the outside world for weeks on end would be by radio back to the Battery for fire missions. It was the Infantry that really fought the Vietnam War, just as it had fought all wars. Yes, we were only a small part of the war, us "Wolfhounds", but some days we felt we were the only ones doing the fighting, even though we knew better. And we wouldn't have wanted it any other way.

We had only been out for a few days when the re-supply chopper dropped off something unusual, a new guy from the Battery was about to join our little band of warriors. At the same time, Sergeant Bowers, our sniper was going to be taking his R&R and meeting his wife in Hawaii. We didn't like to see Bowers go, but we had been listening to him talk about his R & R for weeks now, so at least now we wouldn't have to hear about it anymore.

With our sniper leaving and the Battery sending out a new guy, I got the bright idea that this may be my chance to get the radio off my back and at the same time acquire Bower's sniper rifle and night scope, thus becoming the company's sniper until he returned. I knew I could handle the job, as I'd qualified as an expert rifleman back in boot camp. I wanted something different to do over here besides calling in fire missions all the time. I presented my idea to Lt. White, and much to my surprise he agreed. I guess my gift of some film from the PX had gone a long ways. I greeted the new guy, gave him my radio to carry, and got Bower's sniper rifle. I would stay close to the new guy—as would the lieutenant—for as long as it would take for him to be on his own with the radio, but for the next couple of weeks until Bowers returned I was the company sniper. I couldn't have been happier.

Sniper duty, now that was something I had wanted to do ever since I had met Bowers and had a chance to handle his very special weapon, one of only a hundred or so that were in-country. It was a specially modified M14. This weapon fired a 7.62-mm round in a 20-round clip. It weighed in at approximately 11 pounds fully loaded and had an effective range of 750 yards. The gear that I was to carry along with the rifle included a 3x–9x telescope that mounted on the top of the rifle and a silencer that was just over a foot long, making this sniper rifle one of the deadliest weapons on the battlefield. What was so lethal about this weapon? It was the fact that it couldn't be heard when fired, that was the main reason it was so deadly. That meant the sniper himself would not be detected upon making his shot. At night I would attach a star-scope to the weapon in order to see in the darkness. Here was a weapon that the enemy couldn't hear being fired from up to 750 yards away, which could be shot at night with tremendous accuracy. This gun was the NVA's and the VC's greatest nightmare come true and I was to have complete control of it for at least the next couple of weeks. It would prove to be a very interesting few weeks.

It was late April now, and we were on recon patrol outside of South Dakota. As luck would have it our point-man had surprised three or four gooks cooking up some breakfast first thing in the morning. Normally our patrols wouldn't get started until later in the morning, but this day we had started out an hour or so earlier than usual. We never did surprise the gooks in the morning; as they seemed to have our schedule down pat, as we always seemed to do the same thing at the same time each day. It was something I didn't like, but I was not in charge. We had changed things up a little this day and we got lucky. Our point-man got off a few rounds after surprising the gooks, and as quick as their little feet would take them, off they went running for their very lives.

The rest of the patrol made their way up to the contact point as fast as it could, and what we found there was surprising, as well as kind of funny. There in a little clearing was a very small fire with a pot of rice cooking over it. Nearby lay one pair of sandals and one lone sandal. These guys had left in such a hurry that they had run right out of their shoes. We all looked at each other and laughed out loud. Out on patrol there wasn't all that much to laugh about, but this really got us going. After we calmed down it was time to take a look around and see what else they may have left behind in their haste to depart the area.

Pvt. Mello who was looking up the trail a bit came upon an empty clear plastic holster; this got everyone's attention real fast, for we knew it once held a Russian or Chinese pistol and that was something we all wanted to find in the worst way. One of the weapons we could keep and send home was a Communist pistol. It was the ultimate prize and everyone wanted one. We all fanned out in search of that pistol and it only took us a few minutes to find it. The new lieutenant who had just arrived in the company was the lucky one to stumble upon it. He was only a few feet away from me when he made his find. I would have given just about anything to have found that weapon.

We also found a bag of maps and a lot of Vietnamese money, but it was the handgun that we were all interested in. It appeared the soldiers we had surprised were some sort of gook payroll team or something. They must have also had an officer with them, for officers were the only ones who carried side arms. The lieutenant was proudly showing his prize around to the rest of us when the captain's radio came to life with the call sign "Ten Delta." The captain's RTO (Radio Transmission Operator) quickly grabbed his codebook to see just who "Ten Delta" was and he turned out to be some colonel from division, who just happened to be in the area monitoring our radio transmissions and was curious as to what we had found.

The captain couldn't wait to inform him of exactly what we had found and this included the Russian pistol. I can just imagine the look on that jerk's face when he heard the word *pistol*. He informed the captain that he would be on his way in and for us to secure a perimeter for him—like we just got here yesterday and didn't already know to do just that. These senior officers in Vietnam were really something, they were never in the field fighting the war, but they sure as hell walked around like they were. They were just someone for us to avoid and be laughed at, by the men who were really fighting the war. I don't know if they realized how much disrespect the fighting soldier in Vietnam had for them, but I'm sure that if they had, it wouldn't have bothered them in the least.

Down from the sky came this officer riding shot-gun in a small Loch helicopter, upon its landing he jumped out of it like he was landing at Normandy Beach. His uniform was all starched and pressed. He looked like he was on his way to a costume party. The captain snapped to attention and rendered him the obligatory salute and was saluted back smartly. We stood off to the side, avoiding eye contact with him. If our eyes were to have met we would have had to salute him as well, and we sure as hell didn't want to do that. The captain took over all the things that we had found and gave them to the colonel, so he could bring them back to division headquarters and probably take a bow for taking such a chance in landing his helicopter in enemy territory and all that shit. But what he really wanted to see was the Russian T-54 pistol that the Lieutenant had found; that was the real reason he was there.

The new lieutenant was summoned over to show the colonel his war prize. At this time the colonel informed the lieutenant that he was going to have to take the pistol back with him for intelligence reasons and for him to come by his office and pick it up the next time he was in Cu Chi. The look on the lieutenant's face was priceless. But what was he going to say to such a senior officer—no? I don't think so. He reluctantly handed over his prize to the colonel and after a round of handshakes and congratulations for a job well done, he made his way over to his chopper.

We watched as his chopper lifted off and just like that he was gone. He couldn't have been on the ground for five minutes. We all gathered around the new lieutenant and told him to say goodbye to his war prize, but that wasn't how he saw it. He really believed that the next time he was in Cu Chi he would just have to stop by this guy's office and his Russian T-54 pistol, the most prized souvenir of the war, would be there waiting for him. Like I said, he was new.

A couple of weeks later we were stopping in Cu Chi on our way to Cambodia and the lieutenant and I, along with a few other guys, made a visit to that colonel's office. The plan was for the lieutenant to go in alone and pick up his pistol; we would be waiting for him outside. He was only gone a few minutes and when came out, it was without the pistol. The colonel had already rotated home, his tour of duty having ended a few weeks prior to us getting back to Cu Chi. This asshole had gone back to the States and with him he carried the greatest of all war trophies, to be use as a "Prop" I'm sure, when he would tell his family and friends of his exploits in Vietnam. The lieutenant was devastated, to say the least. His war trophy was long gone and he knew it. But we weren't surprised at all. For we knew these senior officers for what they really were, and it had nothing to do with what they would have everyone at home believe. It had nothing to do with DUTY, HONOR, and COUNTRY.

Chapter 27
Our Trip to Saigon

It was now the end of April and Alpha Company was still making its living patrolling the area southeast of Bear Cat, but the enemy's activity had just about ceased to exist. We were still putting our ambushes out every night and spending the better part of our days cutting our way through the thick jungle foliage looking to engage him, but he just wouldn't show his face.

The new guy Casey, had brought something into the field that I had never seen before out here, a very small transistor radio. This radio had an earpiece with it, so no one else could hear it but him. I didn't think it was a very good idea to have a radio out with us, considering the nature of our business. But the captain didn't see anything wrong with it, as long as he listened to it through his earpiece and never had it on at night while we were out on ambush. Well, what the hell did I care? It was the captain's show and if anything went wrong, because of that radio it was going to be his responsibility and his ass, not mine.

The company was still just outside of FSB South Dakota on May 2 when word officially came out to us to make our way back to Bear Cat. We had heard on Casey's radio just a few hours earlier that the Cambodian invasion had commenced, and even though we were over sixty miles from that area it looked like we'd be taking part in it, after all. To a man we just couldn't believe it; we all looked at each other and wondered, didn't the army have any other troops to send on this mission but the "Wolfhounds"? We had been out of that area for over a month now. Surely they must have filled it with some other battalion by now.

It was going to be a long walk back to Bear Cat and we were still in a very dangerous area. We got our gear together and started out. It would take us the better part of the day to make it back in, and I don't think more than a few words were spoken about the upcoming mission that lay ahead of us. Bear Cat came into view just before sundown. It was an awful place to spend any time at, so we were grateful that we were only to spend one night there and then move on to Cu Chi at first light.

A short briefing was held first thing in the morning, just before we loaded up the trucks that were to transport us up to Cu Chi. But we didn't learn a hell of a lot about our mission, only that we were going to be airlifted deep into Cambodia and would be looking to engage the NVA's Ninth Division. The captain didn't know any more about the mission than we did, but he told us what he did know. And we were grateful to him for that. The more I thought about the army's decision to transport us all the way back to Cu Chi and then send us into Cambodia, the more it made sense. We'd only been out of that area for a month or so, and the company had spent the better part of last year patrolling right along the Cambodian border. As a company we knew the terrain well—we had on more than one occasion been over that border to set up our ambushes at night. Hell, I'm sure we had patrolled it during the day as well, without even knowing it: The border between Vietnam and Cambodia wasn't the most defined of boundaries between two countries in the world, to say the least.

It was a long ride up-country to Cu Chi, and once we got there it was almost like greeting an old friend. Cu Chi had so much to offer us, with its enlisted men's club, massage parlor, and—of course, how could I forget?—The PX. It was a good place to be, if only for a few days, as we got ready to play out our part in the "Invasion of Cambodia".

It was late in the day on May 3 when we finally pulled into the "Wolfhound" area of the base. I personally didn't think we would ever see this area again, considering our new AO (Area of Operations) had been so far away. But here it was and it was a welcomed sight. As a group the "Wolfhounds" always had a great time when they were in Cu Chi Base Camp. The partying would go on day and night. This place was the only place in-country were I felt safe enough to lock my weapon up and let my hair down. Most of the company had been together for five or six months now and had become very close. I had become closer with a couple of the guys than I really had wanted to, but I figured what would be would be and let it go at that.

We still hadn't heard what our role would be in the invasion. The captain said we would be on our own in camp, but we were to stay close by in case we had to move out on a moment's notice. Buzzard, Bernier and I took that to mean that we were free for a while. We didn't know for how long, but we were determined to take full advantage of this unexpected time off. Our first thought was to grab a ride into Saigon, after all it was only twenty miles away. None of us had ever been to the city and we wanted to go in the worst way. Our attitude had changed since we'd received official notification that we would be going into Cambodia to engage the NVA's Ninth Division. The enemy's Ninth Division was a formidable force to deal with, and we really started to get the feeling that many of us wouldn't be coming back. We were going to have some fun while we could and we felt Saigon was just the place to have that fun. Saigon was off-limits to the "Wolfhounds" without a pass and getting a pass was impossible, but our minds were made up to experience Saigon at least this one time while we had our chance, pass or no pass.

Early on May 4, the three of us grabbed our weapons and a bandoleer of ammo and made our way out to the front gate, and waited for a truck or a jeep headed into Saigon that we could hitch a ride with. We knew what would happen to us if we were to be caught; but we figured what was the worst they could do to us—send us to Cambodia? It didn't take long for a corporal from division headquarters to stop and give us a lift into Long Bien, and from there we took a taxi right into downtown Saigon. We were just like any tourist in a large bustling city, except we had machine-guns on our backs. Everywhere we looked, everything was so strange and foreign to us that we really felt out of place and a little nervous. Imagine that: here we were, three guys with over one hundred and fifty air combat assaults between us, and we were still nervous. Saigon was truly a big city. We were out of our element here and we knew it, but we were determined to make the best of it and have a good time.

First up was something I had always wanted to do ever since I was a kid, and that was to take a ride in a rickshaw. We hired three of them, and raced around Saigon taking in the sights for forty-five minutes or so. The next thing on our agenda was some beers and some girls. The rickshaw drivers knew just where to take us: the Rex Hotel. As I look back on it now we must have stuck out like three country boys coming into the city for the very first time—and I guess that's just what we were. The one thing that must have given us away was the fact that we had our M16s on our backs and no one else had an M16 with them at all. Our uniforms were well worn, and we didn't have any stripes or patches on our sleeves either. Everyone else at the "Rex" had a cleaned and pressed uniform, and it seemed to us that every other soldier we saw, was an officer. So this was where all the officers were hiding out, we thought—because they certainly weren't out with us fighting the war.

We walked into the lobby of the Rex Hotel, looked around, and thought we had better get the hell out of this place. The hotel was full of officers, and anyone of them could ask us for our passes at anytime. And if one of them did, it would have been all over for us. As we turned and made our way towards the front door, I noticed a sign that said the bar was on the top floor. The top floor, I thought, now that sounded kind of nice; we could have a few beers and take in the view of the entire city. When we got off the elevator on the top floor, much to our surprise there in front of us was a large bar with numerous working girls just waiting for us. Hell, they were waiting for anyone to get off that elevator, but that really didn't matter to us, now did it?

We looked at each other and our thoughts were the same. Here we would be off the streets and have all the beers we wanted; along with our choice of some very good looking young women. These girls didn't look like the ones working at the cathouse we had visited in Bear Cat. These girls were actually good looking. No wonder all the officers were in Saigon— besides avoiding the war that is. We remained at the Rex rooftop bar for most of the afternoon, our only interruptions being a few side trips with the girls to their rooms. It was truly a most memorable day in Saigon. Upon leaving we all vowed to come back again before our tours were over.

It was getting late and we knew we couldn't stay in Saigon for the night; that would have been inviting disaster. Half-drunk as we were and as much as we wanted to stay, we had to get back to Cu Chi before dark and we didn't have the slightest idea on how we were going accomplish that. But getting back to Cu Chi turned out to be a lot easier than we could have imagined. All we did was go down to the front of the hotel, get in a cab and tell the driver where we wanted to go. He quoted us the price for such a long trip, we agreed and off we went. We arrived back at the base an hour later, just as the sun was going down. We walked through the main gate as if we had just been out shopping at the little stores located right outside. We had made it. We had taken the risk and gone into Saigon and it had been well worth the risk.

Chapter 28
Getting Ready for Cambodia

It was May 5, and we still hadn't gotten any word as to our role in the invasion or the date we would be going in. This day started out just fine, even though the three of us were nursing quite a hangover from the previous day's activities in Saigon. We had just returned from lunch when word came down from division for everyone to gather at battalion headquarters for a briefing. It was about time we heard something. Alpha Company, as well as the rest of the Wolfhounds of the 1/27 Infantry were starting to get a little antsy. We wanted to get going; we knew that some troops were already in Cambodia and we didn't want to miss any of the action. One of the reasons we wanted to have a part in this large mission was that we felt most of the casualties that we had suffered patrolling along the border were inflicted by the NVA's Ninth Division. And this would be our chance to get some of that payback we were always looking for.

The battalion commander gave us one of those pep talks to inspire us, but it really wasn't necessary. We were anxious to get the show on the road. After his bullshit was done, he turned us over to our individual company commanders. It would be up to them to fill us in on our timetable and the exact location of our LZ in Cambodia.

Personally I was caught in a kind of no man's land; I was still the company's unofficial sniper while Bowers was away on R & R, but he was due back any time now. I was also expected to know everything an artillery recon sergeant was supposed to know, just in case he didn't return before we left for Cambodia. I would have to make both the briefing for the artillery and the one for the infantry. It was going to be tough, but I had no choice, as I was expected to be called upon to fill both roles.

Our objective would be the headquarters of the NVA's Ninth Division, whose location was believed to be approximately twelve miles west of the Cambodian border. An area we knew as the "Parrots Beak," it was the westernmost point of Vietnam's "War Zone C". The Wolfhounds had worked this area on many occasions during the previous year and knew it well. The plan was laid out to us this way: Early on the morning of May 9 we would be airlifted to an area referred to on our maps, as Toan Thang 43. As we were being put into this area, elements of the 3/4 Cavalry would secure the roadways north from the border. The following day, troopers of the 2/27 Infantry and the 4/9 Infantry would be airlifted north of this heavily wooded area, while other elements of the 3/4 Cavalry took up positions south and west of the same area. Meanwhile the remaining two companies of the 2/27 Infantry would be put into position east of the woods and this would enclose the entire area, thus preventing the enemy from escaping.

That was the initial plan the generals had drawn up down at division headquarters. Sounded real good to us, all except that "following day" business, which left the 1/27 Wolfhounds to fend for themselves until the rest of the plan went into effect. Taking into consideration the size of the operation and seeing where those choppers were going to be dropping us off, the operation really didn't look all that great to me. We would be dropped off deep into an enemy-held area, one that he'd been in control of with virtual immunity for years, and we would be expected to stay alive until first light, when the rest of the troops would arrive to execute the plan. That was about it in a nutshell. We would be put into such a vulnerable position for the better part of the day and the entire night that this plan had me worried and I wasn't the only one who felt this way. But that was the deal and we would have to make the best of it.

At least we felt we knew the terrain well enough to be able to dig ourselves in and wait for morning and the rest of the troops to arrive. We had great confidence in our fighting ability; now if only the NVA would co-operate, then we would be just fine. And if they didn't? Then all hell would be waiting for the 1/27 Wolfhounds on the morning of May 9, just south of Toan Thang 43.

I looked around the area for Lt. White to see how he wanted to handle the artillery's role in the upcoming invasion. He wasn't hard to find, and he had already hooked up with the new RTO, Pvt. Casey. They had been going over their plans when I sat down with them. I wanted to get a feel for what my function would be. Officially, I was still part of the artillery and Lt. White was my boss. I would never take it upon myself to define my role in the upcoming days without consulting with him first.

It was the lieutenant's opinion that as long as our sniper was away and I had his weapon, I was Alpha Company's sniper, and that was just fine with me. Casey was working out great and that was okay with me, also. If I never had to carry that radio on my back again it would be too soon. The one thing the lieutenant wanted me to do was carry my M16 along with the sniper rifle, in case the company sniper got back in time to take part in the operation. This I had anticipated in advance, for it only made sense. It would be kind of awkward making the helicopter assault carrying both weapons, along with all the ammo and other gear that went with a sniper's role in combat, but I knew I would be fine once the operation began.

The morning of the 6th we would be loaded into trucks and driven up-country to Tay Ninh. This was as far forward as we could go without making our way into Cambodia itself. Tay Ninh was a pretty good-sized base, not as big as Cu Chi but big enough for the whole battalion to spend a couple of days at while it readied itself to be airlifted into Cambodia the morning of May 9. As a company we had been to Tay Ninh on a few occasions in January for a couple of days' rest, so we knew what this base had to offer and it wasn't all that much.

Boy, was Tay Ninh a busy place when we arrived late in the afternoon of the 6th. I was not prepared for the numbers of men and amount of equipment inside the gate, as well as out around the perimeter of the base itself. I guessed they really meant to go in and kick some ass this time.

I had expected to see a few thousand guys, but all the engineers and armor and artillery that had come together for this invasion was impressive indeed. I would estimate that there were approximately fifteen thousand troops getting ready to launch the invasion on the 9th. Tay Ninh was starting to look like something out of the gold rush, with everyone getting ready to line up their wagons and head out for California, except we would be loading up on helicopters and flying into Cambodia.

I settled in for the night feeling as secure as I had ever felt during my tour. With every soldier and his equipment that had been scattered for twenty miles around now within eyeshot, who wouldn't have gotten a good night's sleep? But tomorrow and the following days, with all the troop movements that were about to take place, it would be all I could do to keep track of Alpha Company's location.

As I finally fell off to sleep, I started to formulate in my mind what I was going to do the next day. The first thing I wanted to do was make a phone call home. It would be my first call home since my arrival in-country, five months earlier. The army had set up trailers throughout

Vietnam for soldiers to call home from. These calls home were made using MARS (military affiliate radio station) phones. An amateur radio operator back in the States would pick up a soldier's call and make a collect call to the number the soldier wanted it placed to. The phone call would then be patched into the ham radio operator's system, and the two parties then would be able to speak to one another. The one thing each party had to say after speaking was. " Over." This let the other party know it was his or her turn to speak. These ham radio operators were all volunteers, and I'm sure they patched through millions of calls from the troops in Vietnam. We really appreciated their service, for there was no other way to call home.

I would have to get up real early to get a space in line to make my call, but I didn't mind; I never really slept through the night anyway. My first call home was placed at 6:00 A.M. my time. We were twelve hours behind Brockton time, so it was 6:00 P.M. there. I could hear my mother's voice as she picked up the phone and accepted my collect call from the other side of the world. After the radio operator explained to her how the system worked, I was finally able to speak directly with her. It seemed like a true miracle to hear my mother's voice. It had been so long and so much had happened since we last spoke. Both of us had so much to say that we kept forgetting to say "Over." We found ourselves repeating the same sentences, again and again. We each wanted to know how the other was doing and I asked how everyone one was at home, etc. She asked me if I was anywhere near this Cambodian thing she had been reading about in the newspapers. I told her no, that it was all happening far away from where I was. I didn't want her to know that I would be part of it, for it would have just added to her concerns for my safety.

Much to my surprise, I found I didn't have a lot to say about what I was doing. I wanted to tell her what I was going through, but it just wouldn't come out. I had changed a lot in the last five-plus months, but I didn't want her to know it. I was on a time limit, because other troops were waiting to make their calls home as well and as my call began to wind down I found my eyes starting to well up with tears. I was like a little kid. I missed my mother and family so much it really was starting to overtake me emotionally. I didn't want her to hear it in my voice, so I ended my call home by telling her how much I missed her and loved her and left it at that. I guess I just needed a hug from someone who loved me; I thought a phone call home and the sound of my mothers voice would give me the comfort I so desperately needed, but it didn't.

My call home had ended way too quickly and I was even more depressed after I made it. I really can't say what I expected from this call home. Maybe it was like when we were children and we got hurt or got into trouble, we always went to our mothers for help. A part of me wanted her to come and take me home, but I knew that was impossible. I had been very lucky on more than one occasion during my tour, but this invasion of Cambodia really had me worried. Maybe my call home to my mother was a cry for help. If that was it, it didn't do me any good. I would have to face the unknown by myself and pray my luck would hold.

It was still early as I made my way back to the Wolfhounds' staging area in search of my morning's cup of coffee. My mind was still going over my call home, word for word; I hoped that none of my words had given away how really scared I was of the mission that lay ahead of me.

I found my morning coffee at a mess hall that was just springing to life over by the airstrip, I settled down and started to read some of the letters that I had put off reading for the last couple of days. I still had in my top pocket that letter from my old girlfriend, Janice. I don't know why I had kept it; I guess I just didn't want to believe the words that were clearly printed upon its pages. I would read that letter one last time and then destroy it.

As I watched the letter burn in front of me, I knew I had done the right thing. I couldn't keep hanging on to it; for it was only taking away from the job I had to accomplish, in order for me to make my way out of this nightmare alive. If there was one thing that I had gained from my call home, it was the realization of what was important and who truly missed me and loved me without question. And for this reason alone my call home was well worth making and I was glad that I had made it.

May 8, the day before we were to invade Cambodia began with the usual bright sunshine and high humidity. I don't know how people can live in this place full-time, it was just too damn hot and humid for me. After being here for almost six months now I was getting a little more used to it, but I wouldn't have been able to function without my daily ration of salt pills.

Once again we would go over exactly what our assignments were going to be upon our landing at the LZ. We would also make sure all of our equipment was in perfect working order and that we had enough supplies with us for at least a weeks worth of living in the jungle. We would have to carry on our backs everything that we would need to sustain us for this period. After our last briefing we drew our ammo and grenades, along with all the food that we wanted to carry. At this time we also filled our canteens (eight of them) with fresh water.

I also met with Lt. White to get my helicopter assignment. In the past I had always been in the lead chopper, but this time it would be different; it had been decided to split up the command team of Alpha Company for this mission. I would be in the third chopper with the medic and the captain and his RTO. The feeling was that it was best to separate the lieutenant and the recon sergeant (me) so that if one chopper were to get shot down, the other member of the artillery contingent would be able to take over and complete the mission. After going over everything with the lieutenant I had to agree that that plan was best; it was just that this would be the first time in over seventy combat assaults by helicopter that I wouldn't be in the lead chopper, and it would feel kind of strange.

Lt. White and I also took some time to go over the maps of the area that we would be flying into early the next morning. The area of our landing was quite large, considering the amount of thick jungle that surrounded it. We took note that the clearing the choppers would be landing in had a large dirt road running right through the middle of it. After studying the map for a while, the battle plan that called for the "First Wolfhounds" to come in first and then wait for the other elements to arrive the next day was now starting to make some sense to me. The Wolfhounds needed to secure this large LZ (landing zone), so it could be used as an artillery base to support the operation, once the other troops got into position. We would then be able to advance forward and actively hunt out and engage the NVA's Ninth Division. A couple batteries of artillery and some nine-inch self-propelled guns, along with engineers to clear the field for the instant fire support base would leave Tay Ninh by convoy as we were flying towards the LZ. We just hoped everything went according to plan. If it didn't we would be out there all alone and a Battalion against a Division wouldn't have been a fair fight at all.

Our meeting concluded: I headed over to the small PX to see if they had gotten any film in since the last time I was there. And who should I see out of the corner of my eye walking towards me, but just the guy I was hoping to see: Sergeant Bowers, back from his R & R. I greeted Bowers with a handshake and a pat on the back. It was great to see him. I had not been looking forward to making the upcoming assault carrying not only my gear, but his too. During the up-coming mission it was best that my only concern be that of my job as the company's "recon sergeant". If I was also carrying the sniper gear it would have been a distraction, and any distraction on a mission like this could prove to be fatal. Now Bowers was back and ready to play his part in the upcoming invasion. He said his R & R had been the best time that he had ever had, and I was happy for him. My R & R would be coming up at the end of the month, and I was really looking forward to it. If this mission was still ongoing then I didn't know if I would be allowed to take my R & R, but that was a long way in the future; I would have gone through much before that decision would be made.

Now that Bowers was back, my thoughts began to focus on just what my responsibilities would be as a member of the artillery. I went over and over mentally the maps and the battle plan. I could see it all unfold in my mind and I was satisfied that it would work out just fine. Of course that was if the Ninth Division of the NVA co-operated, as we hoped they would.

The rest of my time until the mission began was spent just like every other soldier who was going to board those choppers in the morning, and that was to have a couple of beers and write a last letter home. As I looked around the company area it kind of reminded me of an English writing class back in high school, the only difference being that everyone was guzzling a beer as he wrote. For the most part, the men of Alpha Company would be in bed early this night, as the sun would rise very early the next morning. It would then be the 9th of May, our day to join the other soldiers already fighting in Cambodia. It was a mission that we were taking with great trepidation, yet every one of us wanted to experience it. If you were a member of one of the United States Army's premier fighting units, the 1/27 Wolfhounds, you welcomed the challenge of going up against the North Vietnamese Army's best, their Ninth Division.

Chapter 29
Invasion Cambodia

I t was the 9th of May, the day that we'd all been waiting for. Alpha Company was as ready as it possibly could be; we had gone over everything we needed to in order to make this mission a success. It was still dark when we started to make our way to the helicopter landing area. By the time everything was in place for us to load up and be on our way, the sun would have peeked its bright yellow face over the eastern horizon, and our day would begin in earnest.

Today we didn't have to wait very long for our flight of choppers to arrive—they were right on time. As they set down to pick us up, the noise of their rotor blades cutting through the air made it impossible for us to hear one another, so we used hand signals to communicate with one another. After the choppers were on the ground all eyes rested on the captain as we waited for him to give the order to load up. Once this order was given it didn't take more than a couple of minutes for the entire Company to be on board and ready to go. This was by far the largest "Eagle Flight" I was to be involved in during my tour in Vietnam. Thirty choppers would ferry the two hundred and forty men that made up Alpha and Bravo Company into combat deep inside Cambodia, this morning. I was in the third chopper along with the captain and his RTO. Also on board were Bowers, Bernier, our Kit Carson scout Tran, our medic Doc, and—last but not least—Corporal Downs from Texas.

Downs and I glanced across at each other before we lifted off, and I'm sure we had the same thoughts going through our minds: we didn't need a repeat of the last time we had been on a chopper together, when we had both been thrown out of it. We smiled at one another and hoped for the best. What would be, would be; it was completely out of our control now as our chopper slowly lifted into the air.

We were airborne now and everything seemed to be going as planned. Looking out over the vast uninhabited countryside that stood between our destination and us, one couldn't help but stare in awe at its natural beauty.

Vietnam is truly a beautiful country, and the difference between flying over it and actually walking around and experiencing it will stay with me for as long as I live. Being on the ground in Vietnam was as close to hell on earth that I ever wanted to get, but flying over it at three thousand feet was another matter entirely.

I looked over to the other side of the chopper and spotted my good friend Bernier. It was just the luck of the draw that he was on the same flight as me; boy was I glad to see him. Throughout my tour whenever he was around things just seemed to go extremely well. For that fact alone I was happy to have him back by my side. This was like no other mission we had been on together, both in size and importance and his presence was a good omen, as far as I was concerned.

Off in the distance we could now start to make out the large clearing that we were expected to land in. From the air it appeared to be a lot larger than I had expected and from our point of view the larger the LZ the better. We wouldn't have to land as close to the tree-line as we had thought and thus our chances of being ambushed on our way in were minimized. The choppers were all flying in a straight line directly across from me and it made for quite an impressive a sight. On past "Eagle Flights" that I had made, the choppers would have all been in a line behind us, so this was the first time that I was able to see what a flight truly looked like from the air. I took my camera out of my shirt pocket. I was not going to miss this opportunity to photograph such a large "Eagle Flight" in action.

The radios were now starting to come to life with chatter from the lead chopper to the rest of the choppers in the flight. We were about to drop down and make our assault. We would come down low and make our way directly into the LZ from the east, thus using the rising sun at our backs to help camouflage our landing. Anytime we had the sun at our backs and could use it, we did. We were only a mile or so out and we would now start to position ourselves toward the door in order to jump out of the chopper the moment it touched down.

The LZ was right under us now and we could see the grass that covered the ground start to spread apart from the down- blast of the chopper blades. Within a minute or so, our chopper was on the ground and we were out.

Alpha and Bravo Company were now on the ground inside Cambodia for the first time and it really felt rather weird. Even though we had been patrolling along its border, this was the first time that we were officially on the ground in Cambodia. We were now fighting the war in a different country. For the men of Alpha and Bravo Company 1/27th Infantry, the Vietnam War had now officially become the Vietnam/Cambodian War.

Once we were on the ground, both companies spread out and took up their defensive positions and dug in to wait for the rest of the battalion to arrive. The choppers had already lifted off and were making their way back to Tay Ninh to pick up Charlie and Delta Company by the time we started to dig in. Going back and picking up the rest of the battalion would take about an hour to accomplish. In the meantime all we could do was wait and hope the NVA wouldn't counter our landing with an attack of their own.

The area of our landing was much too large for us to defend on our own. We waited and prayed the rest of the battalion wouldn't take too long getting here from Tay Nihn. The next hour, as well as the rest of the day would be our most vulnerable time on the ground. We were only at half-strength and we didn't really have any close artillery support to depend on. We could only hope the enemy didn't realize this and attack us, for if they did, it would have taken everything we had just to defend ourselves.

After digging a small trench, we proceeded to fill the sandbags we had brought with us to use as protection. It felt like an eternity, but it had only been a little over an hour since we landed when we began to pick up the distinctive sound of helicopters off in the distance. It was another thirty-chopper lift, making its way with the rest of the battalion to the LZ. As I knelt there and watched so many choppers coming right in on top of us, I couldn't help but feel that we were now more than ready to get going and seek out the enemy and destroy him, right here where he had always felt so invulnerable and safe. Once everyone was down and in place, all we had to do was wait for the Artillery and the Engineers to arrive by convoy via the road that we now had under our control.

The LZ was eerily quiet considering its location, right in the middle of the Ninth NVA's home territory. We hadn't had any contact with the enemy yet, and we'd been on the ground for over three hours now. Where was the enemy? He certainly was keeping a low profile. Oh well, it looked like we would just have to go out and find him, as soon as the FSB (fire support base) was set up.

The day had started out bright and sunny, but some ominous looking dark clouds were now starting to take shape off to our west, and were threatening some serious rain. It was the beginning of the monsoon season, and we could expect heavy rains from now through September. It had been raining off and on for the last few days, but from what some of the guys who were in-country this time last year told me, I hadn't seen anything yet. The monsoons came every year at this time and would make our lives miserable, because our mission would still have to be completed despite them. The rain during this time of year comes in sheets, hitting one area and not another. It can be so localized that one can virtually walk right out of it. The rain would be something I would have to deal with, but for now my main concern was whether or not that convoy would reach us by nightfall.

It was now after 4:00 P.M. and still no convoy in sight. We had been monitoring their radios all day and they were just a few miles away. I wondered what the hell was keeping them.

Finally, a little after 8:00 P.M., the lead elements of the convoy reached the LZ. The sun was starting to set now, but a defensive position for the fire support base would still have to be maintained. The land needed to be cleared and the guns set up, whether it was light out or not. Those engineers and artillerymen worked at a feverish pace until approximately 2:00 A.M., but they got the job done. The base was set up enough to repel any anticipated enemy attacks. I was grateful that we didn't have to defend this half-built base camp this night; for all of us were exhausted from the day's activities. The morning would come soon enough, and a few hours' sleep would give us all a new lease on life.

After what seemed like a short nap—and I guess it really was, as the sun had barely made its way over the horizon—the battalion started to move out. It was time for the "Wolfhounds" to set in motion its plan to seek out and destroy the enemy. Moving the whole battalion into an area that we had never been in before was going to be tricky at best. But from my point of view, the more there were of us the better. This was Cambodia, and I didn't have the slightest idea of what we would be up against—nor did I feel anyone else did. We would have to take it one click (one thousand yards) at a time and face whatever the enemy had in store for us.

The terrain just north of the new FSB (Fire Support Base) was so thick that we were having a very difficult time staying within eyesight of one another. With so many troops working in "Triple Canopy Jungle" it was inevitable that an accident would occur, and it didn't take long for one to happen. Elements of Bravo Company were also making their way north, off our right flank, when the sharp crack of machine-gun fire broke the silence. Our point-man had spotted movement off to his right, he opened up with his M16 and accidentally shot two members of Bravo Company. Thank god, everyone within shooting distance had the self-discipline to hit the ground and hold his fire. But the damage had already done and we now had two wounded soldiers who needed immediate medical attention. There were just too many of us in too small an area for an accident not to have happened. The two soldiers of Bravo Company had each taken more than one bullet to the legs, but at least they were still alive. Everything came to a stop while these men were stabilized and within twenty minutes they were being flown back to Tay Ninh for treatment.

After the incident, the commander of the battalion and the company commanders all got together to formulate a new plan of attack. Why was it that someone always had to get wounded or killed for the lifers to take action? One didn't have to be a brain surgeon to see that we were patrolling too close to one another and the only way out of it was to split the battalion up. Hell, I could have told them that and I wouldn't even have charged them.

The new plan called for Bravo Company to make its way back to the fire support base and provide for its security while the rest of the battalion split up into companies to work their way towards the objective. Now that made a lot more sense.

The rest of the day passed without incident, and by nightfall the three companies were all back together again to form one huge three-hundred-fifty-man ambush. The next day we did the same thing all over again. It took us four days of chopping our way through the jungle to reach our objective, Toan Thang 43. We would wait in an area just north of this small town for everyone else to get into position and then we would move out in force, first thing in the morning.

The evening before we were to move on the objective that we had come for, passed slowly. I'd found myself a pretty comfortable spot on the ground to get my few hours' of well-deserved sleep, before it was my turn for guard duty. I was awakened at 4:00 A.M. by one of my fellow soldiers, who informed me that it was my turn to stand watch. The rain was just starting to fall. The rains in Vietnam would come down so hard that while it was raining it was impossible to sleep. Being out on ambush sitting in the rain was the toughest thing for the soldiers in the field to endure and it made being out in the jungle all that more miserable.

That night's rain signaled the start of the monsoon season, which would last right through September. Five months of pretty much constant rain, and then not one-drop would fall from October through April. This was one very strange and foreign place for guys who were mainly from the cities of America to fight a war in.

The rain stopped just as fast as it had started, and the sun started to show itself off to our east. After getting next to no sleep during the night, it was now time for Alpha Company to move out again.

The area that was to become known to us as Toan Thang 43 was now just a few hundred yards to our front. The battalion would make its entrance to the suspected enemy stronghold from the south. We were prepared to meet the enemy head on and get some payback for the casualties they had inflicted upon us during the previous months of patrolling along its borders, and it didn't take long for contact with the enemy to be made. Numerous bursts of small-arms fire erupted to our front. The battalion had walked right into a large group of enemy soldiers defending Toan Thang 43 and we had taken casualties. How many I didn't know, but there were numerous calls for "medic forward" and that was never a call I wanted to hear.

It was difficult for us to see where the shooting was coming from, let alone who was doing it. The command team ran forward once the call for medics rang out. The captain always wanted to be at the front of his company anytime that it was engaged with the enemy and once he moved forward, then so would I. It didn't take us twenty seconds to get to the front and start to assess the situation. Toan Thang 43 was what we had feared and wanted it to be all in one. It was a huge complex of enemy bunkers with numerous supply drops. Now the calls were coming in from every direction for medics forward, as we were starting to suffer more and more casualties. There were bullets flying everywhere and the thickness of the jungle we found ourselves fighting in, made it just about impossible for us to get an accurate read on just where the enemy was hiding.

The hell with it, we would just call in a fire mission from the new fire support base. "Four Zero," this is "Four Zero Echo. Fire Mission". "Over," the lieutenant yelled into the radio. While he was trying to raise the base I was busy plotting our position and giving him the exact co-ordinance to use for our first fire mission in Cambodia. Raising the base and giving them our location and where we wanted those shells to hit didn't take more than thirty seconds to complete. As a team in the field, Lt. White and I had become very efficient—we had to, as lives depended on our quickness and accuracy.

The artillery shells from those 105s back at the base came flying over our heads and landed right where we wanted them to. We would spend the next half-hour or so adjusting the fire to completely cover every square foot of ground to our immediate front. If I had had my way, we would have called in that artillery all day long.

When the firing had all but ceased and the choppers had been called in to take out our wounded, it was time for us to move forward again. The smell of the artillery shells that had exploded over the last half-hour still hung in the air, as we made our way cautiously into the heart of the enemy base camp that we knew as Toan Thang 43. As I looked around at the objective that we had come to take, it was an amazing sight. The place was vast; it seemed to go on and on. We had never seen anything like it before. The NVA (North Vietnamese Army) had only left a few soldiers behind to protect the complex and to cover their retreat, but we made quick work of them with our small-arms fire and artillery. Not that we were without casualties on our side: we had suffered three killed and nine wounded during the initial firefight. Toan Thang 43 was quite a prize, but it wasn't worth the price that we had just paid for it. It never was.

There were huge quantities of ammunitions and supplies at this location, and a decision was going to have to be made to either transport it out or destroy it in place. This decision would have to be made by someone back at division headquarters, not us. Everywhere we looked there were more and more instruments of war, along with enough rice to feed the enemy for months. Capturing this place and all it contained for the enemy to use against us was by far the best one-day operation that the "Wolfhounds" had while I was with them.

The decision was made for us to move everything that we could from this area to a clearing in the jungle, a half-mile away, from there it would be flown out by helicopter. If it were up to me we would have blown everything in place and what we couldn't blow up, we would have burnt on the spot. But I wasn't in charge, so now the backbreaking work of moving everything that was here to another location would begin. The question was how? The area we were in was quite a distance from any roads, and the thickness of the jungle would prohibit us from getting in any APC's (armored personal carriers). Someone had the bright idea of moving everything by carts pulled by water buffaloes. We had passed a small farming village on our way here, so a squad of guys went back and hired the farmers and their buffaloes to help us get the stuff to the clearing to be flown out. It took us two days to complete the loading and transportation of over a hundred and seventy tons of rice, packaged in two-hundred-twenty-pound bags. Along with medical supplies; cases of AK-47 machine guns, ammo, hand grenades, rocket-propelled grenades; and twenty-seven bicycles. After two days of backbreaking work to move all that stuff to the clearing, it was time for us to get back to finding the enemy that we had come to locate.

Alpha Company would now set out on its own in its quest to locate the enemy and destroy him, all along staying close enough to the rest of the battalion for them to supply additional manpower if we ran into more than we could handle. We spent the next two weeks working our way north to the Cambodian town of Memot. This was a good-sized town, and it was believed that the NVA had control of it and was using it as a rest and recuperation center after they came over the border to attack our fire support bases and ambush us. It was an important objective and we wanted to eliminate it if we could as soon as possible.

The Wolfhounds weren't the only ones assigned to take this strategic town. Along our way to the objective we met up with the Fourth Battalion Mechanized. These guys were always good to have with us, as they supplied some immediate firepower with their tanks and fifty-caliber machine guns. Moving into a town that was known to contain the enemy was always much safer for us walking behind these guys.

We entered the town of Memot at first light, as was our usual operational procedure, but much to our surprise and relief we met no resistance. We told the towns-people though the use of a bullhorn and our interpreter to assemble in the Town Square. One member of each household would remain at home and wait for us to come and search the house. It was felt that some of these people were friendly to the enemy and would be hiding weapons and such inside their homes. Once we had searched each and every home and found nothing of any consequence, we settled in and made the town of Memot our base camp for a few days.

Our invasion of Cambodia had been a disappointment for the most part. We had wanted to engage the enemy, and it seemed like the only thing we were doing was the same thing we had been doing back in Vietnam, searching him out and destroying his supplies and hiding places. These last few weeks in Cambodia had been a very grueling and tensioned-filled time for the men of Alpha Company and we had no idea when we would be leaving. One could never tell what would be in store for us, as our time in Cambodia dragged on.

In the meantime my R & R was coming up on June 1st and I wondered if I would be allowed to take it. I ran the idea of going on my R & R by Lt. White first, as he was my immediate superior in the field. He didn't think it was such a good idea, which didn't surprise me one bit.

One has to put in for his R & R at least three months in advance in order to get the date one wants. It wasn't like I had just picked June 1st out of my hat or something. And I had been looking forward to it for quite a while now. So White didn't think it was a good idea, did he? I would just take the chance that the commander of the "Wolfhounds" would think it was and would over-ride the lieutenant's decision and let me go. Well, I figured what did I have to lose? I went over to the colonel's tent and asked to speak to him in person. Much to my surprise, just like that, there he was standing in front of me.

Being face to face with the Battalion commander made me a little nervous. I then proceeded to explained to him that I was scheduled to take my R & R on June 1st and that I had been out with the "Hounds" since late November. And I felt that I had more than earned this R&R. He asked me why I had been out for so long? (Most RTO's only spent three months on-line.) And I really didn't have a good answer to that question. After a few more minutes of making small talk, he said he agreed with me and if I wanted to go on my R & R, I would have to be ready to go in five minutes. His personal chopper was getting ready to fly back to Cu Chi and if I was quick enough I could catch it. Was I quick enough? I ran over to Lt. White and told him what had happened and that I would be back in a couple of weeks. He wasn't very happy that I had gone over his head, but what did I care. The fact remained that I was leaving Cambodia and going on my R & R and that's all that really mattered to me.

Chapter 30
R & R

I was in the air heading for Cu Chi in the same Loch helicopter that had taken me into the field, for what seemed like a lifetime ago, even though it had only been six months. My R & R had arrived and I was determined to cram as much fun into my five days off as was humanly possible.

The flight out of Cambodia was even more spectacular than my flight in. It may have had something to do with my destination (Cu Chi Base-Camp). We were up around five thousand feet and the view of the countryside was so awesome it's impossible for me to put into words. I had flown on over seventy missions in helicopters but I had never flown at this altitude and it was something I will never forget. Being so high in the air gives you a whole new perspective of the countryside itself. I could see the vastness of Cambodia off to my west and Vietnam off to my east. The great Mekong Delta lay ahead of me. It was all at my feet and I felt like I owned it. Having such a beautiful country at war right below me was difficult to fathom.

We started to make our descent into Cu Chi as the sun was setting. Whenever I came back to Cu Chi I felt that I was coming to another Vietnam. The Vietnam I knew and the Vietnam the soldiers stationed in such a large camp experienced were so vastly different. It was all I could do to keep my mouth shut when I was out drinking at one of the many EM (Enlisted Man's) clubs Cu Chi had to offer. When the base-camp warriors would start with their drunken bullshit stories of their individual contributions and the chances they had taken to help win the war, I just shook my head and moved my seat before I said something I would regret. But this trip back to camp would be different. I would only be there for a day and then I would be off on my hard-earned R&R (rest and recuperation.)

The only question that was left to answer was where did I want to go? A soldier on R & R had his choice of several places to spend his time. I had heard great things about each and every one of them. The only place that I didn't want to go was Hawaii. I wanted to experience some exotic place and I felt that Hawaii was best left to the guys that were meeting their wives and girlfriends. Thailand would be my choice. What more exotic place could there be for a soldier on leave, than Siam? —*The King and I,* and all that stuff?

In Vietnam every day was just like the previous day, but this day couldn't have come soon enough for me. I'd been up for hours waiting to catch my ride into Bien Hoa and from there my flight to Thailand. Upon my arrival at Bien Hoa, the first thing I had to do was check in and get my paper work for the flight, but the second thing was the best, that was my shopping trip to the PX to buy some civilian clothes. I had not worn a pair of jeans and a shirt in over six months, and I missed them.

My flight to Thailand didn't take all that long. Bangkok is only five hundred miles or so from Saigon, but for me it might as well have been on another planet. I had teamed up with another soldier on the plane to help with the expense of the hotel and share the sights and sounds of the city with. Thailand would be one great big party for us, with all the girls and booze that soldiers on leave could ask for.

We hooked up with a different girl each day we were there. Sometimes we would hire one girl to take us shopping during the day and another one to party with at night. Looking back on it now, it seems like one week long blur—much of it I can't even remember. But there is one thing I recall very clearly, and that is that I had one hell of a great time. I don't think I slept for more than an hour or two each day I was there. I figured there would plenty of time to sleep when I got back to Vietnam and I wasn't going to miss one moment I didn't have to while I was on R & R.

My time on leave would come to an end much too soon. It was now time for me to get back to Cambodia and the Wolfhounds. It had been nine days since I'd left the company and I thought it was best to report back in before they came looking for me. A few guys I knew went on R & R and just never came back. They would hide out in Saigon until they were caught and sent to Long Bien Jail, but that wasn't for me. To be honest about it, I kind of missed the action.

I reported back in with my Battery headquarters in Cu Chi to let them know I was back and that I would be catching the first chopper out to Cambodia in the morning. Much to my surprise I was informed that the

Wolfhounds had left Cambodia and were now working an area south of a place named Xuan Loc. I couldn't have been happier—the thought of spending more time in Cambodia hadn't appealed to me in the least. I felt we had really dodged a bullet (no pun intended) by not engaging the NVA's Ninth Division at full strength on his home turf. We all said: how we wanted to kick his ass, but the truth of the matter was I feared that we would have suffered too many casualties, something I didn't want to see happen. I would have liked to have gotten some payback for the casualties the Ninth had inflicted upon us in the past, but I felt the price of that payback would have been just too high for us to pay. And further more it wasn't like we would be running out of gooks to kill, for I was sure that there would be plenty of them to eliminate, just south of Xuan Loc.

So I would be moving to another new area of operations. Nothing new about that, I never stayed all that long in one place while I was in-country anyway. No sense of being in a hurry to get to my new AO. I had already covered my ass by reporting in as soon as I got back from my R & R; what difference would a couple of days reporting back to the company make? A few days lying by the pool at Waikiki East having a few beers sounded just fine to me.

But soon my unexpected extra few days off had passed, and it was time for me to grab my gear and find a flight down to Xuan Loc and rejoin Alpha Company.

Chapter 31

Xuan Loc

Xuan Loc was located thirty miles east of Saigon and just twenty miles from the coast. At the time I thought that I was finally going to get a chance to take a swim in the South China Sea, but that was not to be the case, as the area we patrolled was just too far away. The Twenty-fifth Division was packing up and getting ready to go home in the near future and was now split between Cu Chi and Xuan Loc, and getting transportation down to Alpha Company's new AO was not going to be a problem. I made my way over to the airfield and waited for a chopper going east to Xuan Loc. I didn't have to wait very long, maybe an hour or so. Choppers were coming and going all the time, all I had to do was ask where they were headed and board one headed for Xuan Loc and the Vietnam I knew.

To get to Xuan Loc the chopper had to fly directly over Saigon, and that gave me a great opportunity to get a bird's eye view of the city and take a few pictures of one of the most congested areas in the world. From the air at two thousand feet Saigon looked like one giant mess of shacks populated with people that didn't have a clue as to what they were doing or where they were going. It was one very confusing sight. I was glad to pass over it and get back to the countryside, for it was the jungles of Vietnam that I knew and where I felt most comfortable.

My destination was approaching quickly now, and it was a lot larger than I had expected. Xuan Loc was not just another large camp; it was also a pretty good-sized city in itself. The large camps I was used to had always been located out away from everything else, this was a different situation all together. This camp was located inside of a city. The chopper landed right next to the camp, but I still had to make my way through part of the city to get to its main gate. This setup was very strange, and I didn't feel comfortable with it one bit. It took me a while after passing through the main gate, but I finally found my way over to the Wolfhounds' rear support area and checked in.

The company was out just south of Xuan Loc, and I would have to wait until morning for the next re-supply chopper to take me out to them. I didn't sleep very well that night in Xuan Loc. Who would have, with the constant artillery shells being fired down range? I don't think they stopped firing all night. All night I wondered who was calling in all that fire. I prayed it wasn't the Wolfhounds, as I would be going out to join them at first light.

There was no sun to greet the morning this day, as Vietnam was deep into its rainy season and just as it would be every day for the following four months, the weather forecast was for rain and more rain. Not only did we have to contend with the enemy and all the little critters that made our day-to-day life in the jungle miserable, but we also had to be soaking wet doing it. The monsoon season would take its toll on me, as well as the rest of the troops of Alpha Company.

It didn't take the re-supply chopper long to find its way to the company's location. It couldn't have been more than eight to ten miles out. I was the only passenger on this particular re-supply, and when I jumped out the side-door, Bernier was the first one to greet me. It was great to see him; I had worried about him while I was away, and it was a relief to see him in one piece. I walked with him over to the rest of the company and greeted some of the other guys I knew.

I couldn't stay with them long, as I had to report in with Lt. White and let him know I was back. I figured he would be pissed-off with me for the way I left Cambodia, going over his head and all, so I brought him a small gift of film for his camera, as well as a little elephant for good luck to help smooth over any hard feelings.

The command team had set up shop inside a hooch they had commandeered the day before to take shelter in until the rain abated a little. I walked in, and the only familiar faces that I saw were our sniper Bowers and the captain's RTO. I scanned the room for more familiar faces as I introduced myself to a Captain I had never met before. He reached out his hand to me and introduced himself as Capt. Noonan, the new officer in charge of Alpha Company. He then took me over and introduced me to Lt. Gomes, the new FO (forward observer) from the Battery, who would be my new boss. I was a little dumbfounded by all the changes that had taken place within the company in the short span of fourteen days that I had been gone. For Christ's sake, we had a completely new command team. I was in shock. Where did everyone go, was what I wanted to know?

When the company returned from Cambodia, the division decided some changes were in order. I guess the captain hadn't done as good a job as expected during the Cambodian campaign and had been replaced, because of his poor performance. Lt. White had requested he be brought back into the Battery, as he had been out for all of "three months" and his request was granted. Our medic "Doc" had rotated home, having served his time in-country. I'd had no idea he was as short as he was, but I was glad for him. He had made it and now his tour was up and he was home with his family.

Personally I was glad to be back with Alpha Company even though it had undergone some major changes since my R & R. Corporal Bernier and I were the only ones left of the original command team that I'd been assigned to back in November. Some had rotated out and some had been re-assigned, some had been wounded, and some had asked to be taken off-line; and now here I was, the only one left but one. I thought about asking to be taken off-line also and going back to the Battery, but I really wanted to stay out. I had missed the action while I was on R & R. I had been out now for over seven months. For an artillery recon sergeant that was conceded to be a long time, most guys only stay out for three or four months. But I wasn't ready to go back to the Battery, and I didn't know if I ever would be. Corporal Bernier was still out and I wasn't going to leave him. I would stay out as long as he was in-country, and then I would decide if I wanted to go back in. And besides that, this was a new AO (area of operations) and I didn't want to go back to the Battery without experiencing it.

Rain, rain, and more rain: that would be our lot in life as we patrolled our new AO in search of what was becoming a very elusive enemy. I had been out for two weeks with this new team now and we seemed to be getting along just fine, but the true test would come during our first encounter with the enemy. As much as I may have disliked Lt. White, the fact remained that we made one hell of a team when the company was engaged with the enemy. For some reason we just kind of jelled at those times, and when it was over we would revert back to not getting along at all. During the last two weeks I'd had many conversations with the new lieutenant and we seemed to see eye to eye on just about everything, so I felt we would work together just fine when the time came. Lt. Gomes was new in-country, and even though he outranked me, he respected the fact that I was a lot more experienced than he was. That was a great feeling, something Lt. White and I never had during our entire time together.

The terrain south of Xuan Loc was very difficult and dangerous for Alpha Company to work. It was thick with mangroves and rubber plantations, which were nothing short of horrendous for the company to patrol and set up effective ambushes in. The rubber plantations were of particular interest, as the trees were all planted in such a straight line it was just unreal. These plantations were still being harvested and run by French owners, who used peasant labor to harvest the rubber from the trees. The French had lost their war in Vietnam ten years earlier, but some of them were still here making a fortune off the land and the cheap labor of its people. I had the feeling that regardless of the outcome of this war, these rich French plantation owners were not going to be allowed to stay. And I for one didn't have the slightest bit of sympathy for them.

Patrol and ambush, that was our day-to-day routine, over and over again. We needed some time off and a few days out of the rain before the company had a complete breakdown. It had been over a month now and we hadn't really accomplished anything to speak of, besides a few suspected enemy captured and a hooch or two burnt down. The captain, even though he was new, was starting to see his men lose the edge that they had to have to be an effective fighting force in the field. Once a company starts to lose that, when they do engage the enemy they are not up to par and men get killed. We were only a few days short of our rotation into FSB Swartz and a week's worth of guard duty, when the captain called into division and asked if he could bring his men in a few days early. Thank god he was granted permission to do so, for we had had it. We had been working around Swartz but had never been behind the protection of its barbed wire. Going into the FSB would be extra good for me as it was the home of the Battery I was assigned to and would give me a chance to visit for the first time the FDC (Fire Direction Control) center, as well as meet the Commander of the Battery.

Chapter 32

Fire Support Base Swartz

It took us the better part of the day to make our way to FSB Swartz. The base itself was located right in the middle of a huge rubber plantation. Most of the times FSBs (Fire Support Bases) were located out by themselves with plenty of room all around them, in order to give the men guarding them ample opportunity to see in every direction. But this base was different, as it hardly had any room to see on three sides. It was located too damn close to the rubber trees—so close it made me nervous. The one side facing the road that ran by it was the only side with a good sightline. As far as I was concerned, FSB Swartz was a disaster just waiting to happen. I had been in and out of numerous fire support bases during my tour, but this was by far the worst location of one I had ever seen. I think it had everything to do with the fact that the French owned the plantation and were still making money from it.

Upon entering Swartz, the first thing I did after I put my gear away was to go over to the Battery commander's bunker and introduce myself. I always found it strange to come into a base I'd never been in before and have to introduce myself to a new Battery commander. After all, I was part of the Battery, but no one ever got to see me; I was just a voice on the radio to them. My new Battery commander's name was Captain Chambers, and right from the moment of our first meeting I knew we were going to get along just fine. Chambers, an ex–Green Beret, was in the middle of his third tour of duty in Vietnam. During his first tour he had been a sergeant with the Green Berets up in the Highlands somewhere, and after that tour was completed he went on to Officer Candidates School to be commissioned. We got along great due to the fact that he had spent as much time as I had in Vietnam out looking to engage the enemy. The vast majority of the guys who were assigned to a Battery in Vietnam never got beyond the barbed wire and actually went out and actively tried to find the enemy and kill him. I had never even heard of a captain who had been outside of the wire either, so to have a captain who had been there was refreshing. We had a lot in common and a lot to talk about that he couldn't talk about with the guys that were in his command bunker; that was our bond and the reason we got alone as well as we did.

That first day I also went over to the fire direction control bunker and introduced myself. It was always nice to say hi to the guys I would be speaking with and depending on so much on a day-to-day basis. I had expected to meet up with Lt. White while I was at the FDC, but he wasn't there. It seemed he had been there for a few days after coming in from the field, but he and Captain Chambers didn't hit it off and it was suggested very strongly by Chambers that White find himself a job back at Division Headquarters, which he did. The fact that Lt. White didn't get along with the captain didn't surprise me one bit. They were two completely different types of soldiers; I knew that the captain would be able to see right through White's bullshit and send him packing. The lieutenant was better off back in the rear anyway: He would be able to hang out with all the other jerks that called Division Headquarters home.

A week had passed, and our time at Swartz was up. It was time for us to get back to the war. I would miss my conversations with the captain but I had no choice but to get my weapon, join Alpha Company and move out. I wasn't looking forward to sleeping on the ground in the rain, but I wasn't ready to come back to the Battery either. Captain Chambers walked over to me as I headed out the main gate of FSB Swartz and told me that when I was ready to come in I would be more than welcomed. He would have a job waiting for me. He knew I would be starting my ninth month in the field in a few days, and nine months was a lot longer than any "Recon Sergeant" was expected to be out. He wanted to reassure me that I was welcome to come back when I was ready. Having the commander of the base come up to me and say I could come back in any time I wanted was unexpected and took me completely by surprise. But he had been out for prolonged periods of time himself and knew what I would be facing day in and day out. The more time I spent in the field, the greater the possibility would be that I would not make it home. What the captain said to me that day would weigh heavily on my mind when I finally made my decision to come back in. But for now my place was still in the field with the "Wolfhounds". And I have never regretted my decision to leave FSB Swartz with them that morning.

The company was now well rested and ready to get back to the business of seeking out the enemy that called the area around FSB Swartz home.

We patrolled that entire day in the pouring rain on our way to our first ambush site in over two weeks. Our location was approximately two miles due east of the base. There we found what we felt would be a productive ambush position along a trail that went right through the Michelin Rubber Plantation. Fire Support Swartz had been receiving light mortar fire during the previous few weeks and it was believed to be coming from this area. What the gooks would do is set up their mortar tubes a mile or so from the base, get off a few rounds and then move on. It was our plan to ambush them on their way to their setup point and thus prevent the base from receiving those shells altogether. If we could do that then maybe the enemy would look for an easier target in the future and spare Swartz the shelling that they had been under for the last few months.

The rain just wouldn't stop, it went on and on, making being out all that more miserable. Walking—or should I say sliding? —All day through the rain really takes it toll on the human body after a while. My legs along with everyone else's would be in constant pain from walking so unnaturally for long periods of time. When it came time for us to set up our ambush for the night, the break from slipping on the reddish clay surface of the trail was welcomed. I called in our references points to the Battery and settled back to catch some sleep, for before long it would be my turn for guard duty.

It was just after midnight and the rain still hadn't stopped when my old pal Corporal Bernier reached over and nudged my arm. Everyone was on his highest alert, and not a sound could be heard. Our eyes were squinting through the pouring rain, trying to pick up the slightest movement. It was so quiet that I thought the rain pounding down upon us was making so much noise that it would give our position away, and the seven or eight individuals who were now starting to come into view off in the distance would spot us. But they didn't see us; they kept on coming until they were right in front of us. Not a word was spoken as we opened up on those enemy soldiers with everything we had.

One could almost feel the frustration in the air as we unloaded our clips on these unsuspecting enemy soldiers. We had been out in the rain in this area for over a month now and we hadn't seen shit. This, our first chance at engaging the enemy, allowed us to let loose with everything we had and that was just what we did. We may have overdone it a little, but could an ambush really be overdone? We didn't think so. What we wanted to accomplish was the complete annihilation of the enemy that was right in front of us, in as short a time as possible. That was our definition of a successful ambush and that was exactly what we did.

As was our usual practice, we then moved out of the area and set up a new ambush and waited for more enemy soldiers to come by. We would make our way back to the original ambush site at first light, but until then I would see if I could get some sleep.

I did manage a few hours of sleep after the night's activity, and when morning dawned the squad readied itself to make its way back to the ambush site. We had only gone down the trail a few hundred yards, so finding our way back was no problem. And there they were, eight dead enemy soldiers, lying on the trail just as we had left them a few hours earlier. These guys had been on their way to set up a mortar site; they had two mortar tubes, and each of them was carrying six mortar rounds on his back. We had caught these guys completely by surprise before they had a chance to inflict some potential major damage to their target, which we assumed to be FSB Swartz. We poked around the bodies looking for any documents that may have helped us in the future, but found nothing of interest. These guys were just some enemy soldiers out doing their job late at night, and now they were dead. Looking at them lying there off to the side of the trail, I really didn't have much going through my mind one way or another. The only thing I gave a shit about was the fact that no one from the squad had been injured or killed during the ambush.

We stripped the dead of their mortar rounds and blew them in place with some C-4 explosive. After that we just kind of half-assed covered up what was left of them and moved on. It was kind of a cold way to end the thing, but to be honest about it, to a man we didn't really care how it looked, we were just thankful that it wasn't any of us lying by that trail.

After a few more weeks of walking in the rain all-day and sleeping in it all night, I had to admit I was getting pretty tired of being on-line. My thoughts went back to what Captain Chambers had said to me when I left Swartz, about that job he had waiting for me there. It was now the end of August, and Bernier was scheduled to ETS (end of time served) on September 7th. My mind was now made up: as soon as he left the company to go back to Cu Chi and process out, I would call back into the Battery and put in my request to be taken off-line. I only hoped that the captain would honor his promise to me, and I didn't have any reason to think he wouldn't.

For the first time in weeks the rain had stopped and that gave Bernier and me an opportunity to sit a while and go over the past nine and a half months that we had served together. Bernier and I had hit it off right from the very first day I was assigned to the company. He was an easy going guy, quick with a smile, and always seemed to be there when I needed his support. I don't know if it was something he planned or it was just the way it turned out, but his presence was always welcomed.

The morning of September 1st had arrived, time for Bernier to jump on board the re-supply chopper and get his ass back into Cu Chi. I walked him over to it and shook his hand—and yes, I even gave him a hug, for I would truly miss him. Both of us smiled and said we would get together back in the world, even though we knew the chances of that happening were slim. I watch his chopper slowly lift off the ground and followed it with my eyes until it went out of sight. A tear came to my eyes, for I would miss my friend and my life on-line would never be the same without him.

I was now truly the last one left of the original command team, and I guess my time in the jungles of South Vietnam was also coming to an end. I was starting to show classic signs of being burnt out. During my tour I had seen other soldiers develop this, and each and every one of them had gotten themselves into trouble. One of my greatest fears of being on-line for too long was not being able to leave behind the adrenaline rush that combat gives you. If I couldn't leave it, then how was I going to function without it once I got home? And combat was something that couldn't be duplicated back in the "World". So at this time I concluded it would to my benefit to put in my request to be taken off-line.

I called into the Battery and got the first sergeant on the radio and asked to speak to the captain. Even though it had been over six weeks, he remembered his promise to me of an off-line job anytime that I was ready to come in. It would take a few days for the next re-supply chopper to arrive at our location, and then I would take it back to the Battery.

It rained on and off for the next couple of days as I waited for our next re-supply chopper to arrive. It was very strange being on patrol with Alpha Company, knowing I would be leaving them at any time now. I really hadn't gotten all that close with the new team though, perhaps because I knew I would be leaving in the near future and I didn't want to miss them once I was off-line. I was considered an old-timer now and that in itself felt rather strange. But I had earned it, considering the fact that I had been out longer than anyone else I was currently serving with.

A couple days had passed now and our re-supply chopper was on its way in, shortly it would be my time to leave the team. Leaving was a lot easier on me than I had thought it would be and having only been out with this team for the last ten weeks, made it all that much easier. I gave the stuff I wouldn't be using any longer to Casey, the Battery RTO (Radio Transmission Operator). Among the items he inherited from me was one of my blowup pillows that my mother had sent me nine months earlier. They had lasted that long and he was glad to get one. He had wanted that pillow for the longest time.

I looked around and waved to the men of Alpha Company 1/27 Wolfhounds as I ran to the re-supply chopper that was to take me out of the jungle for the last time. I also whispered a silent prayer for their safety, as my chopper slowly lifted off the ground, for I knew I would never see them again. It only took twenty minutes or so for me to get back to FSB Swartz, where I would finish up my remaining time in-country.

Chapter 33
Up-Country to Visit Billy

It was now the second week of September and I was back at the Battery, but I really didn't have a job description. The job Captain Chambers had in mind for me turned out to be anything I wanted it to be. As I said, the captain and I got along just great. My first night back in the Battery we sat around having a few beers in his bunker, getting to know each other better and talking about the war.

The captain had spent his first tour as a member of the Green Berets up-country searching out the enemy and setting up ambushes at night. Sound familiar? That was the reason we had hit it off so well, right from the beginning. So my time in the Battery would be spent doing just about what I pleased. I'd already paid my dues in the field, according to the captain. Some days I would spend manning the radios over at FDC, and some days I would ride shotgun on the re-supply truck that went into Bien Hoa three times a week. Other days I would just hang around after a night of drinking and playing cards with the captain and his staff. Life for me was good back at the Battery, but I knew it couldn't last. Before it came to an end though, the captain had an unexpected surprise for me in the form of a "five-day pass".

I had never even heard of a pass being given out in Vietnam. I figured that everyone got to take his five days on R & R, and that was it for his tour. But when Captain Chambers came over to my bunker and basically asked if I wanted to go on another R & R—for that's really what a pass amounted to—what was I going to say, no? There was just one hitch though: the pass was good for out-of-country travel only, and if for some reason I couldn't get on a flight out of the country I was to return to the Battery, ASAP.

The next morning the captain and I got into his jeep and headed for Bien Hoa. We made one stop on our way, at the PX, where else? As he wanted to pick up a special gift for his wife's birthday. It seemed like we looked at everything in the store that we thought she might want, finally settling on a beautiful string of pearls. After our little shopping detour he gave me a ride over to the R & R center. As he let me off, he reminded me again, that if I couldn't get out of the country I was to return to the Battery, immediately. I assured him that I would, as there wasn't a doubt in my mind that I would be able to get on a plane and go someplace, anyplace, where I would go really didn't matter to me.

I spent the entire day trying my damnedest to get on anything, going anywhere, but I had no luck whatsoever. All the flights were booked with GIs going on their R & Rs and someone with a pass could only get on a flight on a standby basis. I spent that first night waiting to get out of the country sitting in a bar at the Air Force EM club, drinking beer and trying to figure out a way to get on a flight the next morning. The next morning came and went, and I was still waiting for a flight out, a flight out to anywhere, but none was to be had. Then I got a brilliant idea. I had my best friend Billy Wallace's address. He was with the Marines up at LZ Baldy, twenty miles south of Da Nang. I would catch a flight up there and pay him one hell of a surprise visit. I knew what the captain had said about going back to the Battery if I couldn't get out of country, but I thought I would bend the rules and take my chances that he would never find out.

I couldn't find a flight going north to Da Nang, but I figured I could make the four-hundred-mile trip by hopping choppers all the way up the coast until I got to my destination. It was a little after one o'clock when my quest to find my friend began. I didn't even know the exact location of LZ Baldy, but I thought if I asked enough chopper pilots along the way, then one of them was bound to be going in that direction. I also had no idea what Billy's job was at LZ Baldy, either; he could have been out with the grunts, and then I would have to go out on patrol with the Marines—that would have been something.

The first chopper I approached was going all the way up to Cam Rahn Bay, (my brother Harold's old base while he was in Vietnam) and was glad to give me a ride. This was going to be a lot easier than I thought! But the more the day went on, the tougher it became to find rides. At the end of the day I found myself stuck in the coastal base of Qui Nhon and my trip ended there for the night. Bright and early the next morning, I was standing at the airfield with my M16 on my back and my Bowie knife strapped to my leg, asking the first chopper pilot I saw where he was headed and if I could hitch a ride north. My first stop on this my second day of trying to get to LZ Baldy was Pleiku and from there it was on to Chu Lai. I found myself closing in on my destination, and it wasn't even noontime yet.

Chu Lai was only thirty miles south of Da Nang, so getting a chopper ride there should be no problem. I arrived at the huge Marine base of Da Nang a little after one o'clock; I was probably the only Army personnel there but no one asked me a thing. I proceeded to ask around as to LZ Baldy's location and was told it was ten miles south. Hell, I had probably flown right over it on my way in. I proceeded to the main gate and waited for anyone headed for Baldy. It didn't take long for a jeep to come along that was going my way. It took less than an hour to drive down to where Billy was stationed, and after a day and half of hitching chopper rides, I had finally arrived at LZ Baldy.

The base was a lot larger than I had expected, but I had no problem locating Billy. He had himself a great job as one of the aides to the base commander. A Marine told me where I could find him, and off I went to finish my quest of locating my best friend. I opened the door to the communication headquarters and asked for Sgt. Wallace and there he was over in the corner sitting at his desk. I can still recall the look on his face as I approached him. It was a look of surprise, shock, and happiness all in one. He jumped up and we gave each other a big hug and then stood there for a moment in complete silence just staring at one another. What the hell was I doing there at LZ Baldy and how the hell did I get there? Were the first things out of his mouth. We walked outside and I showed him my pass and reassured him that I wasn't AWOL (absent without leave) or anything like that, and we both just laughed and hugged again. He couldn't believe that I would hitch rides all the way up to spend some quality time with him, but it had been more than worth it, for I had missed my friend. In fact, it was worth the trip up just to see the look on his face—which was something I will never forget. He went in and asked for the rest of the day off and then proceeded to show me around the place that he called home while he was in Vietnam.

LZ Baldy was home to a large contingent of Marines. This was Billy's second tour of duty in Vietnam. After being out on-line his entire first tour and half of his second, he had more than earned his current job back in the rear with the gear. Bill was also an E-6, with over five years in. That alone earned him easier duty, and I know it earned him the respect of his fellow Marines. Bill got me a bunk next to his and asked if I was hungry. Was I hungry? I was starving, I hadn't had anything except coffee for the last thirty-six hours. So it was off to the mess hall for some chow. The rest of the day and into the night we just spent hanging out, drinking beers and telling each other stories of home and such. We turned in early the first night; we had the next day all planned, it would include a trip to China Beach were I would finally get to swim in the South China Sea, as well as some sightseeing around Da Nang City itself.

Bill got his hands on a jeep, and right after we finished breakfast, another Marine, Bill and myself made the trip into the city. Our first stop was China Beach, as this was the best place for us to cool off and check out the nurses assigned to the medical facilities in and around Da Nang. After the beach we drove over to the red-light district for some rest and relaxation, which turned out to be a big mistake. This area of the city was off-limits to Marines not stationed in Da Nang. If I had known that, I wouldn't have agreed to visit there at all. We hadn't been in the area for five minutes, when we were pulled over and questioned by the MPs. (Military Police) after questioning Bill and his friend they came to me and didn't quite know what to make of my situation. Their decision was to take us all in and see what their superiors wanted to do with us. First of all, I was out of uniform—I had borrowed one of Bill's—and secondly, I was way off-limits as it pertained to my pass. They decided to lock me up and send word back to my Battery to have someone come up and get me.

I knew Captain Chambers would be bullshit with me and I felt he would take his sweet-ass time getting north to get me out. I was in deep shit and I knew it. To my considerable relief, a Major who knew Billy came to our rescue. I was let out in his custody and told in no uncertain terms to be on the first chopper out of Da Nang or I would be arrested again. And if I were caught again I wouldn't see the light of day for a very long time, per the commander of the MPs. The drive back to LZ Baldy was far different than our drive into Da Nang. We hardly spoke at all. As soon as I got back to the base, Billy and I would part company, and I would be on the first chopper out. It really didn't matter where it was going; I just wanted out of Da Nang. It had been too short a visit with my friend, but overall it had been worth it and given the chance I would have done it again. It had been great to see him. Bill walked me over to the chopper and we shook hands and gave each other a hug and vowed to see each other at home in a couple of months, God willing.

My visit up north was over, but that didn't mean my leave was over. I still had a few days to have some fun, and I would have that fun back in

Saigon, namely at the Rex Hotel. I got real lucky on my way back from Da Nang; it took me only two chopper rides to get to Saigon. One stop in Pleiku, and I was back in Bien Hoa, where I had started a few days earlier. I grabbed a taxi to the "Rex" and stayed there for the next three days. I don't recall a lot that happened at the Rex, but I do remember enjoying a great deal of booze and girls. I'd been gone from the Battery for nine days. I would have stayed away even longer but my money ran out. There was only one thing left for me to do, and that was head out to Xuan Loc, catch a ride back out to the Battery, and report back in. It had been quite a leave to say the least.

Chapter 34
Thirty Days to Go

U pon my arrival back at camp it was Captain Chambers who was first to greet me, and he wasn't very happy. I had overstayed my leave, and he was bullshit. But I wasn't concerned, for I was now considered an official short-timer: As I had less than thirty days left in-country. The captain and I still got along great; the only thing that changed was the fact that in order for the captain to save face he had to give me a real job. I would now have to ride shotgun for the re-supply truck that went into Bien Hoa three times a week. And I would also have to stand guard at the main gate two times a week. Hell, that wasn't all that bad. I would have volunteered to go into Bien Hoa anyway, just to get out of the Battery. So the captain looked like he had control over his men, and I had a job I could live with. I guess everything turned out for the best in the end.

The ride into Bien Hoa was on the most part uneventful. Corporal Lennon the driver and I would leave early in the morning and get back late in the afternoon. There was only one thing wrong with the whole situation and that was every time we got back to the Base we had a flat tire. It would take us an hour or so each and every time to fix and change that tire, and that was backbreaking work. But other than that, I enjoyed my time away from the Battery. I couldn't wait for my last thirty days in Vietnam to pass—to tell you the truth it was becoming quite boring. I couldn't imagine spending my entire tour of duty driving in and out of Bien Hoa getting supplies, as Lennon had done. I was glad that I had been out with the "Wolfhounds" and had the opportunity to experience Vietnam with them.

On October the 17th, I only had seven days left to serve in-country. Captain Chambers called me over to his bunker to give me the official word that today would be my last day in the Battery. I would be going into Xuan Loc first thing in the morning to start the paperwork that would lead up to my departure from Vietnam on October 24th. I just stood there and stared at him for a moment, as if I couldn't believe my ears, even though it had been expected, counted on even. But to have it finally here—boy, what a great feeling! I had made it; I really had, my tour of duty was finally coming to an end. I had served my time in the rice paddies and jungles of Vietnam, first as an RTO and then as a Recon Sergeant. I had beaten the odds; I had been "lucky" enough to survive numerous encounters with the enemy and come out of it in one piece.

That night I went around and visited all the gun emplacements, along with the FDC bunker and thanked each and every man for his great work and dedication to duty. I told them that their accurate fire and timely response to my urgent calls during numerous ambushes and firefights over the last year had saved not only my life, but that of many other "Wolfhounds" as well.

It wasn't going to be hard for me to leave the Battery the next morning, as I really didn't feel part of it anyway. I had spent nine and a half months out with Alpha Company, and those were the guys I would really miss. Coming back to the Battery was only my way of killing time until my tour ended. Maybe if I had returned to the Battery sooner I might have felt differently, but the time that I had spent on-line with the "Wolfhounds" was far more important to me.

The next morning, I picked up my M16 and my ammo belt for the last time and headed over to meet Corporal Lennon, who was waiting to give me my last ride into Xuan Loc on my way back up to Cu Chi. I waved to Captain Chambers on my way out through the main-gate, and under my breath I said goodbye to the men of Fire Support Base Swartz. I would only have to wait in Xuan Loc until the next morning before I would catch the first chopper flying up-country to Cu Chi.

My last flight in a chopper was a little different than my previous flights. I jumped on board along with a few other soldiers who were also leaving the country and sat right in the middle of the back seat. I also put my seat belt on—hell, I didn't even know choppers had seat belts. Over the last eleven months I had flown eighty-four combat assaults by helicopter, and earned four Air Medals in doing so and here I was just as nervous on my last flight as I had been on my first. Talk about being a little paranoid, but I wasn't going to take any chances now with the end of my tour in sight.

The flight up to Cu Chi only took about forty-five minutes or so, but it gave me ample opportunity to take one last look at this beautiful country from the air. My memories of the bright green landscape and the sun's reflection off the hundreds and hundreds of water-filled rice paddies are still with me to this day, as are the hundreds of days of walking those rice paddies and cutting my way through that thick jungle.

Our chopper landed at Cu Chi without incident. I took one last look around at that chopper as I made my way off the airfield, and my mind wandered back to all the flights that I had made. And I was grateful that this had been my last, even though deep down inside of me, I knew I would miss them.

I made my way over to the headquarters of the 1/8th Artillery to check in and get the paper work started that would allow me to leave Vietnam and the Army itself. My ETS (end of time served) date and the end of my enlistment date in the U.S. Army were one and the same, as I had put in over a year in the States serving my country before I arrived in Vietnam. That meant that once I left Vietnam I would also be out of the military. The last thing I would have to do while I waited for headquarters to process my orders was turn in my weapon. For me, turning in my M16 was a lot tougher than I had anticipated. It had served me well during the dry season, as well as the monsoons. I had carried this weapon everywhere I went in-country; it had never left my side during virtually my entire tour. It had become a part of me, and after turning it in I felt like a part of me was missing. I felt naked and vulnerable without it. But after all, I couldn't take it home with me now could I?

It would take a couple of days for all my paper work to be organized, so I relaxed by the pool at Waikiki East and waited. I was grateful for the few days I had between coming into Cu Chi and actually departing the Republic of South Vietnam. It would give me the time I needed to sort out in my mind, just what had happened to me over the past year and how I would allow it to affect my life once I finally left this place.

Chapter 35

Leaving Vietnam

The date was now October 23rd, and I'd just arrived back at Bien Hoa Army Base after being trucked down from Cu Chi. I was now deep into the process of leaving Vietnam, I was less than twenty-four hours away from boarding my flight home, a flight that at times I had thought I would never make. Being on such a large base as opposed to being in the jungle made me feel like I was just a spectator to the war. I'm sure that being stationed safely behind the barbed wire and sandbags of this huge base made the soldiers who were there feel as if they were spectators to the war as well. The soldiers who had the good fortune of being assigned to such a large base in the rear might as well have been stationed back in the States, as far as the guys who fought the war were concerned.

I took advantage of my situation to go for a long walk around the base, the largest of all the Army bases in Vietnam, and recollect what had happened to me over the previous year. I was right back where I had started my Vietnam adventure, and I felt that sitting out on the perimeter of this huge base, looking out over the countryside would help me put my tour into perspective.

I had so many questions going through my mind that needed answers, and sooner or later those answers would have to be supplied by me. Things that I had done and things that I had taken part in begged for some sort of explanation, if only to myself, from myself, because I was ultimately the one who was going to have to live with what had become a part of me.

My mind went back to that green "new guy" who had taken his first steps along a hot and dusty trail that ran along the Cambodian border over eleven months earlier and how the war had changed him! The changes had come on gradually, almost without notice. I had gone from a peace sign carrying liberal to an ultra conservative during my tour, and as I looked back on it now, becoming a conservative had been inevitable. I would leave Vietnam with one overriding motto etched into my mind, and that was "Live and Let Live". I had been a witness to enough pain and suffering to last me a lifetime. I made a promise to myself that day that I was not going to allow myself to be put into a position of ever again physically or emotionally hurting anyone or anything. I had been there and done that, and I was never going to do it again. If Vietnam had taught me anything it was that all life is sacred and has meaning and a purpose unto itself. While I was engaged in combat and lives were on the line, I was a completely different person; for I had no options and I would have done anything to survive. But that was all behind me now and I would leave that side of me here where it belonged.

My last night in-country passed without incident. Though sleep would not come, the night finally did pass and it was time for me to join the rest of the soldiers leaving Vietnam. The sun had been up for over an hour when I found myself in line at Tan Son Nhut Air Base, waiting for the plane to arrive from the States that would take me home. It had been a long tour for me, as well as the rest of the men in line and we were anxious to be on our way. A couple of hours would pass before the plane that would take us out of Vietnam appeared on the horizon making its final approach to Tan Son Nhut Airport.

I stood there on the airport tarmac with a group of other soldiers and watched our flight home make its landing. It didn't take long for the plane to taxi up to our location and open its doors, revealing a fresh batch of men for the war effort. As they came down the stairs dressed in their clean new uniforms and squinting their eyes to protect themselves from the morning's bright sun, I couldn't help but recall the thoughts that had raced through my mind eleven and half months earlier. It was like déjà vu, except that now I was on the other side, I was one of the lucky ones waiting to board this all-important plane just in from the States. The new men glanced our way as they passed within a few yards of us, but as with my arrival almost a year earlier, not a word was spoken. It wasn't that we didn't have a lot to say, it's just that whatever we would have said wouldn't have made any difference; these "new" guys would have to handle their Vietnam experience each in their own individual way. Each and every man who served in Vietnam had a different and unique experience. I believed then, as I believe now, that how I handled mine was best for me.

For me Vietnam was all about survival and only survival. Nothing else really mattered. I did my best to help the soldier who served beside me to survive, and I'm sure he did the same for me. But surviving Vietnam was a two-fold proposition. First, I had to survive while in-country, and then I would have to survive once I had left. The only way I could figure out how to do that was by leaving a part of me in Vietnam—that part of me that did what it had to do, in order to survive. After my Vietnam experience there would always be two of me: the one who went to Vietnam and was left behind and the one who was fortunate enough to have made it home to live the rest of his life the best that he could.

In order for me to be able to leave part of myself here I would recall Lt. Baker's advice to me eleven months earlier. Lt. Baker told me not to take the enemy's actions personally and to do my best to survive. If I took everything that happened to me and everything I had to do in order to survive to heart, then a part of me would never be able to leave this place. And if I allowed a part of me to continue to fight the war once I left, then I would never truly be free of it and I would carry it around with me for the rest of my days. For my own well-being I would have to leave a part of me here—here, where it belonged.

As we go through life we get all kinds of advice, solicited or not, but Lt. Baker's advice was the best I had ever received. I followed his advice throughout my tour and it still rings true to this very day.

There were things I participated in during my tour of duty that I was not proud of and there were things that I was very proud of. I'm glad I went to Vietnam, and I'm proud of the men I served with. I truly believe that they were the best this country had to offer.

I've been asked on more than one occasion since my return home, if given the same opportunity, Would I do it all over again: Would I volunteer to serve my country in Vietnam?

And my answer has always been the same.

Yes.

Yes, I would, because I have, No Regrets.

###

J. Richard Watkins

MEDALS AWARDED TO
J. RICHARD WATKINS IN VIETNAM:

ARMY COMMENDATION MEDAL (2)

AIR MEDAL (4)

NATIONAL DEFENSE SERVICE MEDAL

VIETNAM SERVICE MEDAL

VIETNAM GALLANTRY CROSS

REPUBLIC OF VIETNAM CAMPAIGN MEDAL

COMBAT INFANTRY BADGE (EARNED)

EXPERT RIFLEMAN'S BADGE

UNIT AWARDS 25th INFANTRY DIVISION

ARMY PRESIDENTIAL UNIT CITATION

VIETNAM GALLANTRY CROSS UNIT CITATION

ARMY MERITORIOUS UNIT AWARD

Epilogue

Back Home

November 1st 1970 and I was finally coming to the end of my long journey home. It had been over thirteen months since I'd waved goodbye to my parents and headed off to Vietnam.

My flight from Los Angles was less than an hour out from Boston when I found myself staring into the mirror of the lavatory with sweat running down my face and butterflies in my stomach, for the first time in quite awhile I was scared, really scared. Why was I so scared? Wasn't this the day I had been looking forward to for so long? As I continued to stare at my face in that mirror so many thoughts began to race through my mind.

I had changed so much since I was home, that I thought my loved ones would see theses changes and not accept me with open arms and the reassurance of their unconditional love that I longed for so desperately, that's what scared me the most. What would I do if they could clearly see I wasn't the same person that went off to fight for his country so long ago. Would they asked me about my war experiences and if so how would I explain to them that I did what I had to do to survive, in order to make it home to them. Or would I just choose to say nothing at all? All I was looking for was love from the only people on this earth that I loved. I didn't think that was asking for so much but I was terrified that it wouldn't be there for me once I had finally made it all the way home and that wouldn't happen until that moment I was back in my mothers arms. My Vietnam experience had changed me and only time would tell if it would be for the better or the worst. I took one last look at that soldier staring back at me from that mirror and turned around and made my way back to my seat in anticipation of our landing at Boston's Logan airport.

The plane only had about fifty passengers or so on board and I was seated in the last row of seats, so I could have a few extra moments to compose myself before exiting. I put on my dress uniform jacket, medals and straightened my tie and with great anticipation made my way to the front of the plane that held the doorway to the rest of my life.

As I made my way down the hallway that separates the plane door and the inside of the airport I was all alone with so many conflicting thoughts running through my mind. I felt light headed with anticipation of what was to greet me once I made it through that final door. Oh please God don't let them see the changes that had taken place within me since we last held each other. I reassured myself that all I would need is a little time to get back to being my old self again. If this prayer would be granted it would be all I would ever ask.

As I walked through the doorway at the end of the walkway that connects the plane to the airport I was greeted by a group of such jubilant friends and relatives that I could hardly contain myself. They all ran up to greet me, but as they did I had my eyes focused on one person in particular and that was my mother who I had missed most of all. We ran the few steps that separated us with the anticipation of the love a child and the love a mother can only share. I had been through quite a lot but it had now all come full circle and I was finally where I longed to be and that was in my mother's loving arms to protect me, at least for a while from horrors of war.

I was home, I could hardly believe it but yes I had really made it. There were many days in the last year when I didn't think this day would ever come but it had, I was home and I am forever grateful to the men I served with for their help in making this day become a reality for me and my family. I owed the men of Alfa Company 1st of the 27th Wolfhounds a lot and I knew it.

Did I ever have the opportunity to get together with Bernier once we both made it home? I'm sorry to say that after that day he left the company outside of Fire Support Base Swartz I was never to see him again.

In fact I was never to see any of the guys I served with in Vietnam again, that's not to say I never will for I plan on attending a 25th Infantry Division reunion in the near future and who knows, maybe some of the guys I served with may be there, I sure hope so.

Janice that's a name I'm sure you remember. Did I ever see her again? The answer to that question is Yes. Unbeknownst to me she was at the airport when I came home. My brother Fred told me when we got home that he had bumped into her at a club during the week and he told her I was coming home on November 1st and if she wanted to see me he would get her the flight information.

After a great coming home party that was attended by everyone that meant something to me I made a call to Janice at eleven o'clock that evening and set up a time to see her the next day. I really didn't know how I was going to feel towards her but I had one very important